The Fermented Man

# The Fermented Man

## A YEAR ON THE FRONT LINES
## OF THE FOOD REVOLUTION

# DEREK DELLINGER

The Overlook Press
New York, NY

*664*
*Dellinger*
*2016*

3  1712  01527  2530

*To John Landis Mason*

This edition first published in hardcover in the United States in 2016
by The Overlook Press, Peter Mayer Publishers, Inc.

141 Wooster Street
New York, NY 10012
www.overlookpress.com

For bulk and special sales, please contact sales@overlookny.com,
or write us at the address above.

Cataloging-in-Publication Data is available from the Library of Congress

*Book design and type formatting by Bernard Schleifer*
Manufactured in the United States of America
ISBN: 978-1-4683-0901-0

FIRST EDITION
1 3 5 7 9 10 8 6 4 2

# Contents

INTRODUCTION
So You Can Eat Cheese?   1

CHAPTER 1
Amateur Jar Enthusiast   15

CHAPTER 2
Life Inside the Average American Grocery Store   26

CHAPTER 3
Fermented Cucumbers Are in a Real Pickle   40

CHAPTER 4
At Least I Won't Get Scurvy   63

CHAPTER 5
Sowing Season   81

CHAPTER 6
Kefir and Loathing in the Hudson Valley   98

CHAPTER 7
How Wild Ales Got Squashed   119

CHAPTER 8
The More It Smells Like a Goat, the Better   145

CHAPTER 9
Differences Between White Bread and Cotton Candy   169

CHAPTER 10
Taking Cartman's Advice   195

CHAPTER 11
Eat Food, Not Too Much, Mostly Rotten Fish   224

CHAPTER 12
After the Fermented Man   249

ACKNOWLEDGMENTS   265

RECIPES   267

# Introduction:
## So You Can Eat Cheese?

STANDING IN MY KITCHEN ON JANUARY 1, 2014, I STARED AT CAB-
inets full of food I wouldn't be able to eat for the entire next
year. In the back of the pantry were cans of beans, jars of jam,
boxes of pasta—the same staples that haunt most pantries in America. Some of them may have first joined the shadows in the back
of my pantry years ago, like the cans of various beans I never knew
what to do with. All of them were now off-limits for my diet in
their current form. The beans might be worth saving for some wild
experiment, at least, and their powers of long-term preservation
were worth noting. The pasta I tossed.

Everything I ate from that point on—for the duration of 2014—
would have to be fermented. With the exception of water, my
sustenance would consist 100 percent of fermented meals and fermented drinks. For the next year, I would make myself the embod-
iment of the preservational and nutritional power of microbe-made
foods, one of the oldest culinary traditions in the world. I would
live off the stuff—or at least try—until I overdosed on sauerkraut.

A few other containers remained in my lonesome cabinets:
some slivers and kernels of various nuts, a bag of sunflower seeds.
I wasn't sure if I'd want to eat vintage seeds in a year, but I left
them anyway. Maybe, I thought, I could throw them in some kimchi. The spices I left untouched. Spices would help season and preserve those foods I could still eat: the jars and jars of gurgling
vegetables lined up on my shelves. Other cabinets and shelves, including most of those inside my fridge, were already well stocked
with the many krauts and preserved oddities that would sustain me

for my year of fermentation. These jars were far more colorful than the cans I was sorting out and discarding—bubbling, alive, and vibrant with the colors of carrots, peppers, red cabbage, and garlic, which had for some reason turned blue.

It was the simple color of an unusual jar of sauerkraut on a grocery-store shelf that launched this whole project of mine. Many months earlier, I had been browsing at a natural food market with a small section—a couple of brands, really—of fermented veggies. I liked sour beers and kombucha and poured vinegar and lemon juice in my water sometimes just for the taste. I enjoyed sour flavors, but the diversity of fermented foods out there had never really occurred to me before. Lately, I'd been cooking a lot of braised red cabbage, which gets a pungent, tangy character as it slowly simmers in its juices and a generous amount of vinegar. And on the grocery-store shelf was this jar of red-cabbage sauerkraut that dared to be a little different. Though not so fundamentally strange, after a moment's thought—why not make kraut out of a different type of cabbage? It seemed like this jar might contain an array of flavors I would doubtlessly enjoy, arranged in ways I had never experienced before. And unlike almost any other food I'd ever seen, this jar was so very proud to assure me that it contained still-living microbes. We are so afraid of mysterious germs, of microbes we don't understand, and here this weird sauerkraut was boasting of their presence.

I had to try it out. At best, I figured it would just taste much like the braised red cabbage I already made. At worst, it would be another forgotten curiosity in my fridge. I'm a collector of condiments, of any novel flavor I stumble across, though half of them go unused. I'm always game for something new.

In the back of my mind, before I even opened the jar, everything was starting to connect. The same bacteria in some of the sour beers I brewed at home was in not just yogurt, but also sauerkraut? And kimchi? And cheese? I'd thrown dozens of different ingredients into my experimental homebrewed beers to see how these new elements would affect the flavor of the liquid, but somehow, the urge to take the bacteria out of the liquid and dump it into other ingredients themselves, fermenting them exclusively, hadn't really occurred to me. The possibilities were fascinating. And endless. If sauerkraut could be so diverse and just about any vegetable could be fermented and there were all these fermented meats and dairy products out there . . . well, you could almost live off the stuff, I thought.

I tried the red-cabbage kraut the night I bought it. It wasn't just the best sauerkraut I've ever had, it was unlike anything I had ever tasted before. I was hooked.

From my struggles to find a fermented meal while on vacation in New Orleans to sampling mucus-y green Century Eggs in Chinatown to my quest to visit Iceland and consume the rotten shark meat that remains a national delicacy, I've found that the world of fermented food is fascinatingly complex and endlessly flavorful. And while most of us may never wish to consume the really extreme examples of fermentation, the ultimate significance of learning about the microbes that make our food goes much deeper. As if creating new and exciting flavors from cabbage and dead sharks isn't enough, fermentation also unlocks all sorts of nutrients, makes foods easier to digest, destroys pathogens and toxins, and sends probiotic reinforcements to restore balance to our microbiome, the unique ecosystem of symbiotic microbes inside us.

At first, I didn't come up with the idea of an all-fermented diet intending to actually go through with it. It started merely as a thought experiment that I couldn't get my mind off of. With research, it evolved from a thought experiment into a real-world challenge. An extreme yet temporary diet—a hard year, January to January. I felt that it would be fascinating for someone to examine the culinary world in this particular light, something that possibly no one had ever done before but which should be perfectly possible, if the supposed health-endowing benefits of fermented foods I kept hearing about were true. I wasn't attempting to address a specific medical issue. But for years I had been questioning much about the general America diet and floundering when it came to understanding what we were supposed to be eating and how we were supposed to be eating it.

More and more, I read about the importance of the microbes that coexist within us and the ways they shape our biological destiny. Our microbiome may steer our health from a young age, determining our allergies and ailments, even having an uncanny bearing on our mental health, food cravings, and weight. The human microbiome is one of the hottest areas of contemporary research.

After decades of sterilizing every surface there is to be sterilized, I couldn't help but wonder: what would happen if you really did live off of food thriving with bacteria? Ingested microbes into your body on a daily basis? Would you become sick, eventually? Would you become healthier, immune to illness? After all, the probiotics I was reading about seemed to claim a solution for just about anything that might ail us. First, we were taught to fear bacteria, to drown ourselves in hand sanitizer so as to avoid "germs." Now, we're supposed to take bacteria in pill form. Something seemed to be missing in the middle of this advice—and someone would have to be stupid enough to consume all the microbes they possibly could to figure out what would happen. Eventually, I realized the person crazy enough to do this was me.

After all, I had become obsessed with microbes and the magic they're capable of, and I wanted to see what all they could do— the humbling range of foods they could transform into something palatable and preserved for humans. After a few obsessive years of homebrewing beer, cider, and kombucha, I was fully enamored of fermentation and the myriad transformational possibilities it represented. One thing led to the next, and the more I dabbled in pouring sugary liquid into buckets to let them gurgle, or packing veggies into jars to let them break down, the more it seemed this infinitely vast culinary world was barely explored in the contemporary American meal. I was fascinated by how widespread the tradition of fermented foods is and how overlooked the connection between them is today. How many people would realize that the yogurt they had for breakfast, the hazy yellow gose-style beer they drank at the craft beer bar, and the pepperoni on that slice of pizza they were craving at 2 a.m. as they stumbled home from said bar are all made by the same species of bacteria?

My diet would invite questions: "Wait, how can you live off of that?" And, "Okay, so what *is* fermented food?"

I've had some version of this conversation dozens of times. Everyone's base of knowledge on the subject is a little different, of course, but it's interesting that there seems to be no single food universally recognized as fermented by the general American public. Alcohol squeaks in there, but many of us have never considered that the same process goes beyond booze.

After someone learns about my Fermented Man project for the first time, the initial response is usually a few seconds of silence. Or they'll ask me why I'd undertake such a diet, and I'll explain. But then they're forced to brainstorm. There may as well be a cartoon thought bubble hovering over their head, a flickering lightbulb next to a sketch of a bottle of beer, and then . . . blank.

Five or ten seconds pass. Then, most people will say, "Oh, so can you eat cheese?"

After cheese, I often have to explain that, yes, bread counts, because the rising power of yeast is a process of fermentation. But once someone has grasped that the subtitle of my book could be "A Year of Grilled Cheese," most have accepted that the project, while still insane, isn't as likely to starve me as they might have first imagined.

At this point, I'll list off a few more well-known fermented foods. Bread and cheese aren't the whole of the story. There are nonalcoholic liquids, like vinegar, kombucha, and kefir. There's yogurt—everyone knows yogurt, even if they don't know how it's made. Kimchi. Sauerkraut is perhaps the most obvious, but one people often forget. We rarely encounter the production behind most of these foods; or maybe the makers of these things use other, more sophisticated-sounding words to describe what's happening. "Cultured" sounds classy and vague enough not to scare anyone away.

The process of fermentation spans an incredibly vast web of foods and cultural traditions, but unless you're into fermentation as a hobby, you probably haven't connected most of these. You've probably never wondered what exactly happens when prosciutto sits around for two years. It wasn't so long ago that I had my own mostly empty thought bubble, holding a jar of lacto-fermented sauerkraut and wondering what else could be transformed by this same process. It turns out, if you really dive into this fermentation business, the possibilities are nearly limitless. In fact, you could fill a book with it all.

*The Fermented Man* is not about trying to convince anyone else to eat *only* fermented foods. If I can lead by example, in taking the extreme road, I want to drive home the importance of eating at least *some* fermented food and being aware of what that means. By doing this myself for a whole year, I hope to demonstrate that it's not that intimidating. It's actually pretty simple. And delicious.


WHAT MAKES SOMETHING A FERMENTED FOOD?

There are textbook definitions. There are simplified answers to this, and I'll explore them all. But they are mostly simple answers that do little to really explain what is a very complex subject. You could write an entire guidebook on DIY fermentation. You could write many, many books about each individual fermented product. Not just fermenting vegetables, but cabbage, specifically. Not just fermenting cabbage, but one regional variant, kimchi, specifically. Every culture in the world has developed its own traditions of fermented foods, and they encompass just about anything you can imagine: from tangy, flavorful condiments to preserved rotten fish to tangy condiments made out of rotten fish.

You don't have to grasp every complexity of every fermentation process to appreciate why it's significant. But if you are daunted by even the fuzzy, philosophical explanations of the basic concept, don't worry. Think of it this way: if there were some sort of invisible, quasi-magical force at the secret heart of the world, operating on everything at all times, it probably wouldn't be all that easy to understand, would it? But you'd want to at least acknowledge it and to be aware of its significance for your everyday life.

For many years, it never really occurred to me that fermentation existed outside of alcoholic beverages (and bread, which is essentially just the solid form of beer), let alone that it produced, say, salami. Salami making, after all, will rarely seem as dynamic as the fermentation of a liquid beverage like beer, where the explosive growth of yeast and their subsequent feeding frenzy creates a stunning, highly visual display. Many a homebrewer has stayed up all night anxiously watching as a more-vigorous-than-expected fermentation foams over the jug that was supposed to contain it, oozing sticky syrup onto the floor. Humans watching a beverage ferment can tell instinctually that some powerful force is at work, even if they don't quite understand what is happening or how. Thinking about wheels of cheese aging in caves, a skin of bacteria and mold accumulating on their milky flesh, it's easy to overlook the common thread.

I would guess that the majority of fermenters start with a beverage of some sort. Beer, cider, wine, and kombucha are all quite fun and engaging to make. In most cases, and probably in most minds, fermentation could be crudely summarized as: when yeast and/or bacteria make bubbles. In most alcoholic ferments, yeast consume a sugary liquid and produces booze and $CO_2$. The $CO_2$, of course, makes bubbles. Such fermentations are lively and active and easy to follow along with. But without an easy visual cue, how does one know if a food is fermented? And what does that ultimately mean?

If one were to live off of only fermented food for an entire year to become a human metaphor, where would one draw the line between food that's fermented by microbes or just rotten? Is there even a line?

In the broadest sense, fermentation is what happens when we let microbes run wild with our food, transforming it through metabolic processes—essentially eating some of the food before you do and leaving behind the gift of little microbial miracles like alcohol, $CO_2$, and tart lactic acid. To quote Sandor Katz, a fermentation guru who has penned some of the most thorough and influential books on the subject, "Fermentation is everywhere, always. It is an everyday miracle, the path of least resistance." It's a truly fascinating way of looking at what happens to the little bundles of calories we call food. What happens to food over time? Something is going to start eating it, and as humans, we have the rare opportunity to guide that process and use it to our benefit. The inevitable path is also the easiest.

Almost all food will ultimately be consumed by some group of microbes, which, in most circumstances, we think of as rot. Fermentation is preservation by select microbes. The distinction is very often blurred, as it's essentially the same process. What matters is which microbes you cede control of your food to, and what they do with it. It's an embrace of the invisible forces around us—forces our industries have been trying to hide from us for decades, removing the unpredictability of wild fermentation in exchange for neat, clean factory production. But there's no hiding the importance of microbes entirely, and waking up to realize how much they shape the world is jolting. If we step away, deny the opportunity to ally with friendly microbes, the warring invisible forces have a free-for-all, entropy reigns, and food decomposes in the resulting frenzy. But with our help, one force wins out over the other, musters behind its ramparts, and an environment is created that allows these friendly, naturally occurring bacteria and yeast to win, to our benefit. Fermentation is easy—we simply let the inevitable happen, but with just enough steering to produce delicious, healthy results.

As it turns out, the implications of this are far more important than just what kind of food you keep in the jars stocking your shelves. We've spent great amounts of energy in the last century learning how to preserve food with chemicals and temperature. More recently, we seem to be entrenched in a long, expensive campaign to smother the entire world in antibiotics, presumably for our health. We aim to be indestructible, and we prefer our food the same way. But for most of the history of mankind, we've already had an easy, reliable technology that preserves through the cultivation of bacteria, rather than their elimination. We've been trained to fear the tiny crawly things we can't see, but so many of them are more than just our friends. They have been with us for so long that they have evolved a symbiotic relationship with us and are likely vital for our health.

I hope the daunting and difficult nature of my Fermented Man diet is enough to grab your attention, because the *why* is far more important than the *what* as far as our embrace of microbes is concerned. Were fermentation just an academic curiosity, a fun hobby for the tinkerers out there, both the *what* and the *why* would bow to the simple *how*. You may have already decided that you're never going to spend a Tuesday night slicing up ten pounds of cabbage and cramming it into jars as sea salt crystals skitter across your kitchen table. That's okay. Fermentation doesn't even have to be DIY. It's more important than just a hobby, as great a hobby as it is; understanding and acceptance is the real endgame here. Reintroducing old cultures in new ways. Finding fermentation in restaurants, on store shelves, and especially in your fridge and cellars and cabinets. It should be made by hand, but it doesn't necessarily have to be your hand.

Fermented foods are not new and are not a fad. They are not a miracle cure-all, nor, really, a diet. While it would probably be far more likely to earn me a lucrative guest appearance on the *Dr. Oz Show*, I am not advocating that anyone else follow my Fermented Man diet exclusively. I want to be upfront: I'm not trying to make the "Only Fermented Diet" into a thing. Consider this an experiment more than a recommendation. My primary hope for this book is that it sparks your interest, educates you, and helps you to figure out how to incorporate these foods into your own diet and daily rhythms.

It often seems that contemporary Western stomachs are being fought over by powerful forces of competing marketing dollars. Be it the forces of industrial food producers and their plastic-wrapped parodies of sustenance or the countless, cleverly marketed programs claiming to help free you from the fattening foods of those same industrial food producers, the only reliable constant seems to be the fact that no one knows how or what to eat for sure. While the aim of this book is not to solve the mystery of the modern diet (though if you happen to feel that it does, please don't hesitate to share these thoughts with, say, Oprah), we will certainly touch on such subjects, as fermented foods are closely tied to issues of health and culture.

However trendy fermented foods may become—and in modern culture, it often seems that we have only fads and fears—they are something that has always been with us. Or almost always. Their near extinction in American mainstream culture seemed entirely possible until very recently. For a couple of decades, cheese and beer and bread seemed doomed to be locked into their new homogenized forms thanks to the heavy stamp of industrialization, reimagined as crude, bland imitations of the life-sustaining goods our ancestors enjoyed. Yogurt had not yet become a billion-dollar industry and a grocery store–staple worthy of an entire section near the milk. Sauerkraut, turned soggy and bland, was mostly just a novelty condiment to be scraped off of hot dogs at baseball games and county fairs.

The forces of industrialization are at work all across the globe, of course. While no one is immune, Americans seem to be particularly enamored of modernization, even hungry for it. With no deep-seated history of culinary tradition to unite us, we're easily distracted by novelties and food fads. We lack the pride for a national dish with a long, historical tie to health. (Apple pie and hot dogs don't count.) One might even make the case that industrialization itself has become the Great American Culinary Tradition, as we have come to value consistency and predictability in our dining experience above all else.

And why not? If fermented foods were lost so easily, what else could their reappearance be but another nostalgic trend? We have no trouble preserving food with modern methods now, so for what possible reason would we willingly choose to consume bacteria?

While I will say again that eating fermented foods is not a miracle cure-all or a secret dieting trick, there are vital lessons of health to be gleaned from learning about these traditional foods. There are broad-reaching, more insidious lessons to be learned about how we see the microbial world and how humans now negotiate with these invisible forces.

And there is also the issue of flavor. Think of a food product with a strong association to a particular country, and chances are fermentation played some role in making it. Whatever they are, fermented foods are neither bland nor boring.

You already associate fermentation with flavor. You just don't know it. Walk into an ice cream shop and you can guess they will have at least two varieties—really, the most basic, popular flavors you can think of for just about anything, ice cream or otherwise. Are we both thinking of chocolate and vanilla right now? Good. No, that ice cream wasn't fermented (though if you're in a frozen yogurt shop, that's a different story), but cocoa beans and vanilla beans both undergo a fermentation process after harvest to develop their flavor.

Enjoy waking up in the morning? No, of course you don't. It's the worst. Thank God for coffee, with its rich aroma and bracing complexity. Those beans are also matured through fermentation. Where would the world be without coffee, chocolate, and vanilla? It would be absolute chaos out there.

Fermentation can take bland vegetables and make them mouthwateringly dynamic in flavor. (They can also take weird-smelling vegetables and make them far more weird smelling in very different ways.) Fermentation touches nearly every condiment you have ever used, as most are simply blends of vinegar (fermented) and spices. Plenty of others take the fermentation all the way.

It is only from our current dismal position seated atop decades' worth of indestructible industrial food products that fermented foods could seem such an obscure novelty, a hot new culinary trend. In cultures across the globe, or moving back through history, fermented foods are more than flavor enhancers or possible health supplements. They are indispensable staples, combating forces of rot and entropy, a means of unlocking nutrients, increasing portability, eliminating poisons, and making those foods we value even more valuable. There is no question for most that a small hunk of artisanal cave-aged cheese is worth more than a liter of milk; that salty, savory slices of prosciutto from Italy should command more desire than mere cubes of cooked ham; or that a sack of raw barley pales in comparison to the desirability of a bottle of barrel-aged imperial stout. Throughout history, these distinctions—the desire to consume the aged and microbe-influenced over the raw and fresh—divided more than shelves in the grocery stores; they have divided classes and kingdoms. Whether for preservation or flavor or status, humans have relied on fermentation for their most precious dishes for almost all of history.

The greatest magic of fermentation, though, is how wonderfully easy it is to perform. With most ferments, the tools required hardly go beyond the raw ingredients. Remember: we are tapping into a natural force. Recipes are less important than a basic understanding of the process, which we'll cover here.

Whatever else you may get from this book, I encourage everyone to try fermentation of some sort at least a few times. Find a night to work it into your routine, to learn its rhythms. Explain it to your friends. Normalize the relationship with microbes that began at the dawn of our species.

After finishing your first batch of fermented veggies, you may, like me, wonder how something so simple could ever be forgotten. Many fruit wines and ciders could be made with about five minutes of preparation using supplies readily available from any grocery store in the world. (And unpasteurized or UV-treated apple cider from the farmer's market will simply start fermenting on its own if you fail to drink it quickly enough.) Beer making requires more steps but is all the more rewarding and creative for its complexity. Homebrew shops are widespread, and assistance is plentiful. In recent decades, homebrewers have been at the forefront of the home-fermentation movement—or at least they're the most visible proponents, due to the surge in craft beer popularity in America. This sudden interest in all types of fermentation is wonderful news for everyone.

When I think about the pervasive mystery of fermentation, the general misunderstanding about how this ancient craft actually works and what it means, I realize that only the art of it has been lost—the knowledge behind it was never very well distributed in the first place. It's no wonder that most of us never tie beer, cheese, and pickles together. Humanity has been summoning these forces for thousands of years without understanding what, exactly, was happening. Sadly, the very knowledge that allowed us to observe and understand the microbes at work all around us also gave us the opportunity, for the first time in history, to fear them and wage war on them. We've seized that opportunity with an unfortunate fervor and quickly ushered in a world where ubiquitous lager beer is a commodity that originates from massive factories. Bread comes from a bag, and yogurt and sauerkraut and all the rest . . . well, we didn't have to envision how those were made at all. There's no need to ever see the process. We just have to navigate to the right section of the grocery store.

But for most of our history, a jug of some beverage fermenting in a cellar and a crock full of kraut, weighted by rocks, releasing gurgling bubbles of carbon dioxide would have as commonplace as grilling meat in the backyard.

A rolling fermentation at its peak leaves a powerful impression. It is plainly obvious that something potent is developing within, under the surface. Touch the sides of the vessel and it will feel mostly cool to the touch, yet the frothing turmoil capping the liquid looks just like a pot of soup simmering, if not more violent. Yeast collects in a thick, creamy head; bubbles dance in fast-moving currents; foam sluices over the lid of a too-small container. Sniff at the surface and a vicious layer of $CO_2$ will bite back, burning your nostrils and leaving you light-headed. A fermentation can look exactly as if it is boiling—an observation that has been made for so long that "to boil," in Latin, is the very root of the word "ferment."

Touch it, and this silent, cold boil will not burn you, though it has many other powers that are equally potent. It is probably no coincidence that the two most powerful and pervasive forces we have to prepare food—the hot flame and the cold boil—are also likely mankind's earliest and most significant discoveries. Each has been theorized to be the first form of technology, but to call them technology seems somewhat off when they exist independently in the world around us. We only learned to steer them, and even that's been dicey work.

Poorly harnessed or not, both forces have mesmerized humans for all of history. Both surround us still in small ways, but for most of us, for most of our lives, we now know these forces only through the fear of their dark sides. We believe our food will soon rot without refrigeration. Without some way to artificially preserve it, some miracle of human technology with powers beyond the root cellar in the basement, would we have food available to us at all? Our love of abundance has eroded our appreciation for the simple, stable foods that have sustained humans for so long.

It shouldn't be this way. And that's why, insane as the idea was, I decided to spend a year of my life studying the curious mystery of the cold secret fire.

# CHAPTER 1
# Amateur Jar Enthusiast

ON A SATURDAY IN EARLY DECEMBER 2013, I SPENT AN AFTERNOON driving around to local farmers' markets and grocery stores, loading up my car with vegetables and spices. Once unpacked, the extensive haul covered nearly every surface in my small kitchen. My year of fermentation would start on New Year's Day, and most ferments take a few weeks to be ready. I had a formidable evening of fermenting ahead of me.

I soon realized I was going to have to pace myself a little better the rest of the year, but at least this way I'd have options to start. Trying so many different things, if I didn't care for how one experiment tasted, or if another didn't come out, I'd have many others to pair with staples like bread, cheese, cultured butter, yogurt, and fermented meats.

Before this marathon session, I didn't have a ton of experience fermenting anything other than beverages. Sure, I'd dumped just about every kind of fruit you could imagine into a fermenting beer or kombucha, but how much crossover could there be between that and, say, fermented fish? Part of me hoped I was already halfway there; part of me craved the wild unknown frontier of whatever I'd gotten myself into. I'd done a few ferments with cabbage and beets in previous months to make sure I wouldn't be a total failure at this stuff, but my relative newness to all this was sort of the point. Whether I would be buying these ferments or making them at home, if I, being nothing more than an enthusiastic novice, could live off of fermented food entirely for a year, that should be a good indication that this ancient art is accessible to all of us.

For anyone's first ferment, I recommend starting with veggies, as they're basically the easiest fermentation imaginable. Fermenting most veggies requires about as much skill as putting a salad together. The only difficulty may be the boundaries of your creativity: deciding which combinations of produce and spices you prefer. Sorting through my haul, trying to come up with novel pairings for a few of them, enhancing others with spices, my knife and arms and cutting board were getting a good workout. But the process itself was very straightforward: just cut up veggies and put them in jars.

For fermented beets—which many refer to as "beet kvass," drinking the juice as a sort of potent, earthy tonic—the hardest part is simply skinning the vegetables. This ferment is one of my favorites, and also one of the easiest, so I make it on a regular basis. After rinsing with cold water and taking off the skin, I cube the beets and drop them in a mason jar. A quart gets a generous tablespoon of sea salt. (Regular table salt contains coagulating agents that hinder fermentation.) Fill the jar with water and screw on the lid—but not too tightly, since the $CO_2$ produced by fermentation will build up pressure and require the jars to be "burped" a few times a day for the first week.

Veggie ferments where you simply make a brine of water and salt to fill up the jar are almost certainly the easiest. Other veggies create their own brine (or *mostly* create their own brine—sometimes it's necessary to top them off a bit). Some, like cabbage-ferments, can take a considerable amount of push-power before the leaves are willing to part with their liquid, though the added salt will also draw out the brine over time. The goal is to leave no piece of veggie exposed to air, so they can ferment within the safe environment of salty liquid. So if you're having some trouble packing your sauerkraut down and under the surface, the only solution is to pack some more. Fermentation is undeniably healthy in at least one tangible way: your arms will get some exercise.

I knocked out beets, carrots, cucumbers, green beans, jalapeños, red onions, and more, spending what seemed like eternity peeling a dozen cloves of garlic. I even attempted some "pickled potatoes" on a whim. I didn't know what I would do with all these fermented creations, or even how I'd eat them. Cook some? Try to whip up novel new "100 percent fermented" dishes? Just pluck veggies out of jars one by one as I got hungry throughout the day?

By three in the morning, I had half a dozen smaller jars filled and a couple of half-gallon and gallon containers ready to go. But I was still pounding away deliriously at a huge batch of red cabbage kraut.

The kraut was proving to be some work. I had decided to make an extra-large batch in the beginning to hopefully save myself time later on—I figured this jar would have to last me through most of the winter. Several heads of cabbage were shredded, their cast-offs strewn around my kitchen table and floor. Salt was everywhere, and a number of impromptu cabbage-pounding implements lay in a semicircle around me on the table. I tried using a clean, label-free glass bottle, a big wooden stirring spoon, a small mason jar, and my own salt-studded fist. It's rather shocking to see how much cabbage will disappear into one vessel as it succumbs to the drawing power of salt, droplets of liquid appearing at first like dew, then rapidly puddling below. Press down and the tide rises, though the cabbage will stubbornly try to float.

The more cabbage I added, the more cabbage I realized I would need. The trick to a successful veggie fermentation is ensuring the bacteria, *Lactobacillus*, can ferment free of oxygen (anaerobically). That's where the brine comes in—with liquid and veggies filling the jar, there should be no room for air bubbles. The fermentation will create carbon dioxide, bubbling up and out of the vessel, so the only opportunity for oxygen and airborne mold spores to sabotage the ferment will be at the surface. That is, assuming you get the salt worked in through the kraut and press everything down thoroughly. A halfheartedly packed jar of kraut might not come out right and would likely lead to a different, less-appealing sort of rot. So I packed and shredded and stuffed and packed, then shredded and stuffed some more.

I had been ready to call it a night hours before. Eventually, I decided I'd just let those hungry *Lactobacilli* get a head start while I got some rest. With a jar full of water weighing down the cabbage in the mostly full vessel, I left it to sit on the kitchen table and went to pass out. I was at it again the next morning after a quick run to the grocery store. More delirious, half-awake chopping and shredding. More packing. More pounding.

I'd been collecting jars for months now—if I'm being honest, I'd become something of a jar hoarder. I would save jars of every shape and size because who knows when you might need just that unique shape and space to store something? This felt like surefire preparation for the difficulties of my year ahead. Old pickle jars; small spice jars; and tall, oddly shaped juice jars all lurked in my cabinets, awaiting their moment, ready to play the ideal host. I acquired a few cases of mason jars, the go-to, traditional jar, highly valued by jar enthusiasts of all stripes. I even splurged on some Fido jars, with a clamp-locking gasket to hold a seal and burp themselves. No expense would be spared in my quest for a fully comprehensive and versatile jar empire.

My jar collection was more than ready for any quantity of kraut. It turns out that I, on the other hand, was not. The smart approach would have been to split my batch into multiple smaller jars from the start, which opens up opportunity for experimentation and on-the-fly modifications. Like not having to keep running out and buying more cabbage because your main jar is just too damn big.

I don't recommend starting out making a huge batch of kraut unless you know you need to feed a large family of kraut aficionados. The effort shouldn't discourage you. As I would learn later, one large cabbage works out almost perfectly most times to one quart-sized jar of sauerkraut, and that's a great place to start. You don't need a dozen jars, just a single well-planned one. A quart of sauerkraut is a great amount of sauerkraut. (Though really, any amount of sauerkraut is a great amount of sauerkraut.)

If you're now eyeing that cabbage with anxiety, start with a ferment that needs only to be sliced, diced, and brined. Without the pounding, the rest will seem almost too easy. With vegetables, the bacteria performing the fermentation are already present. Their native habitat is the vegetables themselves; they're simply waiting for the opportunity to have at it. Without any more action required from humans, their fermentation campaign will begin.

Over the next two days, fermentation became visible in all the jars—some very quickly, some more slowly, subtly. I left the lids to the mason jars screwed on a few turns from tight, to give enough of an opening for gases produced by fermentation to escape. That gas is the most dramatic sign that microbes are at work in most ferments: the cold secret fire at work. Bubbles tracing a path upward to escape.

These are the easy ferments to explain. We are making our food not with the hot flame, but the cold boil. Yet fermentation is not always so plainly obvious, and it's hard to explain just what it *is*, in every case, without delving somewhat into philosophy.

I once had a conversation with a friend about the various diets that shape American eating habits. We talked briefly about the "raw food" diet, and my friend asked whether fermented foods would count in this diet.

"Aren't fermented foods all processed, in a way?" she asked. "I mean, you have to do something to them to ferment them."

"Well, sort of . . . " I mustered my thoughts. No matter how many times I've been called to the task, talking about the base nature of fermented foods always breaks down into caveats and rambling, nonspecific musings.

"Does fermentation happen just . . . on its own? I mean, in nature?"

Turns out, that was a deeper question than my friend probably intended. Most writers addressing the troubling quandary of what fermentation is, specifically, delve into philosophical vagaries. The great question at the heart of it seems to be: "What's the difference between fermentation and rot?" Many describe fermentation as "controlled rot," but that's not the impression one gets when looking at a jar practically vibrating with activity.

It gets complicated. As vibrant as a rising loaf of bread may appear, or the effervescent hiss of $CO_2$ as you open a jar of colorful kimchi, other ferments may steer you back in the direction of rot. Take a sniff of *hákarl*, an Icelandic delicacy comprising shark meat so permeated with uric acid that it must be fermented for months in order to approach nontoxic levels, and you'll likely be back in the "rotten" camp soon enough.

Where do you draw the line? How do you draw the line? Is there a line?

Fermentation is controlled rot, of a sort; it'd be very hard to wiggle your way out of that definition completely. We rely on naturally occurring microbes to partially digest our food for us, but in the process they create an environment inhospitable to even more unpleasant microbes—mold and pathogens that would turn our stockpile of cabbage into a big, blemished heap of foul-smelling produce and, eventually, a pile of fetid brown mush. Many processes that are undeniably part of the cycle of decomposition can also be considered fermentation. That compost pile out back? Fermentation too.

Technical deconstructions of the process typically focus on the absence of oxygen as another defining characteristic, ascribing fermentation to the metabolic process of anaerobic bacteria or yeast. This definition comfortably encompasses your common veggie ferments like sauerkraut and kimchi, as well as beer and wine. But plenty of products commonly considered to be fermented summon aerobic (requiring the presence of oxygen) organisms to their aid, including kombucha and vinegar, and even more curious (to American sensibilities, at least), Eastern mold-based ferments like tempeh and miso.

Most definitions that I've read incorporate the fact that fermentation involves the digestion and conversion of sugar by microbes into acids, gases, or alcohol. This gets a little closer to the heart of it—fermentation is the embrace of microbial conversion of our food into something desirable but fundamentally different—but suffers from the same lapse as the first attempted definition.

Those same aerobic ferments (kombucha, vinegar) remain problematic, as the alcohol of the original fermentation is being converted into acetic acid in what is basically another form of microbial digestion. Is it a double fermentation, or simply the advanced embrace of decomposition?

And if we're going to get philosophical anyway, isn't everything decaying all around us all the time? Aren't microbes responsible for that? The world would be a pile of dead trees and withered leaves without the action of these tiny digestive engines. Wind erodes; microbes decay. Landscapes shift, and the living escape from suffocation beneath the fallen thanks to these quiet invisible forces. Be grateful that sometimes we can guide this process well enough to control what happens.

No, "control" is too strong a word. Anyone who ferments anything regularly has moved beyond thinking we have that much power. Perhaps fermentation could be more accurately described as us forging an alliance in the invisible microbial war raging around us since the dawn of time. By choosing sides, by ceding the advantage to one particular army, we can share in some of the spoils.

Microbes have all evolved defenses for combating and holding off other microbes. Antibiotics were first discovered by stealing a weapon that certain molds produce for defeating bacteria. Alcohol is a potent weapon against all but a few booze-tolerant organisms. Lactic acid deployed by certain bacteria strains will blast competitors out of its path, and acetic acid, deployed by an ectoplasmic-looking Symbiotic Colony of Bacteria and Yeast (SCOBY), practically nukes the competition with such brutally low levels of pH that nothing can survive the aftermath. (Go ahead, try chugging a pint of straight-up raw vinegar.) These weapons were made to fight organisms so much smaller than us that we can't even observe them with our own eyes, and yet they are potent enough to put us on our backs all the same.

I like that, in thinking this way, we move past the notion that fermentation is simply controlled rot. It's more interesting than even that. Sure, we are relying on a wedge of stasis to momentarily halt the forces of entropy. Everything around us will become a reeking pile of mush in the end, ourselves included, but our allied microbes grant us a reprieve, enough time to do some of that digestion ourselves.

By fermenting that cabbage, we encourage our *Lactobacillus* friends to grow, to feed, to live. I doubt those bacteria would think of fermentation as rot, any more than we think of a nice dinner at the local pizzeria as a celebration of rot. No, we are ensuring life.

How safe is the sort of life we're ensuring through fermentation? Or, phrased another way: "How effective is our alliance?" Pathogens deadly to humans cannot survive in a properly fermented environment, and by most reckonings, there has never been a recorded case of death in the United States due to fermented vegetables. (Canned vegetables, which can harbor botulism if improperly prepared, cannot claim the same perfect track record.) Following the basic principles of fermentation—distribute salt evenly throughout, eliminate oxygen—you can be extremely comfortable in eating your funkiest-smelling ferments. Alcohol provides an even more potent weapon against time, and when properly stored and sealed, beer and cider will never go "bad." They will change, maybe turn to vinegar in the worst-case scenario, but vinegar won't kill you. That is why, in the concentrated form of a distilled spirit, the high levels of booze make an impenetrable fortress, a product made from perishable foods that can be left to sit at room temperature for ages without the slightest concern.

The worst-case scenario facing the many jars littering my small apartment was mold. With as many projects as I was tackling at once, mostly all for the first time, I knew I'd have to keep a careful watch for any unwanted growth of fuzz at the surface. Mold is not quite as bad as most of us believe, in our sterile modern age, and our ancestors would have been a bit more relaxed about peeling it off the top of a crock of veggies. I know, it sounds terribly unappetizing, even to me. But it is generally safe to remove white mold and eat what's left below. Colorful molds can be deadlier, and you should pull the plug when you see them. A small patch of mold may not have had time to affect the flavor of a batch of kraut at all, but if its growth goes unchecked, its tendrils will have likely reached into the precious veggies below, releasing an enzyme that will break them down and reduce them to . . . well, to mush, eventually. Even a minor, thwarted mold invasion could still result in a slightly musty, moldy flavor to the ferment, something most of us would really rather avoid.

So my strategy, after that first Great Fermentation Session, has simply been to pamper my ferments at the beginning. Understanding the basic rules allows you to get pretty hands-on with your microbe-veggie friends. You are the server refilling their glass of water, and therefore the occasional interruption of dinner is accepted. Go ahead, open up the jar and push the floaters back under the brine. Use a clean fork or clean hands. Go ahead and swirl the jar of cucumber pickles or beets. Get the brine sloshing around and coating every surface. Mold can't grow without something to latch on to, and it can't grow underwater. (It's also far more likely to grow in summer than in winter, as I would find out later.) If you help ward it off from the start, the rolling boil of fermentation will soon erect another powerful barrier against it. And if all goes well, once the veggies have fermented for a few weeks and can be moved to the fridge for long-term storage, you'll never see any fuzz.

Other things I've found floating on top of my ferments and that you may encounter: white spots, rafts of yeast, large filmy bubbles, and more. I think one of the biggest things to be learned from fermenting your own food at home is that these things are okay, if not particularly attractive.

To my great relief, I avoided any mold in that first batch. It looked like I could have a dozen or so successes on hand, a huge bounty of preserved foods to start me off and hopefully last me through the winter. According to the ground rules my editor and I laid out, I wasn't required to make everything I ate, anyway; the bread and cheese and meat I'd buy would round out my daily rations.

Though I admit, I felt some reservations about a few of those jars. For example, my jar of fermented garlic, which I figured could simply replace the jar of minced garlic preserved in oil that I usually bought from the grocery store. Except: why had all the garlic turned blue?

Well, bluish green. Certainly a color I've never seen garlic be before. Not totally unnatural looking, but in all honesty, not appealing either. Fortunately, I happened to know a garlic expert. I asked a friend who owns a small business called Rockerbox that specializes in garlic powder, garlic dust, and garlic spread. She reassured me that this was a fairly normal chemical quirk, a result of something in garlic that reacts to an acidic environment. (Though I've never witnessed it, apparently this can happen when garlic is cooked a certain way too.) I looked online, and sure enough, there was photo evidence that others had experienced blue garlic of their own. Normal. Or normal-ish.

Not that it made my garlic any less blue.

Okay, so some of my meals might be getting increasingly weird in ways I hadn't anticipated. All part of the wonderful process of letting your food live, right?

If all this effort is required to enjoy a particular type of living-dead food, one might reasonably ask again: Why? The lure of the modern food system is convenience. Millions of options, available year-round with only a trip down the block, a few minutes in a vehicle. For most of us, spending longer than ten minutes in the kitchen to prepare our meals has become more of a choice than a necessity. Spoiled, soggy vegetables might seem a hard sell to some over the sterile, packaged, and convenient.

At first, I thought fermenting was just a fascinating form of food preparation. A curious, forgotten miracle. And there's no denying the appeal of the unique flavors it presents, even if most of us no longer need to understand how those flavors are made. Some may be acquired tastes, while other ferments are nearly universally popular. One culture may find cheese repugnant yet crave fermented black tofu so pungent-smelling it must be consumed outdoors. We are all hooked on one delicacy or another.

It need not even go beyond flavor. If you like cheese, a closer look at fermentation will open up new worlds. Enjoy bread or beer? The more seriously you take it, the more mind-blowing, beautifully crafted masterworks of grain you will find hiding out there. Enjoy cooking, or eating food at all? Fermentation unveils a powerful new tool to literally transform the world around you.

It may sound like I'm throwing down the gauntlet awfully hard, but flavor is the fun part. Flavor is what we can all appreciate.

The deeper into this diet I went, and the more research I did, the more serious this whole thing began to seem. Health, diets, culture, the war on bacteria—my insane project would change my views on a lot of things beyond the proper methods for making a cucumber pickle.

But for those last few weeks of December, my thought process was purely culinary. What was I going to eat this coming year?

And in the back of my mind: What was I going to miss the most?

# CHAPTER 2

# Life Inside the Average American Grocery Store

STANDING AT THE ENTRANCE OF THE SMALL GROCERY STORE IN Beacon, New York, I debated where to start.

These days, grocery stores are pretty much all laid out the same. It doesn't take a special diet or much travel to realize that the industry as a whole seems to have agreed on a certain layout scheme, for whatever reasons of efficiency and shopping fluidity. Produce by the entrance, a deli section nearby with cold cuts and specialty meats and cheeses, more meat at the back of the store, wrapping around to the dairy section, that Less-Special Cheese section (don't worry, cheeses, you're all special to me), and back around to bread, somewhere nearby. In the middle are the frozen foods and . . . well, whatever else it is we're eating.

We tend to think in terms of meals rather than foods. It's how I've always thought about food. What's for dinner? Tacos. Lasagna. Pizza. Grilled chicken salad. A reuben, BBQ, a burger. Pad Thai. Fried rice. Pasta. I'd have to start by thinking in terms of individual components if I was going to make it through the year.

Produce was easy. Just about any vegetable can easily be fermented. Paired, devoted to its own jar, mixed into a kraut or kimchi—it doesn't really matter. Vegetable ferments can be as diverse, simple, or complicated as I wanted. So there was always that assurance.

My primary grocery store didn't have much in the way of kraut—except for the pasteurized, dead stuff that comes in a bag by the hot dogs—or kimchi, but branching out to other stores gave me some options. My local health food store has a small

section of lacto-fermented veggies, mostly variations on traditional sauerkraut. Kimchi hasn't yet spread to every grocery store
in the country, but it's getting awfully close. It could be found,
with some hunting, in every one of the larger grocery chains
around me.

So if I got lazy, or busy, I knew I could get my veggie fix. But I
had to consider that I would not always be eating at home. I was
working at the time as a writer and part-time manager of a local
homebrew shop and exploring a job as a full-time brewer, which
meant I was within a few blocks of home for the majority of the
work week, with occasional commutes into Manhattan. It was
about as flexible a schedule as I could hope for to squeeze a project
like mine into, at least as far as my diet was concerned, though it
didn't afford me a ton of spare time. Of course, there would also
be day trips, road trips, and (God help me) even vacations. There'd
be many times I'd have to eat on the go. There would be many
journeys that would see me at the whim of whatever grocery store
or market I could find.

I've become fascinated by grocery stores in a new and strange
way. They are not generally places to which you give a whole lot of
thought, because there's no need. The restaurants in your town may
vary to every extreme of quality and type of food served, but the
majority of grocery stores are largely interchangeable, by design.

By the produce is the deli (this is fairly universal). I knew that
meat would likely have to play a larger role in my diet than it usually had the last few years, but I had no issue with eating a lot of
fine Italian salami. The American factory farm system has issues
with antibiotics overuse (among many other unnerving issues), but
I figured that couldn't be so much of a problem with meat that relied on living bacteria to acquire its distinctive signature flavors
and preservative value in the first place.

A number of fermented cured meats—with options ranging
from cheaper products of questionable origin to those with legiti-
mate European pedigree—are available in almost every grocery
store. Dozens of brands of pepperoni are available everywhere in

America. Fermented meat products remain probably one of the most popular categories of fermented food in the United States, which is interesting since meat is usually the last thing anyone thinks of when trying to come up with fermented foods. It just doesn't fit into most people's mental image of the same process behind making beer. One hint: if you're looking for fermentation in the deli section, search for the words "lactic acid starter culture" in the ingredients. It sounds innocent enough and doesn't exactly conjure associations between those slices of salami and the six-packs of booze at the other end of the store. Meat purveyors probably don't want you thinking about bacteria when you buy their products either.

Outside of the cold cuts, the basic cured meats you're already familiar with, you aren't likely to find anything really weird in your Average American Grocery Store (AAGS). In most stores, only beef and pork are deemed worthy of fermentation. Fermented chicken just isn't a thing, as far as I could find. Venison or duck prosciutto is absolutely delicious if you can find someone who makes it, but it's not going to be on sale behind the deli counter. And while fish often gets preserved, its fermented forms play coy around the market. In my local store, jars of vinegar-brined herring—preserved and flavorful but not fermented—were all I could find. I wondered then how I would manage to track down something weird in the aquatic realm—the thought of fermenting fish myself, at home, was a bit daunting. But it'd have to be tried. Fermenting fish is one of the oldest traditions in the world, long associated with flavor as much as preservation. Where was all the rotten shark meat in the grocery store?

But we do love the flavors of fermentation, whether we realize it or not, and a journey down the condiments aisle of the grocery store posed an interesting conundrum for me as I debated what I could and couldn't eat during my year. Really, each bottle of mustard and ketchup and hot sauce was a tiny encapsulation of the state of fermented foods in modern America, a mission statement in a neat 8 oz package.

Almost all condiments originated in fermented form at one time or other, and almost all are still based around a product of fermentation: vinegar. The ingredients list for most hot sauces should be pretty simple: vinegar, a variety of peppers, salt, perhaps garlic and some other spices. Blended and packaged, you've got a tasty topping for whatever you're eating. Though, knowing that even the most industrialized condiments can't manufacture their way around the natural fermentation of vinegar to achieve proper flavor, I wondered why they didn't just ferment everything together in the first place.

As it turns out, some do. Tabasco doesn't skimp on the fermentation. Yes, that's right—the ever-popular Louisiana hot sauce so pungent that one commercial from my childhood cheekily suggested its presence in your bloodstream would detonate attacking mosquitoes. In the same Avery Island facility that's been making the sauce since 1868, peppers are aged in oak barrels to ferment for up to three years before packaging.

Worcestershire sauce? Fermented. Soy sauce? Fermented, of course, though there are some cheap imitations out there today that bypass the traditional process. Asian cultures offer a staggering array of fermented sauces and pastes, though only a few, like Sriracha, have nudged their way into the condiment aisle of our AAGS.

Condiments exist for no reason other than to add more flavor to our food, and condiments would not exist as they do without fermentation. Regardless, you probably won't see any live-culture, unpasteurized condiments on the average grocery-store shelf, though since that first day plotting out my store-bought options, I've noticed them popping up here and there in some gourmet markets. (Maybe Tabasco will catch on to the probiotics craze and release an unpasteurized, live-culture version of its traditional sauce sometime soon?) Even so, a sterilized blend of vinegar and spices is still on the fermentation spectrum. Not every ferment can be live-culture by the time it hits our plate, and not everything we eat—or everything the Fermented Man eats—has to contain still-living swarms of bacteria. As far as my diet went, I wasn't going to be able to survive by chugging bottles of mustard all day, so I wasn't going to worry too much about a smear of it on my pretzels here and there. (Another of my ground rules: spices on food were okay. The phrasing of that actually explains it all: spices go *on* food. Spices are not food themselves.)

I'd read that ketchup has an interesting origin story as an Asian fermented fish sauce. It's come a long way since then, and not being the world's biggest ketchup fan, I'd argue for worse. While even the smallest grocery store available to me stocked a number of "fancy" mustards of all flavors and stripes, ketchup didn't seem to be joining in on the artisanal craze. Examining bottles of the few different ketchup brands, it became clear that the red stuff we dump all over our hot dogs and burgers is a bit different from its fermented origins, or even the days, not so long ago, when the term "ketchup" encompassed an entire category of condiments, of which the tomato variety popularized by Heinz was just one. Tomato ketchup traveled a long road to become the default hamburger dressing we know today.

Looking for the ghosts of fermenting bacteria on the sterile packed shelves of a grocery store, I was reminded that fermentation is basically just the pre-digestion of sugar in our food by microbes. Reminded, because once you start reading food labels, sugar pops up everywhere.

The first four ingredients in a bottle of the country's most popular brand of ketchup? Tomato concentrate from red ripe tomatoes, distilled vinegar, high-fructose corn syrup, and corn syrup. The rest: salt, spice, onion powder, natural flavoring.

I'm not blaming Heinz for adding sugar to their ketchup. It's an old recipe, and it makes sense there: the sweetness helps balance out the various contrasting flavors that make the condiment so popular. It's a bit too sweet for my taste—I prefer stronger, spicier condiments, like a potent mustard, hot sauce, or soy sauce—but the sweetness at least belongs. Heinz has also, cleverly, released a new variety called "Simply Heinz," which appears to be the exact same ketchup with only one difference: no corn syrup.

Every other brand on the shelf contained corn syrup. So did the BBQ sauce, another vinegar-based flavor bomb that calls upon some sweetness to balance out the tang. A few feet down from that is the actual vinegar, a condiment I've always enjoyed on its own.

Next, I wandered to the bread aisle to see what I could eat that was actually portable and convenient. Bread would be a lifesaver for me, a sure and constant fallback staple, as it's been to humankind over the millennia. I could take bread anywhere. I could find bread anywhere. I knew that not all bread was created equal, but the majority of it would count for the diet. In this particular store, the bread section was just a sad little annex in the far corner, mostly hidden behind a separate shelf of hamburger rolls, hot dog buns, prepackaged breakfast pastries, and boxes of stale-looking imitations of doughnuts. Most of those pastries would be useless to me, but no great loss there.

But bread, I thought, was indeed going to be easy. Almost all bread and dough-based foods, like pizza crust and pretzels, rely on the activity of yeast to rise and form their texture. The exceptions are anomalies like soda bread, which, as indicated by the name, relies on sodium bicarbonate as a leavening agent, rather than the fermentative action of yeast.

So yes, technically, I could even just live on Wonder Bread for an entire year, if I could stomach it. But even in this small section of plastic-wrapped loaves, there were all sorts of varieties: your good old featureless white breads, your whole wheat and multigrain, honey wheat, potato, oatmeal, rye, pumpernickel. Also, there were bready creations like bagels and English muffins.

I've always been a fan of sourdough. I guess I wouldn't have gotten to the point of even debating living off of fermented foods for a year if I didn't enjoy sour things a little, but sourdough bread seems relegated more often to containing your sandwich at a nice cafe than grocery store shelves. This suddenly struck me as odd, since a good sourdough is supposed to keep longer. That's the whole point of the lactic acid bacteria doing their thing: they create a defense mechanism that holds off the competition. Come to think of it, where were all the bakeries around me making those good whole wheat sourdough loaves? Had we as a society decided that that was exclusively a San Francisco thing?

I picked up loaf after loaf, accepting that I wouldn't be finding a good traditional sourdough here, anyway, in a plastic bag, and noticed an earlier theme returning: corn syrup, sugar, everywhere.

It's no great secret that food producers are just recklessly adding sugar to everything these days. But why bread? The fermentation of bread relies on turning sugar into $CO_2$, because, guess what? The carbohydrates are already there. In abundance. Bread is nothing but carbohydrates and starches to begin with, partially digested for us by bacteria. Does the American sweet tooth simply demand we add more sugar to everything? It seems a bit gratuitous, but apparently so—no wonder sourdough fell out of favor, when its tart character represents the very opposite end of the flavor spectrum. But hey, I could still eat it. Fermentation may have been warped and held hostage by industrialization, but exploring that sad fact was going to be part of my journey too. The good and the bad.

The milk section of the back left corner runs into the yogurt section, which then turns into farmer's cheese, ricotta, and the not-fancy hard cheeses. The whole wall is a nice visual metaphor for the transformation of milk into increasingly stable and solid fermented forms. With far more options than any of the others, though, is the yogurt.

These days, it's hard to imagine a grocery store without an extensive yogurt aisle. It is likely surpassed only by cheese for the title of most popular fermented food in America (assuming we're not counting alcoholic beverages as a food), but either way, we probably eat as much or more dairy in its fermented forms than as actual milk. Yet what is now a multibillion-dollar industry was virtually unknown until half a century ago. As recently as the 1970s, yogurt was still a rare curiosity, considered an ethnic food and known mostly in New York City. Today, the industry is a juggernaut.

How did this one particular ferment manage to achieve domination just as industrialization worked, at the height of its influence, to quietly neuter all other cultured foods?

I had no idea. Regardless, there were a lot of yogurt options in front of me. The seeming ability of yogurt to stand as a base for all manner of dessert-like toppings, fruits, and enhanced flavors was perhaps one clue. We can masquerade the stuff as a hundred other things while still feeling assured that the probiotic dairy underneath is ultimately good for us. To be honest, I had never been a huge yogurt eater, but I would have to start for at least this one year. Examining labels, I was a little surprised and definitely pleased to see that just about all of them were proudly live-culture, their helpful bacteria still intact. A number of them even made sure to include the term "probiotic" somewhere on the package. Mentally walking back through the store, it occurred to me that it might be the only food in that entire grocery to embrace the term and even go as far as to mention which specific bacteria strains were inside. How progressive!

I wondered how many people know how yogurt is actually made or even *what* it is. I definitely recalled a time when I would not have been able to answer those questions myself. I can still recall a conversation I'd had with a friend some years earlier, about a fantasy novel in which one culture was said to drink a fermented horse-milk beverage. We took this to mean alcohol, and the combination of milk and booze caused some kind of circuit to trip in my mind. A discussion ensued: could you actually produce some kind of intoxicating drink with milk? Could you ferment *milk*? What in the world would fermented milk be like?

In my defense, this was a long time ago. And our minds had gotten stuck on the concept of this insane impossibility as some kind of boozy milk-wine. Still, it was a shamefully long time before one of us turned to the other and said, "Oh. Fermented milk would be . . . cheese, I guess."

I'm not even sure we ever even thought to include yogurt. We definitely weren't aware of kefir, a sort of drinkable yogurt, or the fact that beverages like the boozy milk-wine that so confused our thought bubbles was indeed possible.

A few weeks after I first told her about my book project, a phone call from my mother helped solidify why this remains so confusing to so many people.

"How can you eat yogurt?" she asked. She'd become fascinated by uncovering things that I could eat and would usually call me to share the discovery. This time, though, it sounded like she thought I was trying to pull one over on everyone.

"Why would yogurt count?" she asked. "Isn't it cultured?"

Ah, an easy question, at last.

"Cultured and fermented mean the same thing in the yogurt world," I told her. "'Cultured' just means it's made with bacteria cultures."

"Cultured" sounds so much friendlier. More elegant. Perhaps for no other reason than in English, culture also means . . . well, culture. Class. Worldliness. Sophistication. And saying a food is cultured sounds undoubtedly more sophisticated than saying it sat around for a while with bacteria growing in it.

I had always considered myself a relatively healthy eater, even if I probably couldn't have explained specifically what that meant. I have always, also, been skeptical of a lot of the advice swung out year to year by the health media. Eggs are bad. Eggs are back in. Fat is bad. Carbs are bad. Certain things found in carby foods are bad. Certain fats are bad. Certain fats are more bad than others. Alcohol is bad, except exactly two glasses of wine per day is good. MSG, it turns out after fifty years, might not actually be bad after all—a lot of that was just racism. Whoops.

It's exhausting. I am deeply skeptical by nature and mostly ignored acting on the advice I read, figuring my diet of primarily tacos and pizza with creative toppings would work itself out, being by necessity of composition a varied blend of food groups. Since college and subsequent efforts to become not completely incompetent around the kitchen, I considered myself a moderately savvy food consumer.

But until planning out my Fermented Man diet, I wasn't really the type to walk around a grocery store reading food labels. Gut intuition is more my thing. Trying to make most of my food myself, from basic ingredients. Suddenly I was the type of person who had to be hyperaware of how things were made. Partly for practicality, partly for research, partly out of sheer curiosity. The specter of fermentations past will always linger in our grocery stores, no matter how completely industry grasps our food production, and suddenly I was trying to understand how this one way of making things had slowly, efficiently been warped, altered, forced into this new way of making things.

Usually with more sugar.

One neat rule of fermentation that I learned early on, thanks to a few years of homebrewing and feeding sugar-tea to the glass jug of kombucha beneath my kitchen cabinet: fermentation and disgusting amounts of sugar do not go hand in hand. Kombucha starts as sugar-tea but doesn't have to end that way; a fully-fermented kombucha would contain very little sugar in the end. Just acid. I'm often asked how to make cider so that it comes out still sweet (ugh, Americans and their too-sweet cider), because the natural trajectory of the yeast in the beverage will leave apple juice minus all its sucrose. And that's how these things are meant to be— it works out well for all parties involved. The process of fermentation directly consumes sugar, leaving us something else in its stead. Alcohol, gas, acid. True, beer still contains carbohydrates in its finished form, but not simple sugars. Kombucha is often flavored with fruit or even back-sweetened, but its microbial agents of change tackle those simple sugars too, if allowed.

Most ferments can be broken down into alcohol ferments and acid ferments roughly by how much sugar they offer up to the microbes. Sugar-rich sources like grains and fruits favor yeast, which drowns out the competition in an explosion of booze. Vegetables— not so sugar rich—still contain enough carbohydrates to please the hordes of bacteria that live natively on their skin, waiting to perform their own harvest. If cabbage contained as much sugar as grapes, you can bet that getting drunk on cabbage-wine would sound like a typical Friday night activity. Home fermenters are known to make wines out of every and any fruit imaginable. Banana wine? Been done. Banana beer? Of course. Very little that grows on this planet has not been thrown into somebody's bucket of homebrew.

Not that I'm not fond of many sugary foods myself. Growing up in central Pennsylvania, doughnuts were practically a daily staple of my diet. And sure, even as my tastes skewed more and more toward savory, dry, and earthy flavors, I still got cravings for snacks. I'm a sucker for Double Stuf Oreos and ice cream and whoopie pies and probably always will be. We can't all be perfect.

But I always felt that there was an important distinction to be made: these things are snacks. Not necessarily going to kill you if you indulge in them occasionally, but not part of a regular diet. That's the important distinction: snacks are not food. Snacks are an indulgence.

Taking an aggressively critical view of all the food I was examining, it was starting to seem like the vast majority of these aisles in my grocery store were devoted to snacks, and snacks trying to pass themselves off as food.

In the center aisles were plenty of snacks, and plenty more semifood offerings in all manner of cans, jars, and bags. Sauces of every kind. Crackers and chips in every shape conceivable. Potato chips in every flavor imaginable, from salt and vinegar to cappuccino. (Seriously, what the hell are you thinking, Lay's?) Bags and boxes of pasta. Plenty of pickles to choose from. Canned beans. Canned fruit. Canned vegetables.

Among the canned vegetables are a few lonely vessels of sauerkraut. Bags of it are strategically located next to the hot dogs in another section, but here, the few available options look more like the sad novelty sauerkraut has become. More a relic of tradition, a shrug of a condiment, than a side dish legitimately enjoyed. The jars I examined were dosed with high fructose corn syrup to sweeten them up, to help them appeal to American taste buds. They were pasteurized and dead, so the extra sugar would be consumed by us, instead of by the microbes that made the kraut in the first place.

A walk around the modern grocery store is secretly an education in the many ways we have devised to preserve our foods. A dozen different methods can be observed, but we have gone to great lengths to obscure the oldest and perhaps healthiest.

MANY TIMES SINCE BEGINNING THIS CHALLENGE, I HAVE PAUSED TO consider what life would be like without electricity. Food that basically makes itself naturally evokes this thought experiment, I guess. You consider a life without cooking. Without refrigeration. Without the modern grocery store.

Life without fire or the ability to cook would be a challenge, but a lack of refrigeration might be the ultimate setback for most of us. In this hopefully hypothetical scenario, I suppose it would depend as well on what other resources might be available to us. Are we truly isolated and living from scratch, or can we hop down the street to the market? So much of what stocks the AAGS seems destined to rot within days if we don't keep it in the safety of the fridge, but part of this is mere training—decades spent viewing our refrigerator as some magical box into which almost all food must go. Store in one magic box to keep it cold, then cook in another magic box to transform with heat.

Fermentation, of course, takes care of both the preservation and the preparation, a fact that hit home when I spent a week, later on in the year, camping in northern Vermont. I'd given a lot of thought as to how I'd take vacation while forced to eat so particularly, and relaxing in a remote lakeside cabin, I had no fridge or ice chest, none of the usual conveniences. It rained every day, hard and steady, so I had no fire. I could not cook. I hardly even thought about it.

Of course, I could still go into town, to the market, and buy supplies. I wasn't living completely off the grid, but it felt strangely refreshing to be disconnected from so much of it. To decide it was dinner time by simply picking up some food and taking a bite of it, not having to think at all about what sort of "meal" I might want to prepare. It was among the most relaxing, tranquil vacations I've ever experienced—I look back on that week now as one of the best weeks of my recent life. I had some salami and prosciutto, a variety of cheeses, kefir, yogurt, cultured butter, a modest loaf of bread, and beer. I would eat them each as they were, without bothering to take that extra (and ultimately unnecessary) step of actually slapping the cheese and bread and butter together and applying flame, transforming them into a meltier, warmer, toasted version of what I already had. No grilled cheese. No pizza. Just a week of eating simply; a small blip in my year of eating simply.

Admittedly, I had some advantages that week, given the weather. It would have been somewhat harder to pull off in sweltering July humidity. While the constant rain storms caused drastic temperature swings, the highs and lows alike remained on the cold side, with a few of those chill evenings cold enough that I could see my breath. Other days, the afternoons were just pleasantly crisp, maybe a little damp, but hospitable enough that I could sit under the cabin's awning, out of the rain, with only a T-shirt and a hoodie.

Even through the warm afternoons, my yogurt was happy to sit out on the picnic table without an ice bath, perhaps digesting a few more of its remaining sugars. Being in Vermont and all, I'd picked up a large tub of maple yogurt. The bit of syrup that'd been blended into it added a nice balance of rich, earthy sweetness to contrast the tangy dairy, but this balance shifted throughout the week. Each day, I noticed, the yogurt was a little less sweet as the temperature spiked high enough for it to continue to ferment.

Otherwise, most of my food remained unchanged from day to day. I ate my loaf of bread quickly—it was the only thing likely to go stale in that span of days. While tasty, the loaf started to get brittle pretty fast. I was eating it by tearing off chunks and shoving those chunks into my face, the way bread is meant to be eaten. In the mornings, I'd smear delicious Vermont cultured butter over the crags of its interior. In the evening, I'd pair it with cheese. But with a quarter of the loaf left, it'd gotten too hard to be palatable, just chewing the stuff untoasted, un-warmed.

No matter the quality, no matter how natural or how preserved, all food goes bad eventually. With some food, this is okay. Even fermentation is sometimes about transformation more than preservation. Bread is meant to be eaten fresh, and this simple fact cuts to a glaring flaw in our modern food system. The centralized food market has done wonders for our schedule—being able to buy all we need in one location saves us hours of time—but it has its costs. Fermented or otherwise, foods like bread were never meant to sit in box trucks and on shelves for days before we bring them into our kitchen. How many foods do we still buy from the people who actually produced them? Not just farmers, but bakers and butchers? If we buy all our food from the same place, in all its magically sterile and prepackaged forms, how connected can we possibly be to how our food is made, transported, and preserved?

# CHAPTER 3

# Fermented Cucumbers Are in a Real Pickle

CENTRAL PENNSYLVANIA IS A LAND OF FARMS, PROUD TRADITIONS, and respect for the handmade. We adore our bake sales and Amish furniture. We have more cows and corn than you can shake a stick at (even a fine handcrafted Amish stick custom-built for shaking). And yet canning vegetables won out over fermentation in that area some time ago—in this land of German immigrants, I could never recall crock-fermented sauerkraut being the ubiquitous staple you might assume it'd be.

I asked my grandparents why they never dabbled in fermentation. How did they, two Pennsylvania Dutch farmers who can still speak low German, not at the very least grow up on sauerkraut? My grandpa was never the cook. My grandma is an excellent one, but adventurous eating isn't exactly their speed. They stick to the familiar. I couldn't believe they never made anything with milk—their milk would have all been raw at the time and would have begun to clabber on its own rather quickly. But they told me they just kept it cold and drank it quickly.

Hadn't they ever made some kind of kraut, at least?

Once or twice, my grandma thought, maybe she had. Hard to remember the exact process from so long ago. There were a few things she thought she may have prepared in their fermented forms—like the traditional Appalachian pickled relish known as chow-chow—but she had eventually switched over to canning without really thinking too much about it. She could recall there being a big crock, and while she wouldn't have really understood what fermentation even was at the time, it seemed like real fermented kraut was a likely result.

If even the people who made the stuff couldn't tell you what exactly they made, maybe it's not so strange that fermentation poses so much confusion to us today, decades from when it was forgotten. My grandparents lived in a transitional period. Canning was easier and more predictable, but even packaging your own food for storage through the winter suddenly became a thing of the antiquated past, so much more labor intensive than simply shopping at the "super" market that only folks like farmers in rural Pennsylvania might take the time to do it.

Modernization was filling every cupboard of every home in America.

BACK IN 2013, ONE OF MY GOOD FRIENDS WRINKLED HER NOSE AS I described my plan for the year. She cut me off halfway through my explanation of the elaborate diet: "I'm sorry, there's no way putting that many bacteria inside you can be healthy."

I had explained why bacteria were important to our bodies, but she was convinced that, even given the excellent ratio of friendly versus unfriendly bacteria among us, something would eventually prove to be dangerous. If you're eating so many bacteria, what are the odds that, at some point, something unsavory wouldn't eventually slip in there?

Really, it all comes down to pickles.

You see, not only do pickles taste great, they make for a wonderful explanatory tool. For as many times as I've had to discuss the basic concepts of fermentation, I've had to explain why I couldn't eat most pickles under an "all fermented" diet. The impression I've gotten, after dozens of such conversations, is that most people assume anything that comes in a jar or can is pretty much prepared the same way. Sauerkraut tastes sour. Pickles taste sour. They must have been fermented, right?

If I unknowingly slipped in my Fermented Man diet in 2014, it was likely due to someone telling me, innocently enough, that the veggies they had made were fermented, when, in fact, they were actually pickled in vinegar. I learned early on that I couldn't trust that the basic tenets of fermentation were understood even by people already interested in the subject. People would repeatedly insist they'd made some fermented whatchamacallit or what-have-you, but when they revealed the process they used, it was clear the stuff wasn't. Remember that guy who lived off of McDonald's for a month? Imagine if people kept driving him to Subway instead, then insisting it was basically the same thing anyway so what did it matter? In practice, yes, they're right. But we're trying to prove a point with an annoyingly restrictive dietary platform here, guys; we have to stick to the plan.

Part of this confusion probably arose because fermentation, pickling, and canning exist along a spectrum. Food can be more or less fermented, and canned foods can be prepared in a few different ways. And while we've been fermenting food for a very long time, it hasn't actually been that long that we've known exactly what was happening during fermentation. But the basic premise is this: in fermentation, the microbes already present are given the chance to activate their natural defense mechanisms (creating lactic acid, in most cases), souring and preserving the food.

Canning might refer to anything in a sealed container—regular old tins cans come to mind, but the process applies to home canning in glass mason jars as well. If the fundamental premise of fermentation is "food preserved by microbes," then the premise of canning is "preservation of food by elimination of all microbes (and sealing off the container so that no more microbes can enter)." Once again, mankind relies on the two oldest of elements: the cold fire and the one that scorches and kills.

Many canned foods are also pickled in vinegar. Take the case of the noble cucumber. So commonly associated with preservation and sour flavors is the preserved cucumber that almost all of us will think of pickled cucumbers when we hear the term "pickle." Originally, cucumbers were simply one pickling option, as almost anything can be preserved similarly, from eggs to fish, veggies to fruit. Today, Americans eat almost as many cucumbers in pickled form as in their raw state. Pickled cucumbers are right up there with French fries for snacks you can track down just about anywhere.

Almost anything can be preserved through either fermentation or canning, and as far as simply preserving the food, pasteurization through heat is usually enough to do the trick (in canning).

Except in the case of botulism. When the bacteria-averse expressed their fears to me, the various horrible ways (in their head) by which I might die, botulism was the specific bogeyman most people could name. Hardly anyone these days actually knows someone who's gotten botulism, of course, but somewhere along the way, the horribleness of it has been imprinted on us. Like shark attacks and clowns, it's just one of those things we humans instinctively know to fear.

Here was the logic of my concerned friends: if I'm inviting bacteria into my food, wouldn't I *have* to be increasing my chances of contracting botulism or some other horrible ancient plague? The chances of consuming the wrong bacteria would have to be greater from eating *some* bacteria than from eating *no* bacteria at all. Seems like basic common sense. While we're all fairly unlikely to be eaten by a shark or a clown, statistically speaking, our chances must improve somewhat if we go swimming in the ocean, and would be even worse still if we regularly sneak backstage at the circus.

But don't look too surprised when I tell you that the opposite is actually true. (Well, in the case of bacteria, at least . . . maybe not so much with the clowns.) With the exception of meat, which can blur the lines between fermentation and rot in unique and special ways that we'll tackle later, it is near to impossible for pathogens to exist in a fermented environment. Microbes have had innumerable generations to hone their weapons, and when given the opportunity to muster overwhelming odds against invasive foes, they do not fail. Practically speaking, only mold can encroach on this territory, and it must attack from above, from outside of the domain of the fermented goodies. Experiments have shown that hostile strains of *E. coli* introduced to a wooden barrel of cheese will be utterly snuffed out by the cheese-making microbes resident in the wood. When fermenting (just about anything that isn't meat), we don't have to worry about which bacteria are safe and which aren't.

Remember: bacteria are present on almost everything in its native state, and even innocent-looking vegetables can harbor both friendly and unfriendly ranks, especially in some recent, highly publicized cases of raw veggies contaminated by run-off from factory farms. In the best-case scenario, fruits and veggies are just fermentations that haven't started yet, and you're very likely to have consumed plenty of bacteria from that salad you had for dinner last night. Bacteria are omnipresent. They're already on your vegetables, whether you allow fermentation to begin or not. Until one strain is given the chance to dominate, the native ecosystems of microbes will continue to coexist side by side, waiting. "In light of recent outbreaks of foodborne illnesses traced to spinach, lettuce, tomatoes, and other raw vegetables, I think it would be fair to say that fermented vegetables are safer than raw vegetables," writes Sandor Katz in *The Art of Fermentation*.

Canning, on the other hand, has a catch. Pasteurization through heat *should* work, as common sense would suggest that nothing could survive a journey through boiling water. How could fire possibly fail to kill all?

Botulinum is a toxin produced by *Clostridium botulinum* bacteria. While recent cases of death from botulism are quite rare, almost everyone is at least familiar enough with the deadly neurotoxin to fear it, perhaps simply because of its status as one of the deadliest toxins known to man. A mere microgram—one millionth of a gram—is enough to kill you. One can dodge a mold invasion just by keeping your eyes open. Botulism, on the other hand, hardly needs a foothold at all. And being completely odorless, you might never know it's there until it's too late.

How can this particular bacteria survive the pasteurization temps of canning? Well, the bacteria itself can't. But a high-temperature, low-oxygen environment will stress the bacteria into producing its toxins, which are, unfortunately, the substance that's so deadly to us, rather than the bacteria itself. While boiling may kill off bacteria, the toxins can survive temperatures up to 250°F (121°C). And since we've done botulism the favor of killing its competition by boiling everything else to death, there's nothing to destroy the toxins that remain in the food.

Botulism will not survive in a highly acidic environment. Few things will. Our friendly bacteria and yeast can eventually choke on too-high concentrations of their own weapons, be that acidity or alcohol, which explains why distilled fermented beverages are virtually eternal. So while fermentation is generally an anaerobic (oxygen-free) environment, a jar of fermenting cucumbers will never allow C. *botulinum* to gain a foothold due to the immediate acidity it creates. Even beer, wine, and other alcoholic beverages are too low in pH for the deadly toxin, and they enjoy the added protection of alcohol.

Acidity also explains why vinegar pickles are perfectly safe to make at home. Vinegar itself employs a complex fermentation that results in an ultra-low pH, an environment where botulism won't have a chance. That blitzkrieg of acidity eliminates almost all concerns. Home canning *is* easy and safe when a sour flavor is already associated with the food. Vinegar adds both a safety net and a new dimension to preserved, canned cucumbers.

Or pickles, if you like. Semantics. These pickles also make it very difficult to explain why not everything that tastes sour is fermented. After all, a *Lactobacillus*-pickled cucumber and a vinegar-pickled cucumber both taste more or less like, well, a cucumber pickle. What else are you going to call them?

To add to the confusion, canning vegetables and fruit implies that pasteurization through heat is being used to ensure a safe environment, and, in most cases, boiled vinegar is also added. Boiling-hot vinegar is surely a bath nothing can survive. But if one were to simply brine vegetables in vinegar, without heating it up first, could native bacteria survive? Theoretically, if the acidity of the vinegar were not too severe, or if it were raw vinegar, still containing its own blend of microbes, could, technically, some additional fermentation occur?

Probably, yes. Is there a way to tell just how much something has been fermented? Some sort of measurement of degrees, maybe a scanner to indicate Bacteria Power Level? Sadly, not that I'm aware of.

Here's a quick cheat on your quest to find fermented pickles: skip anything at room temperature in the grocery store. The pickles labeled "half sour" or "full sours" in the cooler are almost certainly fermented the old-fashioned way, and whole pickles are a much more likely bet than those in slices or spears. Another way to know for sure is to check the ingredients list. If vinegar is listed, those pickles are likely not fermented, as the vinegar did the souring instead. No vinegar listed under ingredients, and you are almost certainly holding some fermented cucumbers.

I warned you that this was complicated. So many questions in fermentation are best answered intuitively, by gaining a general understanding of how these forces work, but the lack of cut-and-dried explanations can be frustrating. If you simply haven't thought to tie the word "fermentation" to one time-honored, traditional process spanning many foods, it's easy to miss its connection to the bigger picture. Early in the year, seeking out new sources for good pickles in my area (pickle browsing: a normal way to spend a Sunday afternoon), I stopped at a fledgling flea market in a cavernous, half-empty old mall. Most vendors were selling trinkets and quirky antiques, with a few food vendors tucked in the back. One, though, occupied a prominent position right inside the entrance, virtually unchallenged in offering snacks to shoppers. It was a pickle stand, and I caught word that this gentleman's pickles were particularly renowned. At other locations where he set up shop, I was told, the line often stretched so far back as to block other vendors.

Whole pale-green pickles floated in plastic-lined barrels brimming with murky brine flecked with garlic and spices. You could practically see the bacteria in there. These had to be fermented. Just to be sure, though, I asked the man behind the barrel: "Are all these pickles fermented?" I knew the question would quickly begin to sound obnoxious if I asked it of every server of every restaurant throughout the year, but it seemed like a fairly reasonable question to ask a professional pickle maker.

He stared at me for a moment, then looked away, as if ready to move on to the next, less-prying customer. A shrug. "I'm not really sure."

I pressed on; I had to make up my mind whether to order some. "Do you add vinegar to them?"

"Oh, no. No vinegar."

"Okay, cool. So they ferment themselves."

A slightly more curious look. "Well, if you say so!" He turned to his teenage assistant. "Guess you're never too old to learn something new."

So, all you amateur jar enthusiasts can take comfort in this: you don't even need to know what fermentation is in order to make great pickles.

And, unfortunately, vice versa. Being able to sniff out fermented things from non-fermented-but-similar things—while a fun party trick that will no doubt earn you scores of new friends and an unassailable reputation as a fun guy to be around—does not automatically make you a master of DIY fermentation. There's another reason vinegar pickling of cucumbers took off and outpaced the old-fashioned way: fermented cucumber pickles are actually somewhat tricky to make. While vinegar-pickled cucumbers tend to stay crisp and crunchy for a long time and can easily be packaged in well-packed slices, fermented pickles lose that expected consistency fairly quickly. Not a big deal if you're preparing whole barrels that will sell quickly at the market, but it's a bit more of a challenge for those of us making just a couple of jars at a time at home. Especially when, with a dozen other ferments lining your shelves due to some crazy book project you took on, you forget to eat them until a few weeks later.

Okay, so I'm admitting here that my first batch of pickles was a bit of a disappointment. No one promised that fermented foods have to come out perfect every time. Frankly, part of the appeal is that you're attempting to harness the chaotic entropy of the world around you. In this case, entropy manifested itself as a jar of too-soggy cucumbers with a pungent, aged garlic flavor permeating their flesh. I was not a fan. I ate the contents of one jar, somewhat reluctantly, and let the other sit on top of my fridge for an undetermined period of aging. Maybe I'd see how they were holding up a year later, at the end of my fermentation quest.

While fermented veggies may offer numerous benefits that their pasteurized and canned brethren cannot, there's no denying the appeal of pickling. A preference for consistency in our food is hard-wired into our brain; our animal instinct wants to know we're consuming something previously established to be safe. But pickling in vinegar is limiting in many ways, too. And truly, nothing beats the ease and satisfaction of homemade sauerkraut.

My first batch, that giant jar of red cabbage kraut, actually turned out excellent. After a month, I repackaged it into smaller jars and let them hibernate in my fridge until summoned as a side dish. One advantage of fermented foods: they age well. Remember, these foods are alive, quite literally. Flavors and textures develop, shift, expand. Sometimes in intriguing and beguiling ways. Other times in slightly odd ways. Radishes fermented whole lose some of their pungent kick, but after soaking in brine for days, they pick up a mushy, soft texture that's disconcertingly different from the snap one expects when biting into a radish.

If some of these quirks sound off-putting, remember that we're diving into an entirely new genre of flavors here. You may love some, and you may hate some. But let's not lie to ourselves: we love variety, or at least the illusion of it. We are familiar with so many categories of food these days, to the point where even our most basic, no-frills grocery stores have to be broken down into dozens of different categories of cuisine. It's time to add a few lost categories back to the shelves and embrace the funk.

An early favorite of mine—perhaps the first veggie ferment I ever attempted, before I actually started this project—was fermented beets. Or perhaps I should say fermented beet juice, as the liquid was what I was really after. You'll hear this ferment referred to as beet kvass, especially if you go researching it via the various health and nutrition blogs documenting its numerous health benefits. It's supposedly derived from an old Eastern European traditional recipe.* If you hate the flavor of beets, then perhaps you won't like this one, because it comes out pretty much exactly how you'd expect sour, salty beet juice to taste. Some of the earthiness inherent in the beets is curbed a bit by the briny funk that emerges, but you can also spice it up, add some ginger or herbs, if a pure blast of beet doesn't sound as appealing to you as it does to me.

Anyway you dice it, beet kvass is so incredibly easy to make on its own, requiring no more effort than peeling and quartering some beets, that it may be the ideal introduction into the world of sour fermented vegetables. Beets contain plenty of sugar, which results in a dynamically visible fermentation. Watch, in the first few days, as this vibrant, intensely purple liquid bubbles and froths, and you will quickly understand the fundamental magic of fermentation. You may not be able to see the microbes themselves, but you will certainly see what they're doing. Just don't seal that lid too tightly.

Mold is even more easily avoided in liquid ferments than with solids like sauerkraut that tend to poke their way above the safety of the brine, but a few harmless corollaries to the fermentation process may still spook you if you aren't prepared. Internet message boards covering fermentation bloom with novice fermenters snapping murky pictures of some strange patch of color and asking, in panic: "Is this mold?" Often, the suspicious patch in question is not mold, and there's no cause for fear. Mold is fairly easily to identify. It's got that distinctly fuzzy texture that makes us cringe at the sight of it . . . or even as I think about it, writing this sentence. You know it when you see it, as they say.

---

*Most of the Eastern Europeans I've talked to have never heard of fermenting beets this way and are only familiar with kvass made from bread. Regardless, the name seems to have stuck.

If your mysterious patch is a flat white raft on the surface of the liquid—usually there are a couple of these clustered together—chances are you've just got some innocent yeast. Yeast and bacteria, while as different on the tree of life as humans and turtles are (*Note:* that is an approximate, not scientific, analogy), have nonetheless joined forces for much of their history to mutually consume a common food source. Most ferments tend to favor one or the other, but it can be hard to break apart that long, strange alliance, especially when you're presenting the microbes with an appetizingly diverse food source. Raw beets contain quite a bit of sugar for a vegetable, and other starchy plants like potatoes also favor both bacteria and sugar-hungry yeast.

The result is something called a pellicle, and it's truly a sight to behold. It's easy to see how one might mistake the colony of microbes for mold or something more ominous: it is a floating mass of bubbles and ropey white canyons, something that looks like it might be found deep within a cave. Yet a pellicle is totally harmless, a mere physical manifestation of the microbes already in your food.

I first encountered a pellicle when brewing beer. They're a common, even expected sight in the world of sour beer makers. Home-brewers are so proud of the surreal skin of bubbles floating atop their beverage that there are whole forum threads online devoted to sharing "pellicle porn." Strange as this may sound, you might begin to understand when you see how varied and fascinatingly bizarre these things can get. I've been guilty of oohing and ahhing and snapping photos of some particularly badass pellicles on my own beverage ferments from time to time.

When a pellicle popped up on my jar of sweet potato wedges that were intended to become "fermented French fries," it was a jarring sight, even for me. Most of my veggies prior to this had simply fizzled and gurgled for a few days, with maybe a few patches of yeast floating to the top at their most dramatic. But this here was a pretty serious pellicle; I had an aggressive culture of something going, whatever it was.

If I hadn't seen a pellicle before, in a more expected context, I certainly would have been horrified. Anyone less well versed in microbial habits might have immediately tossed the contents, and one could hardly blame them.

The fries still tasted good. As with many fermented variations on ordinary foods, the texture is slightly, almost disconcertingly different from the stuff you're used to, but the flavor poses an impossible-to-describe twist.

One has to wonder at the reaction from the various humans throughout history who have opened up a vat or jar or crock of sugary, starchy liquid, only to be greeted by the alien landscape of a real funky pellicle. And furthermore, the curiosity and guts of those brave gastric explorers willing to consume something so strange looking, with no real idea whether it might kill them or not. How could a monk at a brewery operating in the 1300s possibly know that this mass of solid, caked-over bubbles was actually a membrane of yeast and bacteria, all of them friendly to humans, happily munching away at the sugars below? You'd have to be brave enough to reach in for a sample. Fortunately, people did. Perhaps their gut instinct simply told them, "Well, it doesn't look like a fuzzy mold," and that was enough. Perhaps a month without anything to drink seemed like the worse alternative.

Usually, fermentation isn't quite so dramatic. In the winter, most ferments tend to be tame, as the cooler weather favors more of our desired lactic acid–producing bacteria, and encourages them to work more slowly, with less of a show. The heat of summer, on the other hand, can bring a frenzy of activity as the ecosystem of bacteria diversifies considerably, and all of them work at a more frantic, sweaty pace.

Summer also tends to make those fears of mold far more likely to become real. Warm weather stirs up activity in any kind of life, just as the cold inspires hibernation. Yet I found mold fairly easy to avoid, with a few exceptions. Early on, mold got to one batch of veggies: the only batch I lost to the fuzz. It was a jar of green beans, and after contemplating the density of the white, nasty mass squatted atop them, I didn't even bother trying to salvage the batch.

Sure, maybe I should be a more adventurous eater, but the smell was thoroughly unappealing and it was only a small jar. I hadn't been looking forward to the batch *that* much, I decided.

After pondering it later, and checking my notes, I knew exactly why those green beans succumbed to mold. I had bought them along with a whole roster of other veggies for a second big fermentation session in early February. The beans were a bit past their prime (actually, well past their prime). The midsections and tips had already begun to break down, leaving a pasty, dark-green mush that rubbed off on my fingers as I cut them up. I tried to avoid the saddest-looking of the bunch, using only the beans that remained crunchy, but apparently it didn't matter. On the microbial battleground I had tried to stake a claim in, the opposing forces were already too far along and weren't about to be driven out by the *Lactobacillus* counterattack. My beans were already on the path to decay.

And so I got a bit of both. They fermented, but decay wasn't about to be held off for long. It was a simple mistake and a good lesson to learn: the quality of what you're fermenting matters. It's almost never too late for fermentation to occur, but one has to understand its limits and your own willingness to embrace the forces of both life and rot simultaneously.

But understanding these few basic concepts, you can pickle just about any vegetable. Some, of course, more easily than others. Some may be prone to gnarly pellicles, which can take the ferment in a more interesting direction than you might like. Some may simply warp in the direction of strange textures, strange consistencies. Other ferments may bring out harsh, bitter flavors or just lose what made them appealing in the first place.

When people asked me throughout the year what I most looked forward to eating again after my fermented-only diet was over, I had a hard time coming up with an answer that felt really genuine, at first. Half the "catch" of this project, to me, was that I could recreate practically anything with enough effort. French fries and pizza were almost too easy, but it made for a bit of fun explaining how and why.

A burger would be a bit more of a challenge, though corned beef is on the spectrum, and Reuben sandwiches were one of the few readily available on-the-go meals I could count on. Not exactly a burger, but at least it was something similar that I could enjoy.

So what did I really miss? A burger and fries and milkshake had been a fitting last meal, but I wasn't absolutely dying in anticipation of having them again. Maybe something sweet, maybe a sleeve of leftover Christmas cookies and cupcakes. But to be honest, the less sweet stuff I ate, the less I missed it. Overly sweet treats had begun to seem cloying to me for a few years now, and while I wouldn't turn down a cupcake upon my return to normalcy, it really wouldn't be my first choice, either.

There was one food that had been a particular favorite of mine that I'd already assumed I wouldn't be enjoying for the duration of 2014. One food, right at the onset, I missed a whole lot.

I love avocados. They've become trendy lately, one of those versatile throw-em-on-anything foods that everyone seems to decide they love feverishly all at the same time, like bacon and pumpkin spice. But for good reason. Despite actually being a fruit, avocados are the perfect vegetable package: portable, easy to chew and digest without any sort of preparation, creamy in texture, and packing a lot of energy without a lot of sugar. And let us not forget: we couldn't have guacamole without them. Where would we be without guacamole, I ask you?

So why didn't I just ferment avocados? Sure, it can be done. I found a few recipes online. The results, I'm afraid, didn't look terribly appetizing. The avocado's fatal flaw is that it suffers from enzymatic browning when exposed to oxygen. We've all encountered the party bowl of guacamole after it's been out for a few hours— craters carved out by chips, all brown and ugly at the surface. Avocados are one of the few foods that are really best consumed fresh.

Sadly, this is a bit contrary to the goals and methods of fermentation. Some things work; others just don't. With some it can simply be hard to find the balance, as in the case of the mighty pickle, another frequent victim of over-sogginess. And it's all personal preference. It's all one fun experiment until you find that which blows open new doors of flavor and that which doesn't. I love the transformation of tough, indigestible cabbage into the texture of its fermented state. Baseball stadium kraut, that sad mass-produced stuff slopped onto hot dogs, is all mush. But homemade kraut can strike a perfect balance between its original crisp crunch and a more weathered, wilted state. There's still resistance in your mouth, but only just enough. Maybe it's why cabbage is one of the most popular bases for fermented veggies in the world: it's almost like it's designed for it.

But aged avocados? Brown and gooey or soggy, thinning, floating sadly in brine. Neither really sounds like how I want to remember and cherish my favorite vegetable-that's-actually-a-fruit. But it turns out there are other ways to ferment veggies than just brining them. I was thinking too small, and I'd have to leave the comfort of my gurgling mason jars to find it.

MY FIRST BIG TRIP OF THE YEAR WAS TO NEW ORLEANS, IN FEBRUARY, for Mardi Gras.

I wasn't looking forward to this trip for a number of reasons. New Orleans is a swell-enough town, but Mardi Gras in particular struck me as very much not my thing. I am not what you would call a "party person." I am more of a "hermiting myself away on a mountain to get some writing done" type of person.

Disliking massive drunk crowds hurling cheap plastic jewelry at each other is one thing. But logistically, the parades made the city extremely difficult to explore. Floats bisect the town, shutting you off from sections of the Big Easy like a moat. Situate yourself strategically on one side, or you aren't going far. Add the sheer chaos of Mardi Gras on top of this, and I assumed I would be spending most of my time stationary, making the best of whatever grilled cheese sandwich I could dig up at the nearest pub.

One day, exploring the city on foot when the trolley was too busy to be bothered with and no taxis could be found, I realized my calorie intake for the day was likely to consist of no more than the bottle of strawberry kefir I was carrying around. I'd begun a demoralizing relationship with mealtime.

Fortunately, New Orleanians do enjoy food from time to time, and I stumbled across a few specialty shops even on my limited travels. Some delicious cheese and charcuterie were had. In the mornings, fantastic iced coffee and more could be found in Stein's Market & Deli, a sandwich spot with a fantastic selection of cured meats, good beer, and other delicacies.

All in all, I would have come out fine. Limited as my options were, I could more or less survive on the common menu items that counted so long as I ignored some sharp, hunger-induced mood swings.

That was my goal for those three days in New Orleans: survival. I expected no revelations. I certainly didn't expect to be won over by the gaudy parades. If I made it out without getting clobbered in the face by a twirling mass of purple beads, I would count the trip a reasonable success.

But the fermentation gods would smile upon me yet. At the end of a trip on which I expected to drown in cheese, I ended up discovering an entirely revolutionary fermentation method—a technique I almost certainly would never have come up with on my own.

At Carmo Cafe, in the Lafayette Square Historic District, I caught a glimpse of a fascinating-sounding menu item: a daily *shio koji* platter. While I was (and remain) no expert on the many diverse and complex Eastern approaches to fermentation, I recognized koji as the common term for *Aspergillus oryzae*, a mold used to make sake, soy sauce, and miso.

Utilizing koji, from their descriptions, could mean only one thing: fermentation. You don't get mold all over your food on purpose without aiming for a bit of edible entropy. How does one make a platter of substantial foodstuffs out of moldy soy and rice, anyway? I was dying to find out.

Clutching the menu like a treasure map, I hurried to the counter to order.

"Let me check to see if we have any left . . ." I was told.

A brief moment of panic.

"Just one more. You're in luck."

No one has ever been so excited to hear that a restaurant had some moldy food left over in the back as I was just then.

As I waited, I pried for details. The koji-master himself wasn't there at the time, but so far as I could glean from talking to the staff, the contents of the platter were buried in a mass of koji and allowed to develop in the snug embrace of this moldy incubation chamber. Because they are dunked in a well-established culture that's already embraced a life of fermentation for some time, it doesn't take long for these new guests to be properly fermented themselves.

It was a technique that, before walking into that restaurant, I had only a vague inkling of, a poorly formed sketch in the back of my mind from mentions in the fermentation guidebooks I'd read previously. It helps to think of the microbes doing the work of fermentation as inhabiting a medium. Be that a salty brine or a sandbox of soybeans, the microbes are swimming around our food in order to work on it, to digest it. The workings of *Aspergillus oryzae* are quite complex, but in this case, I wouldn't be eating the medium itself—as I would if I were eating miso, which is reduced to a brown, creamy, umami-rich paste during its long koji-hosting lifespan. Instead, I would be eating brief guests the koji had hosted and influenced.

The process seemed intuitive to me, the goals and basic principles similar to those of other vegetables I might ferment at home, but the concept of using some sort of semisolid quicksand as an incubation culture was kind of mind-blowing. An entirely new medium in which to ferment things! No longer was a jar filled with salt brine the only option, a potential soggy death for so many textural foods. With this method, almost anything could be fermented, I figured: cucumbers, sweet potatoes, eggs, sharks, Double Stuf Oreos, etc.

The server set down the platter in front of me.

"Today's platter consists of tofu, fermented for two or three days."

The white slivers looked more or less like normal tofu, but less crumbly, with a mozzarella-like consistency. The transformation was subtle but evident.

"Coconut slivers, fermented for about twenty-four hours. Zucchini, for two days. And avocado, fermented for four days."

Avocado. Fermented avocado. I had found the Holy Grail. The server could not have possibly understood the look I gave the food before me.

"Almost everything gets between one to four days in the koji," he went on. "Hardly anything needs more than four days, but with some things, it can be interesting. The tofu just becomes really cheesy if you leave it in there too long."

Old cheesy koji tofu sounded amazing to me, but alas, it wasn't on the menu that day. Couldn't complain. My happiness at finally finding a novel dinner, and the last of it left for the day, was now dwarfed entirely by my excitement at finding a real, live fermented avocado.

There was a small dish of soy sauce for dipping—another cleverly paired koji creation. It added a final delicious layer to the tofu. The coconut slivers were lovely on their own. The avocado was as avocado-y as I could hope for. Its texture was soft and overripe, slightly mushier in consistency, with a frazzled surface that hinted at its koji bath. There was just a hint of funk in the flavor, a slight background tang, and a deeper impression of rich umami character. It was different from a regular avocado in some exciting yet imperceptible way. Hardly any enzymatic browning. Hardly any indication that this avocado had been peeled and left to sit out for a number of days.

After all, it had simply been transposed from the cocoon of its hard shell into another cocoon, ripe with microbes.

It was delicious.

Back home, I researched the various methods of these Eastern-style pickles with microbial incubation chambers. For all my conviction that fermenting vegetables is one of the easiest things in the world, I had not accounted for the various ways other cultures have found to ferment something. It's not always as easy as shredding and cubing and plopping into a jar.

The shio koji platter I had enjoyed at Carmo Cafe in New Orleans fell under the scope of a broad Japanese fermentation tradition called *tsukemono* ("pickled things"). But while Western picklers almost always rely on a liquid salt brine, the Japanese employ various media in which to grow their cultures. That shio koji platter was host to koji, naturally, and "shio" just means salt. But koji, in the form of moldy rice bran, requires some work to produce in the first place, and I was already juggling a daunting number of fermentation projects. It was growing hard enough to keep track of all the different jars sitting around my house, and the more distinct cultures I began to use, the more likely I was to botch something (or just forget about it for a few days too many).

Hoping for a simpler-but-similar alternative that didn't require tending to koji first, I investigated the list of other tsukemono ferments. *Misozuke* means that something has been fermented in miso, while *kasuzuke* uses sake lees as a fermentation medium. *Karashizuke* jumps off from kasuzuke by adding mustard to the lees. But *nukasuke* sounded the simplest: a fermentation method for vegetables buried in rice bran that used nothing more than the vegetables themselves as the starter. That sounded like a reasonable escalation in difficulty: same as my usual process, just with rice bran instead of water, I figured.

I ran into my first hiccup when I couldn't find rice bran locally. I read online that wheat bran could be used instead, though, and a local natural food store did carry that. A bowlful of bran, the hard outer layer of a wheat berry, kind of looks like a bowl full of cereal from a distance. I read that one can often source it from a local bakery, as its tendency to go rancid quickly makes it an unwanted accessory to flour, and thus it's often discarded. Except wouldn't the high oil content and that whole rancidification thing be an issue if I was fermenting with the stuff too? I wondered. Only one way to find out.

Nukasuke, while easier sounding than the miso method, still requires an additional first step: prepping the bran. To give the bran full credit, it really exists as its own individual fermentation in this process, with whatever vegetables you add simply joining the party. And thus it earns its own name on the growing list of nomenclature I would have to learn: *nukadoko*.

Every guide I read told me that to get that nukadoko started, I first had to roast it until it just begins to change color, for reasons I didn't quite understand. Some said that the roasting temperatures were meant to kill "bad" microbes nesting in the bran, but the temps wouldn't be warm enough to hurt the good bugs. I didn't think that sounded quite right—*Lactobacillus* starts to get uncomfortable above 120°F and won't survive for very long above 140°F—but maybe the roasting was some simple flavor enhancement that had become tradition without anyone really remembering why. Regardless, I made the mistake of overloading my pan, making a mess and roasting the wheat bran a bit unevenly. The stuff began to smell, unexpectedly, exactly like popcorn. Transferring it into the large glass bowl I planned to ferment in, some clumps came out a too-dark brown, while the rest was just dusty tan powder. Close enough, I hoped. I still wasn't entirely sure what my goals here were.

But a bowl of bran powder wouldn't create an anaerobic environment entirely conducive to fermentation on its own. It can't become vegetable quicksand without some water. The goal is to get it to the consistency of actual wet sand, so I measured out an estimate of the water I'd need and boiled it with some salt. While that cooled, I poured into the bran half a bottle of a sour beer I'd made a few months earlier. I'd read that adding a bit of beer is often done for an additional layer of protection, and this one happened to have a healthy population of *Lactobacillus* in it for some bonus bacteria.

I'd decided to go with radishes for the trial run of my *nuka* pot. Some sources suggested simply discarding the first vegetables to run through the ferment, as they were more of a starter for the bacteria than anything else. I hadn't been loving the other radish ferments I'd tried so far, which was bumming me out, as I love radishes in their raw form with a bit of salt and spice. These mildly fermented, salted radishes shouldn't turn out too different, I figured, so long as it didn't develop an overly soggy nuka. When the water was cool and I poured it into the bran, the resulting texture was somewhere between wet sand and a half-melted snowball. It didn't pack the way I imagined, and the consistency now looked quite a bit different than the pictures of slick wet rice bran I saw online, which seemed to sink into a uniform paste-like consistency that perfectly molded to its environment. Mine felt a bit more like I was a kid piling some leftover stir-fry together and trying to hide a piece of food they didn't want to eat.

I added a bit more water to try to get a more pliable texture, though it didn't help much. The radishes were submerged, certainly, but they didn't feel buried so much as clumped together with some soggy wheat bran. It seemed like an awkward marriage. I tried not to grow skeptical of my success with this experiment, as some will tell you that microbes can feed off of vibes. Didn't want to prematurely kill their self-esteem if they were really ready to surprise me.

Vegetables fermented in brine are incredibly easy to tend to. Depending what kind of fermentation vessel you're using, they may require zero action on your part after the initial preparation, and at most you'll have to burp a lid a few times a day or prod some floaters down back below the brine. Nukasuke, on the other hand, requires twice-daily maintenance. Best practice suggests you stir up the pot with your hands, imparting your own bacteria as you mix up the action happening in the bran. As mold has a much easier time forming on a solid surface, regular stirring is required to keep it at bay, too, especially in the pot's early stages, before it's had the chance to develop a strong community of good microbes.

Gradually I remembered why I had never gotten very good at making sourdough bread, why I haven't had a pet since moving out of my parents' house, and why I remain slightly daunted at the thought of having children in the future: I am not very good with keeping a schedule of regular daily responsibilities. I'm more of a "wing it" spontaneous type. Keeping a sourdough starter or a nuka pot is very much like having a pet, except that if you forget to feed a pet one afternoon, it will be happy to remind you of your neglect. Forget to tend to your nuka pot for too long and it'll just quietly go south on you.

The radishes I pulled from the pot after two days were disappointing as pickles, though that wasn't unexpected. The nuka was too young to do a whole lot of fermenting, but the radishes came out soggy, like wrung-out sponges. They'd managed to soak up an impressive amount of liquid, especially considering the bran still seemed too lumpy to me, too limited in its submersive capabilities. I still felt like it was too dry and unworkable, and yet my radishes were just the opposite.

I composted the radishes and prepared Occupant Number Two: some weird little minisquashes from a local farm. They looked like tiny pyramids stuck to each other base-to-base, but also, you know, like a squash. They were too cool-looking not to buy, but I had no idea how else to eat them, so I figured a sacrifice to the Pit of Bran was not a bad plan. Even if they wouldn't make for very much food, however they came out, they would still provide plenty of microbes to the nuka.

Considering their firm, tough exterior, I was a little surprised when these, too, emerged a soggy, strangely textured version of their past selves. Everything on the platter at Carmo Cafe had maintained a graceful consistency. Whether it was the different method I had chosen or some failure on my part when I assembled the nuka pot, this was not looking like a quick path to fermented avocado. I wasn't even sure I was looking at fermented veggies that had much more appeal over their brined cousins, especially considering the amount of effort required.

For round three, I tried cucumbers. Soggy perhaps, and not very fermented-tasting, but not a disaster. Round four was green and red peppers. They were, we'll say, all right.

I carried my nuka pot with me to work a few times, which was, as you can imagine, cumbersome. But it couldn't be neglected. Extract vegetables, add new vegetables, every couple of days. Introduce new microbes. Cater to existing microbes. Check moisture and salt levels. The nuka must be stirred. Every day, twice a day. Religiously. Faithfully.

I hope you can understand why eventually I maybe started to get a little neglectful. It was a lot of responsibility. And I had no lack of other things going on in my own life, which seemed to have reached a peak fermentation of its own. I was diving deep into research for this very book, while taking on writing projects and workshops to help spread fermentation knowledge whenever I could. I was mulling over a career change and trying to ride out the skepticism of my friends and family and my significant other at all these grand ambitions of mine, some of which resulted in me skipping lunch while at the same time carting about a pot of inedible mush. I was taking it on faith that I would somehow ride out this wave of anxiety and stress, no small amount of it due to the ludicrous difficulty I was facing with my diet. My schedule and my time-management skills were fraying. My life, I was beginning to sense, might continue to bubble along at this frantic state of activity, or just as easily slip into decay. So while it made me more than a little sad, I didn't feel as if I had failed too greatly when, a few weeks into my nuka pot experiment, white patches of mold appeared. Game over.

This wasn't the lesson I'd hoped to learn. I'd hoped to learn how to make fermented avocados. Instead, I was gifted another important lesson: sometimes things just don't work out. Fermentation can be unpredictable. It can result in failure. But when is "predictable" ever interesting, anyway? The hard road is often worth taking, for reasons that may not become clear all at once.

# CHAPTER 4

# At Least I Won't Get Scurvy

'M NOT LIKELY EVER TO MEET ANYONE ELSE WHO FOLLOWED A 100 percent fermented diet for an entire year, much less as a genuine way of life. Without a book to write, it just doesn't make much sense to avoid a lot of the things I had to avoid. I got this deep into my mad fermented quest to prove a point. But then again, I'm not the first to follow an insanely constrained diet of some kind, either out of exploration or necessity. I became fascinated by finding examples of those who followed some similarly narrow food pathway or took up a diet that sounded, to me, much like a microcosm of my Fermented Man journey.

In 2011, J. Wilson undertook the challenge of living off of beer as his only source of calories for the forty-six days of Lent, in a nod to the historic tradition of fasting practiced by Bavarian monks. Of course, Christians throughout the ages have often given up alcohol for Lent. Wilson's sacrifice went the other way—giving up everything but water and four kegs of a specially brewed dopplebock-style beer.

He did just fine on the diet, too, at least as far as not-starving goes. (Whether he was an entirely productive employee at work those afternoons remains unanswered.) He'd lost 22.5 pounds by the end but described his energy level as high. Of course, the pledge was more spiritual fast than brave new diet, and Wilson never intended to show that someone could live off of beer indefinitely. Could I simply imbibe nothing but beer to cruise my way through the Fermented Man diet? I suspected not. Forty days of drinking only a single style of beer sounds a bit exhausting.

We modern eaters are a finicky bunch. Most of us crave endless variety in what we consume, as evidenced by a stroll around a suburban grocery store. Never before in history have humans had the option to eat so many different things at any time.

Such a drastic change in my diet required abandoning (for the most part) the total variety of options I had grown accustomed to, the infinite combinations of dinner dishes, the easily prepared lunches and on-the-go snacks that had always been staples. Rather than simply having to avoid this or that, eating only fermented food for one year felt like learning how to eat from scratch. Shrink one realm of the world down considerably, narrow yourself to a small window of choice, and you begin to see whatever is left quite differently. Rather than assembling food on the fly, meals had to be planned out in advance. Days, maybe even weeks in advance. If I didn't have something ready or waiting in the fridge, the tempeh Reuben I was planning on for dinner wouldn't happen.

Maybe, I'd begin to think, I'll just have a grilled cheese for dinner. Again.

In the city for a day? Thank goodness I can get a grilled cheese at the deli.

A bowl of sauerkraut not filling me up? Obviously, I still need calories in addition to microbes. Let's round that out with a grilled cheese. I felt myself falling into a rut of my own making. And it was only the end of March.

This first curveball to hit me was, I knew, almost entirely psychological. Eating a variety of foods is fairly deeply ingrained in us. We may not be aware of an internal motive for this, but it's likely something instilled in us by the eating habits of our ancestors. Varying our diets, rather than eating just one chunk of steak again and again, proved a good strategy for ensuring our nutritional needs were met. Societies that once lived mostly off meat—including the Inuits, Icelanders, and Scandinavians, all in frosty northern climates—were able to get their full nutrient fix by consuming the entire animal. Whatever you have to work with, taking the path of maximum variety is going to be the best option.

We've lost this habit, preferring to consume lean, aesthetically pleasing chunks of meat and leave the wasted scraps of the animal for our pets or hot dogs. But we haven't lost our desire to eat a lot of different things.

Traveling really drove this point home. Sometimes I might find an unexpected fermented treat, something I wasn't already eating. This required some hunting, however, and required a lot more time and effort than I usually had. Hunting down exotic foods wasn't my full-time job, and since I was committed to doing this diet for a whole year, I still had to eat whatever was available at the time. Preferably three meals a day's worth. I began to crave variety fiercely, while at the same time, some part of my mind kept insisting it was all a trick. An illusion. Had my diet, our diets, ever really been that much more varied to start with? Wasn't I able to eat all the major food groups whenever I wanted?

Many of my meals began to resemble a charcuterie and cheese plate—maybe some bread, Spanish olives, and sauerkraut on the side. Delicious, gourmet even, but a nagging concern haunted me every time I surveyed my inventory: were my meals too monotonous?

It wasn't that I couldn't eat a variety of foods: protein, fat, carbohydrates, and all the vitamins and nutrients in between, all were easily represented, just maybe in different proportions and forms of delivery than my body was accustomed to. I wasn't worried about getting scurvy. Fermented veggies contain more nutrients than their raw counterparts, and as the story goes, Captain Cook discovered that sauerkraut offered a solution to keep his sailors in good health and scurvy-free when fresh foods remained a distant memory on long sea voyages.

I never doubted, before I began the diet or anytime after, that my nutritional needs would be met. It was simply difficult to eat enough to feel truly satisfied. My artificially limited diet had become inconvenient and labor intensive.

It takes a drastic change in perspective to recall that eating was not always so convenient. Consider the absurdity of the modern war on calories from a historical perspective. Our food system now often implies that foods are "healthy" for having the least amount of calories; that high-calorie foods, therefore, are inherently unhealthy, by virtue of the fact that they do their job too well. Indeed there are other flaws in many of the high-calorie foods we eat— that blooming onion is an undeniable monstrosity providing no real nutrition—but the basic notion that calories are somehow inherently bad is a uniquely modern concept. In previous eras, "empty calories" from packaged, processed food had simply not been invented. Calories themselves were not even a concept, though any poor peasant returning from a day's labor in the field would agree that you needed as many of them as could be obtained, whether from beer, cheese, or a fatty cut of meat.

Make it difficult to eat, establish a diet that takes a good deal of effort to land your next meal, and the whole modern conception of food will begin to seem somewhat backward. It was the first of many unintentional eye-opening experiences in my year, even though I'd seen it coming. On the go, or on vacation, I was spending more time discussing what I could eat with my traveling companions than spending time actually eating.

"What's something you could eat there?" a friend would ask, spotting a new restaurant.

"Nothing." (Slight undertones of frustration).

"What about Thai? Shouldn't they have something?"

"Most likely not." (Subtle shades of bitterness).

"There's a Korean place."

"Kimchi isn't a meal." (Thinly veiled despair).

"Italian? Pasta . . . oh, no. Hmmm."

Did I regret agreeing to this project on a number of occasions? Yes, most definitely yes. Did I sigh loudly and with great exasperation after investigating the fifth restaurant in a row where I couldn't eat anything except maybe a few scraps of white bread? Indeed. I apologize to all my patient, accommodating traveling companies with whom I was maybe sometimes a bit curt. While I continued to feel surprisingly healthy, I was definitely not always in the best mood.

There were afternoons where I simply went without eating due to the sheer inconvenience of doing so.

And thus had I discovered a bit of a conundrum. From the beginning, I wasn't meant to be creating a new fad diet, or even claiming that eating this much fermented food was better for you than eating just *some* daily servings of fermented food. Clearly, by any logic, the diet wouldn't be any more optimal for health than if I had simply agreed to eat sauerkraut, yogurt and kombucha every day, on top of whatever else I ate. It was the inclusion of fermentation that was the point, not the exclusion of anything else.

Accidental and unforeseen, this drastic overhaul of what I was allowed to eat, and how restricted my calorie sources suddenly were, would give me new ideas about a lot of things. But for a while, my daily anxiety was how I could fix my hunger pangs when I wasn't at home. Endless grilled cheese? Grilled cheese all the way down?

One day in late spring, I neglected to pack anything for lunch before heading into the office. On my lunch break, I headed straight to a Trader Joe's, figuring their selection of specialty foods was my best chance for a decent meal. I returned to my desk half an hour later with a light shopping bag containing a few wedges of cheese, some bread, and a pouch of kimchi.

I decided the kimchi was close enough to a salad to make do for my lunch. This spicy Korean fermented cabbage is a staple of all Korean diets, consumed with every meal. It is both condiment and side dish, more ubiquitous (and far more versatile) in their cuisine than even French fries or ketchup combined would be to Americans. But it is not, I noticed, considered a meal. Served in dumplings or with some rice, sure. But there is always a foundation beneath it.

For one, an entire bowl of kimchi is not the easiest thing to consume in one sitting. While I love spicy food and probably have a higher threshold for pepper-induced pain than most people, shoveling pepper-coated forkfuls of cabbage into my mouth soon brought about a surge of sweating and tears. Looking at the calories contained in that pouch of kimchi, I realized I'd probably burned more calories chewing and sweating through the (tasty, tasty) stuff than I would earn from digesting it. Cabbage is not a filling food. The ten calories per serving in that pouch were, sustenance-wise, about as helpful as eating a tablespoon of ketchup.

Vegetables in general are not exactly calorie-packed. Perhaps that's why salads throughout history were viewed as a supplement to a meal. Without some non-vegetable topping to bolster the calorie count, most people couldn't live off of salads. Leave out the dressing, the nuts, and the croutons, and there are only a few calories to be gained from your chewing efforts. Nutrients? Sure. But actual energy? Not so much.

While there are hundreds of variations of kimchi, the standard mix is a blend of Napa cabbage, carrots, daikon radish, garlic, and gochukaru red pepper. But recall that sleight of hand that fermentation performs, swapping those few grams of carbohydrates and quietly replacing them with lactic acid and carbon dioxide. Carbon dioxide, you may be surprised to learn, has even fewer calories than a bowl of iceberg lettuce.

For months I couldn't shake a fundamental question: what was I actually *living* off of? What are other people living off of? What did people in the past live off of? Is there a distinction between nutrients and calories, and have we in modern society lost our sense for it?

People would ask: "How do you stay thin when you're eating so much cheese and drinking so much beer?" The thing is, most of these fatty, calorie-packed foods made the proper way are rich and heavy and filling. Believe it or not, it's hard to eat *that* much cheese when you aren't eating all that much else. Believe me, I tried. Cut out the processed stuff, the fried stuff, the easy snacks, the sweet pastries made with bleached white flour, and most of the other normal stuff that makes up our diets . . . again, it's hard to eat *that* much cheese. And I'm positive that it's physically impossible to eat that much cabbage. There was zero chance I'd gain any weight during my year of fermentation.

A grilled cheese for every meal could theoretically do it, I suppose. Grilled cheese is probably the easiest way to pack down fermented calories. That gooey melted stuff, paired with good toasty bread, some mustard, and of course butter to get the right shade of brown on the bottom—fair enough, it would be easy to overindulge in grilled cheese after grilled cheese, certainly one of mankind's greatest inventions. Before beginning, I joked that the subtitle of *The Fermented Man* might end up being "A Year of Grilled Cheese," and once again, an offhand joke threatened to inch toward seriousness.

I tried to use a trip to Philadelphia to break the endless cycle of grilled cheese. Wandering the aisles of a massive farmer's market, I stocked up for breakfast, lunch, and dinner. Despite my best efforts, the three meals, as usual, looked pretty much the same. I picked up some local kefir, a nice surprise to see from Pennsylvania's extensive dairy country, a ball of mozzarella cheese, a baguette, and a quarter pound of Jamón ibérico—Spanish cured pork eaten in thin slices similar to prosciutto. Dairy, meat, bread; breakfast, lunch, dinner. Eat and repeat.

That night, I walked around the streets of downtown Philadelphia eating a ball of mozzarella cheese the size of my fist as if it were an apple. I must have looked unbearably cool to anyone who noticed. But apple-sized balls of cheese weren't going to be enough to get me through the year. After my koji failure, I needed to find some easier ways of thinking outside the box.

Fortunately, I still had a few tricks up my sleeve. Much as vegetarians switching from a meat-filled diet will often seek out substitutes of what they ate before, I figured I could manage a few 100 percent fermented reconstructions of some of my favorite meals. First up: pizza.

Tell people about your plans for fermented pizza, and you can watch gears turn as they picture a traditional slice floating in a jar of brine or maybe, better yet, slices of pizza packed like cabbage leaves all the way to the top, fermenting in their oily juices. Actually, it's not as strange as all that.

Pizza is both a great example and another scapegoat of our post-cultured dietary habits. Consider how close pizza is to an entirely fermented meal already, even in its current commoditized state. The crust is merely bread of a different shape. While sadly few pizza doughs are sourdough these days, even a quick rise with yeast relies on fermentation. The main other component of pizza is that greasy cheese, of course. Another lesson here in how our preparation methods have changed: mozzarella may not always be fermented the way it once was, as much of the cheaper stuff these days is prepared with vinegar. In less than an hour, an enzymatic reaction from the acid transforms our ball of cheese into the stringy, solid form we love. But no matter: mozzarella can be fermented too, and it tastes better for it. And as a nice bonus, the topping so picturesque and inseparably associated with American pizza parlors? Pepperoni: a spicy, fermented sausage.

Pizza is practically defined by fermentation. The only ingredient that remains is the red tomato sauce. And as a simple veggie ferment, that part is incredibly easy. Puree, add spices, ferment, apply to pizza. Or, as I would begin to do later for even greater simplicity: ferment whole cherry tomatoes in brine, then cut up atop pizza, foregoing the "sauce" for a more chunky Italian version that conveniently required less work.

Pizza is easy. And pizza is endlessly versatile, which is perhaps why Americans have adopted it as one of their national foods. We've made a habit of tossing just about anything on a pizza, so it fit just fine into my routine. It's an easy way to consume fermented vegetables like red onions, tomatoes, olives, and peppers, or even sauerkraut and kimchi. They would no longer be live-culture after baking in the oven, of course, but they'd still be delicious. Fermented sauces and pastes could be added sparingly for more flavor impact. Toppings as simple as prosciutto with balsamic vinegar are especially delicious.

The concept is incredibly easy, and the subtle changes potentially dramatic. While I can't claim to be an expert sauce maker, at least not yet, the magic wrought by fermentation, especially with the right blend of spices, promises to open up an exciting new realm of flavor potential. Perhaps it's a culinary trick that will one day catch on. Pair a fermented sauce with a whole grain sourdough crust, and you've got yourself a formidable fermented meal.

Pizza helped to restore some illusion of diversity into my diet, while at the same time reinforcing how psychological this all was. Wasn't I still just eating bread and cheese with some veggies on the side? What did it matter if it was laid out before me as a basic wooden-board cheese plate, bread and butter on the side and a dish of kraut or pickles to pair with the rest? Why did the pizza seem so much more like a meal?

Maybe it's habit, or maybe it's another ingrained evolutionary hint. Cooking (most) food is generally a beneficial if not vital step to unlocking its full nutritional potential. Not only are we modern eaters big fans of varied, complex flavors, but we enjoy lots of flavors combined, all together, in some sort of prepared dish. The rare foods we still frequently eat on their own—slabs of meat, mainly— are heavily seasoned and transformed in both flavor and texture by heat.

We are inclined to cook. And by cook, I don't just mean the use of a stove or microwave to prepare food. I mean that we modern eaters are not only trained on variety, but complexity.

Maybe it's not just modern eaters, come to think of it. Tales of varied and elaborate feasts can be found in pretty much any ancient text with a long-enough word count. We have always fetishized our meals, and without cable television, previous cultures simply wrote out their food porn at length.

At some point, this type of literary tangent started to die out in mainstream prose. Food was too abundant, this sort of overindulgent smorgasbord too obtainable and everyday to be titillating. Why read about it when we could just go to the all-you-can-eat buffet down the road?

But there is a noticeable difference in the tone of "feast literature," something that doesn't seem to have an equivalent in modern storytelling, or even our contemporary fascination with food television. Clearly, a fundamental shift occurred in those intervening generations between village feasts and celebrity chefs. Our obsession with food did not necessarily lose sight of fetishizing abundance and variety—those things simply became so ordinary for much of the world that we needed a new culinary lens to feel justified in our salivations.

Having worked previously as a server at an establishment with well-hyped all-you-can-eat seasonal specials, I can tell you that comically unnecessary quantities of food beyond any human's daily needs no longer inspire reverence and awe. This is now expected, ordinary; it is a basic demand of our food supply. (And, still speaking from personal experience here, we do not tip well when presented with this new bounty). High end restaurants are often parodied for their undersized portions, so assumed is the normality of unlimited feasts.

So the narrative of food fetishizing has shifted. It is now the ingenuity and complexity of a meal that we mythologize, that we want tempting us from our television screens, theoretically inspiring us to attempt such culinary feats ourselves. Are we now obsessed with mastering such dishes in our own kitchens? Perhaps some of us try to invest the time; most of us likely become frustrated by how challenging it all is, however easy the professionals make it look. Perhaps a few of us actually have the time and skill to succeed at making our own elaborate meals on a regular basis.

But the desire has been planted: at heart, we crave abundance, variety, complexity, and, above all, elaboration. We want to cook, to prepare something new, to create a mélange of flavors and textures. Or, failing that, to have someone cook for us.

And who do we turn to for that? How do we satiate our lifelong desire for elaborate and varied food? Those who can cook, and cook really well, are always in demand. The restaurant industry is one of the most tumultuous yet unmovable industries in America. It is one of the riskiest types of businesses to open, yet that doesn't stop thousands from giving it a try each year, all to meet our desire for new options, even of the same basic genres of cuisine. But for those of us without the economical or practical option to eat a hand-crafted meal of this sort on a regular basis, the food system has ways of fulfilling our desires anyway. Chain restaurants offer the assurance of familiarity and consistency, the reassuring illusion that some Tuscan chef, somewhere in Italy, is working in the background to conceive these uniform dishes. It seems odd that fast food would be required to offer variety and complexity to meet expectations, yet bless their go-getter attitude, national chains still find novel ways to sell you the same five ingredients wrapped up in a new shell and given a punchy made-up name.

Even fast food seems like a better fallback option than so many of the prepared meals lurking on grocery store shelves—undying, unchanging, squatting in their final form, the supposed shape of a meal. Something prepared. Something slightly elaborate, even if, really, it would take about the same amount of time to combine those three or four basic ingredients and put them in the oven. However lazy those packaged foods may seem, they at least promise that you're getting a meal. A balanced combination of ingredients carefully thought out; the embrace of warm red sauce and something resembling cheese to lift you above the chaos of this world. We'll eat anything as long as it's presented in the guise of a meal.

All through my fermented year, I couldn't believe how difficult it was to escape the gravitational pull of the meal, the illusion of cooking something to make it more interesting. But consciously I knew it was often redundant: fermentation *is* a form of cooking. It not only preserves but prepares food, with microbes, rather than a microwave.

Many intellectuals, writers, and anthropologists over the years have attributed some significance to the fact that we are the only animal that cooks its food. Clearly this sets us apart from animals, but so do many other things: culture, complex language, art, architecture, a desire to continue wearing watches even after they've become completely irrelevant, Led Zeppelin, etc. But more recently, scientists like Richard Wrangham, in his book *Catching Fire*, have argued that it was cooking itself that first started us on this path, before even factors like tools and language and music.

Raw food necessitates a significant increase in time and energy for the body to process it into something useful, resulting in fewer calories obtained for the effort. Raw food is an expenditure in energy in both its acquisition and its digestion, which is why most animals spend a significant portion of their day in both the pursuit and internal processing of it. One of our closest relations in the animal world, chimpanzees, spends ten times longer chewing and eating than we do—48 percent of the day, compared to a scant 4.7 percent of our human hours. Wrangham, a Harvard biologist and anthropologist, estimates that our ancestors spent about half their waking hours simply chewing their food. Chimps, fellow meat eaters that they are, have under half an hour per day left to hunt, Wrangham estimates, making meat a rare investment in time, an occasional lucky treat.

The body is an engine that is never idle, and while it may seem counterintuitive, the very act of digestion poses a huge caloric cost. Other big hits are keeping the heart pumping (as the writers of many emo ballads can attest) and putting our big brains to use (occasionally). Even when we are resting, and regardless of what we are thinking about, one-fifth of our energy is being funneled into keeping our brain humming. The human brain may be the most sophisticated computer ever created, but it doesn't come cheap.

Evolving a bigger brain, one that would necessitate such a huge allotment of energy, would have required either diverting energy from some other function, or a massive jump in caloric intake. A bigger brain is a great way to solve the riddle of cooking, but in order to get there, well, you need the brain first. A classic chicken versus egg scenario, except we needed to eat both of them to get to the other side of the road ourselves.

And it's too late to back out now. Whatever came first—the thinking, the fire, or the craving for steak—we have little choice. We are invested in cooking. It is, maybe more so than even language, the defining trait of our species. We signed on for bigger brains, our bigger brains taught us to cook better to better feed the brain, and on and on, a cycle of eating and thinking and cooking and killing that's brought us all the way to bacon-flavored everything and chicken nuggets in dinosaur shapes. Doesn't matter what we want to use our brain for, now: we're stuck with it.

If cooking is a necessary part of human life, what happens to us when we stop? You may have heard of the raw food diet, and you may rightly wonder how such a thing could be. There are certainly many foods that are just fine eaten raw, and many foods that might be better for it. Salads are great! In fact, giving up salads was one of the most frustrating aspects of my diet in 2014. And truly, there are few simple joys greater than a sliced ripe avocado sprinkled with salt, an apple plucked from the tree in September, or a tomato fresh from the garden. The raw food diet locks adherents into consuming heaping piles of plants and nuts. Plants are good. Nuts are good. The diet has its heart in the right place but succumbs to the same problem that all modern diets seem to have, what I'm going to dub the issue of "dogmatic exclusionary dieting."

Almost all modern food trends seem obsessed with excluding something in order to fix ourselves. They play to an apparently instinctive suspicion in humans that "good" and "bad" exist within clear-cut boundaries in all things, and by avoiding some category of "bad" foods, we will achieve health. And so, followers of some modern diest are told to avoid [foodstuff] with the devotion of religious zealots.

You may rightly be thinking that I am writing this after months of following one of the silliest, most arbitrary, and most highly exclusive diets one might imagine. It was not without a sense of irony that I began this crazy experiment—more than irony, honestly. From the beginning, I wanted to explore the nature of the extreme diet itself. I set out to prove a point (several points, actually, if we're counting). Not just about the lost art of fermentation, but also about the tedious and arbitrary nature of the modern Western diet.

I'm eating this cheese *symbolically*, you see. (At least, that's what I tell myself so I can sleep at night.)

Unfortunately, the basic, decent advice at the heart of the raw food diet misses the point that things like the concept of a raw food diet wouldn't exist without cooking. Wrangham, the Harvard biologist, notes that in spite of convenient modern technologies like juicers and blenders and year-round access to bananas, nuts, and other high-quality agricultural products (which, most likely, the consumer did not have to expend any energy in growing or harvesting), raw-foodists are often worrisomely underweight. Everyone's body and metabolism are different, and it must be noted that the raw diet may work for some but pose a debilitating threat to others. Some may simply be attempting the diet in order to lose weight, in which case, well, they will very likely succeed. But there are alarming warning signs about the diet's sustainability: one study found that half the women surveyed stopped menstruating due to malnourishment.

Indeed, it is actually possible to starve to death while filling your stomach with raw food. All of which is simply to note that the ability to transform food, the ability to cook, is the foundation of humanity, the root triumph of our species. Keep that in mind the next time you feel stupid about burning your popcorn.

Fire and fermentation both transform food, as we know. Predigesting our food through either method unlocks nutrients that we could not otherwise access, or that would take us an afternoon of chewing to unlock. Heat denatures proteins, allowing our digestive enzymes to tackle them. Only a fraction of the calories in raw starch and protein are absorbed by the body directly via the small intestine. Heat gelatinizes starches, especially helpful in the manufacture of booze. Heat, when put to use by a skilled hand, can improve texture and taste. As can fermentation.

The heat and the microbes are two sides of the food preparation coin.

Both fire and fermentation exist independently in the world around us; neither is an invention of man, but a fleeting natural phenomenon captured, harnessed, and utilized as a tool. The first difference is in the sparks. Whereas mankind likely stumbled upon fermentation by accident, observing its spontaneous occurrence in nature and then adapting that into a controlled, repeatable process, fire is more elusive. Without our intervention, in many parts of the world, fire in nature would be a relatively rare sight. When it happens naturally, it is often as a deadly inferno, as dangerous as it is uncontrollable and unexpected.

While we are so used to the presence of fire in our everyday lives now that we have lost some of our fear of it, the primitive hunter gatherer inside us still feels a primal rush of adrenaline at the staging of a gratuitous fireball—the exploitation of which has defined many a Hollywood career. But try to imagine an era before fire had been harnessed, when all you would have known of the stuff was, every few years, a wildfire tearing across the horizon, ravaging fields and forests and anything you had known briefly as home. Fire would have been a truly distressing phenomenon, as mystic and puzzling as it was deadly. A force of nature that fed insatiably and grew exponentially.

Now imagine the first person to take the leap and suggest that this same terrifying force, capable of leveling a good portion of the world around you, might be an acceptable tool for preparing dinner with the family. You would have chased him out of your tribe on account of his obvious madness.

Conjuring fire is not particularly easy and not particularly intuitive. Given only the raw tools of nature, you are unlikely to ever do it by accident. How many of us have ever actually performed the old Boy Scout trick of rubbing two sticks together to make a spark? I certainly haven't, and I'm an avid camper and hiker. I use matches and newspaper to start my fires because, hey, I don't have that much free time to sit around rubbing tree branches together. I've got writing deadlines. I've got beers to keg.

The sparks of fermentation, unlike the sparks of fire, are easily conjured. They are already there, pending no chemical reaction at all, and indeed are happy to get to work even without you around. The whole world is poised on the edge of fermentation, always. Rather than hours spent smashing wood together, fermentation needs only a nudge.

And then there is the issue of fuel. Fire, meant to cook our food, needs an outside energy source, which can be a problem. As primitive man, as a farmsteader or voyager, as a modern hiker or even a backyard cook, we may have only so much fuel to feed our fire—maybe because there are only so many trees surrounding our small prairie home, or maybe because we're running low on dinosaur fuel to burn. Perhaps even worse, if we aren't careful, this same tool of fire can get away from us, once more demanding fuel from sources we may not want to burn.

Fermentation, as we've seen, requires no outside energy source. The food itself is the fuel. Self-starting and self-fueling, it is the perfect package, a near miracle of sustainable technology.

The raw food diet does address some real and very important concerns with cooking meat. Few subjects are as complicated and fraught with tension, emotion, and gut reactions as the consumption of meat. We love our meat, and for all the flack vegans receive about trying to convert others to their views, I can't imagine there's any group as loud and hair-trigger defensive about food as people who really, really love bacon. But for all the moral complications and politics inherent in our meat, the shifting advice over what causes heart disease and what doesn't, it's starting to look like the improper cooking of meat may actually be the largest issue as far as our health is concerned. Charring meat when cooking generates compounds known as heterocyclic amines, which are carcinogenic. These compounds only form when meat is cooked above 300 degrees, to the point of being well-done. As far as society's recent conviction that meat itself is unhealthy, studies that are able to parse apart cooking method indicate that it's the type of preparation, not the meat itself, that strongly correlates with disease.

That doesn't rule meat out, of course, it just suggests (at least pending more research, as is the way of Good Science) that we should be thinking more about how we prepare our meat. From antibiotic-fueled factory farms packed wall-to-wall with sickly, miserable animals, to our primal instinct to blow stuff up real good with a big hot flame, we need to rethink how we consume. One doesn't have to commit to eating only raw vegan food to accomplish this, just as one doesn't have to give up salads in order to gain the probiotic benefits of sauerkraut. I ate a great deal of meat during my year of fermentation, but looking back, I realize that rarely was it ever near a fire. Sure, the occasional pizza topping got some heat (though not direct flame). But as a calorie-packing and easily portable fix, perfect for hiking or day trips or simply on-the-go snacking, most of the meat I consumed in 2014 was never cooked at all.

While the probiotic bacteria living in the food get all the buzz these days, when discussing the merits of fermentation, the so-called "prebiotic" effects of fermentation may in many ways be of equal importance. Since eating all of our food raw would require a significantly greater investment in resources, we've employed fire and fermentation to do most of the work for us. In fermentation, microbes are literally predigesting our food. But rather than stealing all our energy and nutrients, these microbes often leave more than they started with, at least as far as our digestive systems are concerned. Fermentation can pull many of the same tricks that fire does in unlocking what's already there, and often more successfully, with fewer negative side effects, as in the case of those fermented meats. All the neat and convenient transformations that heat can pull on starches, fermentation can accomplish also. And where fire might scorch certain nutritional components, fermentation generally makes a food that's better for us.

Almost any category of fermented food opens up an avenue of enhanced nutrients, or the removal of something our bodies have a hard time processing. Soybeans, it turns out, are actually rather difficult for the body to digest, making tofu a less-than-ideal meat substitute. And unfortunately, that's the optimistic view. Unfermented soy products contain anti-nutritional factors, components that block our ability to process or utilize nutrients, which can be outright harmful to the body. Soy is a major cash crop in the United States, and even if you've never consumed tofu in your life, you've been eating lots of soy in some form or other. It poses a risk of brittle bones, thyroid issues, memory loss, vision trouble, and more. Try tempeh instead: a slab of soybeans fermented by mold. Or take miso: a nutrient-rich, highly flavorful paste from soy that's fermented with a different species of mold. Same base ingredient, wildly different outcome, and thoroughly transformed in both nutrition and texture by microbes.

And then there's that question of energy use again. Simply cooking the soybeans to make tofu takes about six hours. Fermenting the soybeans into tempeh takes just, well, the mold. It's a theme we'll see again and again: fermentation unlocks the full potential of foods and often does so with greater efficiency.

While my diet may be more ridiculous and arbitrary on the face of it than the raw food diet, there's another big thing the two have in common: how much more difficult gaining weight becomes when you've blocked out a huge percentage of your options.

I didn't want to lose weight. Not getting enough calories on so many random days is not healthy, regardless of your weight goals. Calories are actually the point of eating food in the first place, as you may recall. If you aren't getting calories, it doesn't matter how nutritionally dense what you're eating is. That jar of sauerkraut or kimchi can have all the vitamins in the world, it might even help to prevent cancer down the road, but if it doesn't have calories, your body is going to be running an energy deficit.

It's a concern I know my vegan friends must face on a regular basis. Diets that exclude one or two categories of food can be hard, especially when eating out. But diets that allow only a few categories of food mean eating in some places is simply impractical, if not impossible, and a matter of great effort (or extensive Googling). Not eating for eight hours because there's nothing you *can* eat is probably counter to the whole notion of a basic healthy diet. The madness inherent in these situations was glaring from the start, and there were many weekends where I questioned my sanity, while doing my stomach no favors.

Still, the monks could survive many more days of fasting than the afternoons I endured. If nothing else, I'd survive.

# CHAPTER 5

# Sowing Season

ALL YEAR, PEOPLE LOVED TO ASK ABOUT MY LAST MEAL AND MY first meal. I realized, with a mild sigh of relief, that people responded to the artificial construct of my diet, even understanding that it was more statement than science. Immediately latching on to the exaggerated and absurd lengths of my one-year dogmatic exclusionary dieting, people wanted to pry into the framework of the thing, the borders and boundaries, more so than what was left inside the fence.

My last unfermented meal prior to New Year's, by the way, was a burger and fries and milkshake. I figured I should go hard in the direction of American classic before the next year got real weird. Most people would nod in approval at that. But they rarely followed up to ask what the first thing I ate the next day was: the first fermented meal. They didn't try to pry into the routine of my daily lunches. They weren't as interested in the daily grind of eating, which, it turns out, just gets tedious when examined too closely. People are interested in the big symbolic meal. They wanted to know about what I was giving up.

I can't shake the feeling that we humans love just the construct of diets, to the extent that, for whatever reason, it's built into our psychology. Maybe it's that small insinuation of abstinence that tickles our brain: you can have everything but food containing _____. Do we just get off on withholding?

Was I sneaking hamburgers and salads on the sly? Perhaps I just don't seem very trustworthy (it's the beard), but most seemed surprised that I wouldn't be. Who would possibly know, after all? I seemed to have most people's tacit consent to cheat.

The thing was, I was pretty sure cheating wouldn't make

things any easier unless I was prepared to just really blow it all up and cheat full-time. I didn't need reminders of what I was missing, save for, maybe, that fondly remembered koji-fermented avocado. A burger is no more than bread and cheese and meat, all of which I could already eat. French fries are no more than potatoes, and I could ferment potatoes. Sure, my fermented sweet potatoes got a little strange with their funky pellicle coating, but once they went into the oven, they turned into fries all the same. It was the mental rearrangement, the struggle with the concept of *the meal*, that really ate at me for much of the year. The monotony. The constant cheese. The desperate sprints to the store to restock bread and yogurt.

I didn't really miss any particular thing. I just missed the variety and convenience. Being a lifelong vegan seems harder to me than my diet in the grand scheme of things (one year can only crawl by so slowly), but at least vegans have, by now, small segments of the food industry catering to them.

I missed having the option of eggs for breakfast, rather than just bread and butter and a yogurt smoothie. But how else was I supposed to start the day? How many minimum-effort options did I have?

Pickled eggs are a divisive food, which has always surprised me. I love pickled eggs, especially beet-pickled eggs, which are fairly popular among at least a small crowd of us in northeastern farm country. I don't really understand on what grounds they even need defending: they taste like eggs (good), but pickled (good), and sometimes with the added character of beets (good). No brainer.

I figured I'd re-create this classic recipe, except with fermentation rather than vinegar pickling. In some sense, it'd almost be easier. I tossed in a cup of kombucha to make sure the pH was low to begin with, a dash of various spices, and then just cubed a beet for the fermentation. Hardboiled eggs won't ferment themselves, so I'd be relying on the *Lactobacillus* from the beets and the mixed culture of microbes from the kombucha to get my fermeggtation going.

The fermentation was the easy part. The hard part was actually hard-boiling the eggs.

In retrospect, I realized it'd been some years since I'd actually made hard-boiled eggs myself at home. It's not that it's hard to do, but there's some finesse required to keep the eggs elegant and intact, which was far more important than usual, given my endgame for them. Peeling them haphazardly or inexpertly would result in a botched egg missing a large chunk of itself. It also turns out that eggs that have sat in your fridge for about a week peel much easier, and I'd used fresh eggs right from the farm store.

My second mistake: I started this little egg project at eleven at night, thinking it would be a quick chore before bed. One thing led to another, and soon two in the morning rolled by, finding me still in the kitchen, cursing at the miniscule flakes of shell that peeled off one at a time, stubbornly, taunting me. I left a crater in one egg as its flesh detached along with the shell, and so I set it aside, not sure if this would be a hindrance to safe fermentation. A few eggs later, it happened again: a huge mortal wound rendered the entire oval end of an egg deformed and craggy.

Exhausted, hungry, and growing annoyed with my comically inept egg-peeling skills, I reflexively held the egg up to examine it, and then took a big bite out of it. Just a boring, plain, hard-boiled egg. Except— oh no, oh no—it wasn't fermented. My worn-out brain had simply determined that eating it was the best way to dispose of the blemished thing and didn't bother to consult with me first.

I looked in panic around my kitchen, over my shoulder, as if someone might be waiting to pop out and point an accusing finger at me. No one was. But you must judge as you see fit, dear reader. I will say, it ate at my conscience for the rest of the night.

I gave the eggs about a week before I began eating (the rest of) them. At first, nothing too remarkable happened—it could have been a standard beet brine ferment, except with more egg-shaped stuff floating within. But all in all, it wasn't weird. A little funkier smelling than vinegar-pickled eggs, and not as overtly sour. I used a few of them in kimchi fried rice, a dish which really highlighted how much effort could stack up in preparing some of these meals. Kimchi had to be fermented, the rice had to be soaked and fermented (plus cooked), the eggs had been fermented, and then all were fried together to make the dish.

So I ate most of the rest of the eggs on their own. They aged over time, slowly turning an interesting shade of grayish purple. It's hard to imagine "grayish purple" as a color, I know, but these eggs somehow managed to place on that curious slice of the color spectrum. On their own, or even as a supplement to a dish, they were a fun experiment. Not one of my favorites, and maybe not worth the effort (given my horrid peeling skills), but something I was glad to have tried. I could do better. I could do weirder. But I could also use something more versatile. Or better suited to standing on their own than okayish, weird, mildly fermented eggs.

They were, like so many things, not a meal.


As it turns out, I grew up eating 100 percent fermented meals for lunch almost every day, though I hadn't the slightest idea at the time.

Up until high school, the meal I most often packed for lunch was entirely fermented. It was not probiotic and probably not even particularly healthy. Yet it was all touched by the magic of fermentation, albeit of the less-than-wild sort. But this was just a sandwich, not a whole lot different from the square, floppy sandwiches many of us ate for lunch as children, packed in aluminum foil or purchased at the school cafeteria in a protective sheath of plastic wrap.

The fermentations that produced my lunch had been carefully monitored, dialed in, controlled. The bread, while cheap and mass produced and white, was still a product of yeast. The cheese, while unnaturally yellow, was still microbe-born. The meat deserves far more praise in retrospect than the other components of those lunches. Despite the fact that this meat was named after the town in which I grew up, it never occurred to me until college that Lebanon bologna was almost completely unknown outside of central Pennsylvania. Why wouldn't it be universally known? The stuff was delicious, far superior to the other sad excuses for sandwich filling available.

This special Lebanon sausage is made from coarsely ground beef that's cured, seasoned, smoked, and fermented. If that sounds like a whole lot of steps for a simple lunch meat destined for sandwich slices, well, it is. And maybe it helps explain why the stuff was a staple of my childhood; it's far more flavorful and interesting than most cold cut alternatives. The combined forces of cold smoking and fermentation give the meat a slightly tangy, pungent, gamey flavor.

One reason our sausage tradition in Lebanon may not have caught on elsewhere: it unfortunately shares a name with a far inferior product. Ours is spelled Lebanon bologna. It's called Lebanon "ba-low-nah." The other stuff, that pale, unflattering precooked deli meat, is "baloney." And it's disgusting. Barely fit for human consumption. Lebanon bologna bears no similarities to it whatsoever.

We are proud of our properly pronounced deli meat for good reason. So proud, in fact, that every New Year's Eve, the city of Lebanon drops a 120-pound sausage to ring in the New Year. It might be the defining achievement of my hometown. And it certainly shaped my love for fermented foods.

The Lebanon Valley is in the quirky Appalachian heart of Pennsylvania, about an hour and a half outside of Philadelphia, in an area where horse-drawn Amish buggies remain a regular sight. For the first ten years of my life, I lived on a farm.

My parents were bankers, not farmers. They just happened to rent a section of a house on a farm. The farmer himself lived up the hill, a cow pasture separating the two residences. It was no wonder he chose the house on the hill: not only did his perch offer a much better view of the open countryside, but the house he rented to us was adjacent to a large cow barn. A very traditional looking barn; you can probably picture it quite easily. Out back, just a few feet away from where we parked our cars, was the manure pit for the cows.

Are you familiar with manure pits? Everyone should be. Just as everyone should be required to work as a server at a restaurant for at least a year of his or her life, everyone should have the opportunity to live next to a manure pit, at least briefly.

If you need help envisioning what a manure pit might actually be like, try to picture a large concrete swimming pool full of cow shit. It's exactly like that.

Our farm must have gotten a reputation for being a good place to dump unwanted cats, so one defining quirk of my childhood was that we'd have a new pet every few months. A car would pull over, pull away, and we'd start brainstorming adorable names for a feline. At the height of our cat kingdom, we had thirteen living with us. Some indoors, some outside. We more or less let them do whatever they want—not that there's any corralling cats.

A few of the cats, every now and then, would attempt to leap onto the metal grate that covered the manure pit. The grate was solid enough to support the cows but not their excrement, you see. This way, the cows could carry out their business without having to stand around in it—it all just dripped through and pooled below in that big concrete pit. After successfully joining the friendly cows, the unfortunate cat would realize that the spaces in the grate necessary for allowing the poop to fall through also made it an incredibly difficult surface to traverse for a much smaller creature, even one as graceful as a cat. The younger, nimbler cats usually made it back to solid ground okay. A few of the older, less-nimble cats, their vision fading and their reflexes no doubt dulled by the noxious fumes wafting around them, occasionally fell into the pit.

What happens to a large mass of organic matter in an oxygen-free environment? Everything has to break down eventually. Dust to dust. But when your pool is so nutrient-rich (yummy) and favorable to anaerobic bacteria, what's happening is actually fermentation. Poop to fermented poop, then to dust.

I fondly remember that farm and the summer nights spent with my mother rescuing our pets from a large pool of aromatic brown sludge. Those were formative years.

My family eventually moved up the road a few miles. This time, to our own house on our own property, sadly abandoning the idyllic farm life. (Still surrounded by fields on two sides, though). Ten miles away from Hershey, PA, the occasional morning breeze would now bring in the subtle roasty aromas of chocolate, another fermentation inspiring potent fragrances. The Dellingers were moving up in the world.

The Pennsylvania Dutch culture that saturates this region is thoroughly, unmistakably German, in spite of the name. The "Dutch" comes not from the Dutch, but from "Deutsch," the German's word for their own country. Central PA even maintained its own low-German dialect, which my grandmother can still speak.

I've always loved German food. Sure, it may not have the pedigree or charm of some of its culinary neighbors, but it's probably that very matter-of-fact, unpretentious directness in the stuff that wins me over. I think of traditional German food as down-to-earth, rustic, relying on a few humble ingredients for rich, strong flavors. It's farmers' food, and Central PA remains farm country.

Pretzels? German in origin, brought to America by the Pennsylvania Dutch. Eighty percent of the nation's pretzels are still made in central PA. I maintain as well that the region is the doughnut heartland of America until demonstrated otherwise. Most of those traditional, Old World–inspired doughnut recipes also rely on fermenting the dough, like the incredible potato *fasnachts* my grandmother makes on Fat Tuesday. And Lebanon bologna, outside my childhood bagged lunches, was also particularly delicious at the county fair, grilled and served in a pretzel bun, with mustard and sauerkraut.

Sauerkraut was definitely not an uncommon accessory to meals when I was growing up. But to be honest, I don't remember it as being revered, either. It was traditional, enjoyed on a semi-regular basis, but at least among the people I knew, it was just . . . sauerkraut. Maybe it came from a cooler in the grocery store or a can on a shelf, or maybe someone at church made it in her basement. I must have had homemade sauerkraut on a number of occasions. Briny, lactic, live-culture sauerkraut still teeming with microbes. I don't remember any discussion of why there might be a difference between that and the store-bought variety.

I was back at my parents' house for Christmas just a few days before I began my year of fermentation, walking through one of the larger grocery stores in my hometown. I was on the lookout for local foods, especially sauerkraut. In an area with such a rich, deep love of its unique traditions (especially our ludicrous array of desserts), wouldn't even the most basic grocery store cater to this legacy? Growing up, the doughnuts in even the chain stores around me were well above average, incomparable to the sad excuses for doughnuts now available to me in New York. (Don't even get me started on the grotesque petrified cake rings they pedal out of a certain large coffee franchise.) Wouldn't we Pennsylvania Dutch still have the same appreciation for kraut, the defining foodstuff of our German forebears?

Apparently not. My options were almost entirely plastic-packaged and bland-looking and certainly not originating from some Mennonite family's fields and crocks. Lebanon bologna is available in every grocery store and deli section, but even that is rarely made the old-fashioned way these days, on a small scale, packed into wooden barrels. Yet a few miles down the road, I could find live-culture jars of properly made sauerkraut at the local natural food store. Miso, kombucha, fine cheeses, and cured meats were also available. Not because it happened to be in Pennsylvania Dutch country, but because it was a natural food store, stocking the same artisanal products that anyone in the Northeast would expect from such an establishment.

There is a strange separation inherent in the way Americans shop for food today. Across most of the country, grocery stores are practically identical, stocking the same products from the same brands. So why the sudden rise of the natural food store phenomenon? The labeling—that "natural" before a market's name, slipping in there in opposition to whatever the other options represent—is a pretty strong declaration that something on the other side is wrong. It's not even controversial at this point to suggest that the average grocery store favors industrialized food. It's simply the price we accepted in the name of consistency and steady availability.

But natural food stores have their own reputation. One gets a general sense that these are the stores for health freaks, people who would never miss a yoga class, crunchy-granola hippies, twenty-something hipsters, and writers following obscure, tedious diets for a book project. Counterculture weirdos.

This shouldn't be weird. Sterilized, processed food, food that can maintain a facsimile of "freshness" days and weeks after preparation, is what's truly weird. Prepackaged lunches of crackers, coldcuts, and mystery cheese are weird. Hand sanitizer might actually be more evil than weird, but the basic concept: weird. Thinking we can escape bacteria, wash them out of our lives and bodies with a bit of soap, is deeply misguided.

Going to any extreme is weird, and often dangerous. But I figured, if I have to go to the opposite extreme just to prove a point, so be it. I'm a little weird myself.

If you, like me, are a human being living in early twenty-first-century America, then you, like me, live in a very unusual period of history in very unusual culture. An unprecedented place and time. Reliable refrigeration extends only a few generations back. Hand sanitizer was not even a concept until the late 1980s. Food was largely available based on how long it could be preserved, not how far and how quickly a company could ship it.

One thing has not changed much: humans, at least those with the resources and time necessary to spend time thinking about such things, have always argued about what makes up a healthy diet. At least among the wealthy, fad diets are not a modern invention, even if most humans simply ate whatever they had available and could store safely. But whatever we were eating, rich or poor, feast or famine, a nagging uncertainty about our diets seems to haunt us always. Perhaps it's the direct connection of sustenance to life, and our inescapable fear of mortality. If we could just figure out how to eat a little better, could we live a little longer?

When it was discovered that germs cause disease, and some germs are bacteria, it would seem a logical conclusion to think that avoiding bacteria would, in general, allow us to live longer. In the case of many specific, deadly bacteria, this is true. Unraveling the germ theory of disease has saved countless lives. No one is arguing that.

Why, then, would we still want to make some of our food with microorganisms? Or even allow them to come anywhere near our food supply?

It seems disingenuous to purge our hands of microbes (at least the 99.9% of them promised on the bottle) with a glob of hand sanitizer and then eat some pickles crawling with them. So, over generations, we began to favor these foods in pasteurized jars and cans, hiding the process that made them behind a curtain of industrialization that most of us can go our whole lives without ever getting a glimpse behind. Bread became fluffy white loaves with the softest of crusts, and cheese became gooey orange squares. Beer became fizzier and lighter until even brands competing fiercely for a slice of a billion-dollar industry were selling identical products. Milk, ultra-pasteurized, is no longer the foundation for dozens of rich and nourishing live-culture creations, but just a thing that goes bad and smells foul if you let it sit in your fridge for too long.

All these things still bear the stamp of microbes and fermentation somewhere along the line. Even the flimsiest, flabbiest loaf of bread employs yeast to rise and give it texture. Even the most sparkling, filtered light lager would contain no alcohol without fermentation. Our bagels and cream cheese, the pickles accompanying our sandwiches, the Hershey's Kisses adding their essence to the fall breeze across my lawn—impossible without microbes. But we've realized that, even when we don't quite want to pasteurize and sanitize every one of those microbes out of our lives, we can confine them to the safe stainless-steel vats of our food-producing factories.

Does food taste better that way? I would suggest an emphatic no, and the massively booming craft-brewing industry, ushering hundreds of varieties of lost beer styles back into our culture, offers a compelling case that we don't all prefer uniformity. We're in the midst of a revival in many ways, across many foods. If nothing else, the concept of gourmet is back. For many, natural food markets are just that.

But in most contexts, for most humans, safety would certainly have to trump flavor. Are we safer for scrubbing and spraying and rinsing every gleaming surface, every inch of our skin, with anti-bacterial suds?

The bigger the question, the more complicated the answer tends to be. And fermentation touches on many big questions—more than I could have ever realized from the beginning. There are many types of fermented foods, many ways of preparing them, and many ways of consuming them. And beyond eating them, there are reasons why a better understanding of our relationship with microbes may be vitally important for the continued health of the human race.

There are plenty of convincing health-based arguments for why we should all be consuming more fermented foods. Probiotics are gaining popularity in pill form, because I guess that's a bit more marketable than telling people to eat food rich in living bacteria. Make no mistake, though, it's the same concept either way: those pills really are just encapsulated bacteria given a more nutritional-sounding name. And while I personally feel you should just skip designer pills and break out the sauerkraut and kombucha, either way, the complex relationship with the microbes inhabiting our own body is one of the most important fields of research under way right now. What we eat has been shown to affect the composition of our microbiome, our unique ecosystem of microbes coexisting with us and themselves, in multiple ways, though researchers are still attempting to determine how drastic those changes might be.

For once, folk wisdom and peer-reviewed science seem to agree on what might sound, to the uninitiated, like wild health claims. From the Romans to Confucius to the guardians of kefir grains in the Caucasus Mountains to the Turkish eaters of yogurt, cultures around the world have associated living, cultured foods with long life and health. Some extreme and very unsubstantiated claims have been made about the benefits of fermented foods, but underneath the hyperbole lies a simple truth: our bodies rely on a balanced microbiome to survive. Many of these microbes are involved in our digestion—up to 30 percent of the nutrients we absorb would be impossible for our bodies to access if microbes did not first unlock them for us. It is a symbiotic partnership older than our species.

The more we research this relationship, the more it begins to look like our health and the health of our microbes is one and the same. Consuming a variety of live-culture fermented foods and beverages, as our species has done throughout history, may be a way of calling in reinforcements. We give them food, and they give it back to us—better and longer lasting.

And yet in spite of feeding the microbes first, fermented foods often contain *more* nutrients than in their original form. Fermented foods are, in almost any light, nutritious. Maybe in ways we are only just beginning to understand. Research on our relationship with bacteria is at full krausen right now (sorry, beer metaphor—you can read that as "at full steam ahead"), and numerous, groundbreaking studies are dropping all the time on the significance of probiotics, prebiotics, the human gut, and our complicated microbiome.

It might have been a bit of an understatement earlier when I suggested that microbes maintain a vital balance within us that helps us to digest our food. For one, that balance is being violently assaulted. Hand sanitizer is hardly more than a metaphor in our war on bacteria: antibiotics now pervade our medical practices and prop up the foundations of our food-production methods.

To this day, I vividly remember when, in my childhood, I heard that our sun was just another star. Utterly convinced that the sun could not possibly be just the same thing as all those other dots in the sky, I even entered into a bet with my friend John about the nature of stars. John, of course, was the wiser of us. Or at least the better read, as far as second graders go.

Sometime after that, I heard our bodies were composed of "cells"—individual living pieces. To my young mind, the very fabric of reality was suddenly rent. Picture, for the first time in your life, understanding that the world around you can be broken down into smaller parts, each alive and ignorant of the fact that it's a part of You, whatever that even means. Try to conceive, as if for the very first time, realizing you are not one whole solid unit but a composite of many living things.

There were a few days where I began to think of myself as a swarm of tiny animals acting in unison. Like the giant man in the parade: three or four smaller beings squatting on each other's shoulders, relaying curt messages to enable locomotion. I had a very strange sense of self until someone told me that cells didn't quite work this way. The human body is a bit more intertwined than just millions of tiny animalcules working in chaotic unison. They couldn't exactly decide to just bail on me and swarm off independent of each other, either. From there, my notion of how the body's cells worked grew more complicated until it was just no more than background noise in the weirdness of life.

Except, in retrospect, I was actually closer to the truth as a child than I could have realized. A collection of tiny little animalcules, working together? I was only really off in the percentages. Upwards of 70 percent of the cells in and on your body right now are bacteria, rather than human cells. Your brain weighs about 3 pounds. All the bacteria sharing your body with you weigh about the same.

Treating every conceivable ailment afflicting us with antibiotics, including propping up the poor health of our factory-farmed livestock, sounds a lot less like a solution after you learn that, in human bodies, bacteria outnumber cells containing our own unique DNA 10 to 1. A significant percentage of these bacteria, perhaps up to 100 trillion of them, can be found in our intestines. You know, the things that do the stuff with the food we eat. So by sterilizing, pasteurizing, and homogenizing all the calories we consume, we aren't exactly avoiding bacteria. And we may even be starving the ones our bodies have come to rely on.

There are around 10,000 species of bacteria found in the human body, far more than could be found in a jar of sauerkraut. But research increasingly indicates that keeping even small numbers of these friendly bacteria in our lives, and diet, can have varied positive effects. In some cases, it may be as literal as calling in reinforcements, replenishing some of the diversity wiped out by the antibiotics we take throughout our lives. The more friendly bacteria in us, the better: by allying with us in the constant war of life at the microbial level, they are a vital line of defense, out-competing and neutralizing pathogens that would harm us. As they are such an integral part of us—essentially another vital organ, dispersed throughout our body—our continued health is very much in their interest too. They provide nutrients like vitamin B and vitamin K. In some cases directly: the dregs at the bottom of a bottle of unfiltered beer? That yeast is rich in B vitamins. The ability of microbes to use almost anything as fuel means that we, too, have more options.

Even the moment of our birth brings us close again to a jar of sauerkraut: *Lactobacilli*, the same genus of critters that transform our cabbage, also inhabit the human vagina, secreting lactic acid that discourages pathogens, creating a foundation for reproductive health and a healthy birth.

If we are so intertwined with bacteria, how is it that we've gotten so good at fending off disease by killing them? And if so many of these microbes are on our side, why have their cousins been so very skilled, throughout history, at killing vast numbers of us?

The microbial world is complex, and, unfortunately, human beings seem to have an innate desire to reduce complex things down to simpler terms. We've been taught about "good bacteria" and "bad bacteria," but that's an oversimplification of a complex network of life forces. Confusing, too, is the popularity of the term "germs" to describe the invisible world of microbes. It is the only term most of us hear applied to disease-causing microbes, featured heavily on those omnipresent antibacterial soaps and gels, but the term is virtually meaningless. Not all bacteria are germs (as hopefully I've shown), and not all germs are bacteria.

More confusing still, many bacteria can be both good and bad: species like *H. pylori* have been associated with health problems in humans, yet separate health issues seem to arise in their absence. Terrified as we are of *E. coli* outbreaks, most people probably don't realize that the average human already carries *E. coli* in our intestines, where the bacteria remain harmless so long as no outside invaders upset the balance of things. The reality of the world is that so much is ultimately about balance—but balance is hard to market.

Viruses, which are even more closely (and more appropriately) associated with disease than bacteria, are not affected whatsoever by antibiotics or antiseptic hand gel. Most of our weapons are banking upon fighting a certain type of enemy, but these types of weapons are not tactical: they destroy indiscriminately. While a few here and there may be foes, the majority of the bacteria killed by your 99.9 percent effective hand soap are friendly, helpful allies. Many others, like the viruses responsible for most of our modern ailments, escape entirely unscathed. This isn't just bad aim. It may be cultivating problems we're only beginning to notice. We launched a great new war without really understanding what we were fighting. In trying to purge ourselves of microbes, even friendly ones, we may have inadvertently created a new breeding ground for the strongest of our enemies.

If germs are so terrible, so inescapable that we need to wash ourselves of them before touching anything, how do children on farms remain healthy? We are scared to even shake hands with one another, and yet some of us grow up next to swimming pools of bubbling cowshit crawling with bacteria and somehow survive. Not just survive: a 2014 study by the University of Gothenburg showed that Swedish children living on farms that produce milk had one-tenth the risk of developing allergies as urban children. A separate study by researchers in northern Indiana found that Amish children were even less susceptible to allergies and asthma than their European counterparts. Only 5 percent of Amish kids had been diagnosed with asthma, compared to 6.8 percent of children on farms in Switzerland, and 11.2 percent of other Swiss children. When given a given a skin-prick test to determine whether they were predisposed to having allergies, 7 percent of Amish kids had a positive response, compared to 25 percent of the farm-raised Swiss kids and 44 percent of the other Swiss children.

We seem to do just fine when we grow up alongside bacteria; maybe even better. But for the first time in history, children can be sheltered from this microbial world to a great extent. Our food is a clean slate; our bodies are welcomed into the world of a sterile hospital, and we are washed, scrubbed, coddled, and treated again and again with reassuring prescriptions of antibiotics to knock back our every illness. The meat we eat, which spends most of its sad, squalid life sick to the point of collapse, is treated with huge doses of those same microbe-clearing cure-alls. We can't escape. We have chosen our bodies as the frontlines for an antibiotic war.

My region of Pennsylvania has, sadly, been the subject of aggressive, widespread development for the last decade or so. Whether it's due to our relative proximity to Philly and the reasonable cost of property in the area or to our delicious Lebanon bologna (I'm guessing it's mostly the lunch meat), the region has become a magnet for clusters of townhomes. I haven't lived in central Pennsylvania for over a decade now, and the part of New York that's adopted me is mostly small towns interspersed throughout the hills and fields, many of them surprisingly self-contained, without an excess of the sprawl that typifies suburban America. Returning to the far-reaching cornfields of Pennsylvania to visit my parents has often been a jolt. Year after year, it would be all the more unsettling to spot three or four new complexes of identical suburban-development homes encroaching on the fields that form the scenery there, replacing those old farms with cookie-cutter houses.

Between visits, I would see the forces of human design wipe the canvas clean, bulldozers clearing a field or forest and leaving nothing but acres of lumpy, rock-strewn dirt.

These mounds of dirt, this ruined earth, would often sit for months, sometimes years, as the financial engine of development switched gears. And the first thing to grow back whenever a field or forest has been cleared, whether by fire or bulldozer, is not the trees. It's never anything we'd consider nice. The first things to rear their head after you level the playing field are weeds. The hardy, mean, nasty stuff.

We are doing this to ourselves, often from birth, and yet for decades have been failing to plant the seeds of the microbes that may actually benefit our bodies. We are leaving our bodies to the weeds.

# CHAPTER 6

# Kefir and Loathing in the Hudson Valley

HALFWAY THROUGH SUMMER, STARTING TO FEEL LIKE I'D FOUND some footing in the daily routine of my strange diet, I realized that I had yet to eat anything truly exotic. I'd fermented some weird things, consumed a lot of funky flavors, scraped off suspicious white molds, and thoroughly scrutinized any number of unexpected pellicles. But before tackling century eggs, I don't think I would have described anything I consumed as outright terrifying.

The first terrifying thing (maybe even the most terrifying thing) about century eggs is the price. I obtained my carton of eggs in Manhattan's Chinatown, where there are numerous brands available. For six eggs, prices range from two to three dollars. This just doesn't seem right for an aged, fermented Chinese delicacy, but okay. I got one of the most expensive brands, hoping that the prices were at least mildly correlated to quality.

A plastic window offered a glimpse of the contents. Still inside their shells, they seemed harmless enough, almost exactly what you'd expect an eggshell to look like. In this case, a grayish, spotted quail eggshell rather than a plain white chicken eggshell, but still.

A reassuring tagline on the side of the box hinted at the wonders therein: "Vacuum fresh. Lead free. Health."

Later, back home, I gathered two friends to tackle the century eggs with me. This was not a quest I needed to see to completion on my own. None of us were mentally prepared to dive in headfirst, so we sampled a few of my other finds first: fermented sweet rice, an unusual dessert that appeared to be simply white rice brined in a jar, and *baijiu*, an enormously popular Chinese spirit. The rice was surprisingly delicious, swimming in its own boozy syrup, while the baijiu boasted an incomprehensible but intriguing flavor that proved to be a love-or-hate kind of thing. It smelled like mothballs and tasted like distilled melted Skittles with a kick.

On to the eggs.

Century eggs, which can be duck, chicken, or quail, are preserved in a mixture of clay, ash, salt, quicklime, and rice hulls for several weeks to several months. They are the rare alkaline transformation, in which the pH inside the egg raises dramatically, opposite of the trajectory taken by most lactic acid–creating fermentations.

We peeled off the shell, which is where things started to get weird. The alkaline aging process thoroughly changes the internal appearance of the egg. Most ferments are still recognizable as themselves. Not here, not quite. Sure, century eggs are still egg shaped, but you've never seen an egg of a color and texture like this. It's like someone took a regular eggshell and swapped out the insides with a brown geode. There was even a cool fractal pattern on the egg's surface, completing the rocky illusion. Odd for an egg, but all things considered, the outside was kind of cool looking. Of course, we had yet to cut the thing open.

Within lies the true horror. The yolk. My god, the yolk. The puss-green, mucuslike corpse of a yolk at the center of the century egg will haunt you. It is the sort of sight that would inspire H.P. Lovecraft to retreat to a cabin and feverishly pen volumes of cosmic horror. Tentacled, loathsome Elder Gods would hatch from an egg that looks like this.

We split one egg three ways. One of us could barely get a bite down. My other friend was apparently fine with it all and went back for seconds. Which, honestly, was better than I fared. I did okay with the first chunk, but that vision (see above, re: green yolk) wouldn't get out of my head. You couldn't unsee it. And the second the creamy, gooey yolk was in your mouth, you weren't tasting it. You were just seeing it, again, still, in your mind. Staring into it. And unable to look away as it stared back. At the second bite, I started gagging.

The strange thing is, century eggs don't actually taste bad. I've heard varying descriptions, but my personal impression was that the flavor basically resembled that of a normal hard-boiled egg. Granted, I was trying very hard not to focus on what I was eating and may have missed some of its finer nuances, but there was a hint of something aged about it, a slightly musty, earthy, almost cheesy quality. Overall, flavorwise there was nothing dramatic. The texture was a bit odd, like a very solid gelatin that just broke into smaller chunks in my mouth. The more I chewed, the more disconcerting this became. The globular texture triggers memories of the appearance, and the fun begins.

For once, the question of *why?* struck me as a bit less unnecessarily stodgy than usual. If the flavor isn't significantly altered, and we no longer need to bury eggs in the ground in order to preserve them, what's keeping this bizarre tradition alive as a delicacy?

There is weirder stuff than old eggs out there, to be sure. Whole herring brined, stinking, in its own juices. (You don't cook with these fish, you just eat them whole.) Rotten shark meat, buried under the Icelandic soil for months at a time, said to be one of the worst smells on the planet by the time it's done fermenting. And yet it remains, in Iceland, a national delicacy.

I'm just guessing at this point, but I would speculate that traditions like century eggs and fermented shark meat have not persisted due to longstanding, if vaguely understood, associations with probiotics and health. A fun way to torment and disgust tourists seems like a more likely explanation for their survival. Do we eat these foods because, however extreme their flavor, at least a few of us will learn to genuinely enjoy and savor them? Because it's tradition? Because of health? Because at one point, we were too desperate not to, and we just never stopped?

Why, in this era of industrial wonders, do we continue letting microbes do our dirty work for us when it comes to our food?

LET'S TAKE THE WAR ON BACTERIA TO ITS LOGICAL CONCLUSION. What would happen if we won?

Victory could take various forms: elimination of just those bacteria that are harmful to us, or maybe, to be really thorough, the elimination of all bacteria. We'd certainly have conquered our bacterial fears in either scenario.

Antibacterial soaps and gels go for the carpet-bombing approach, killing indiscriminately (and often leaving the nastiest stuff behind, as we've seen). Why sort out the good from the bad, the thinking here goes, when there's no way to easily identify the enemy. Nuke the entire site from orbit. It's the only way to be sure.

Say we had that option. Say we could divorce ourselves from our microbes. What would happen? Would we be healthier, free of the risk of contracting many or most diseases?

Sure, microbes likely do us some good. We've evolved to cooperate with them, live with them, mutually benefit each other. Some good microbes help to fight off other bad microbes, and viewing the microbial world as a battlefield of shifting alliances, this makes some sense. But what if we could just dodge the issue altogether—not just end the war, but disband the armies and dissemble their arsenals? Would we skip the risk entirely?

Could we live in a world without microbes?

It turns out, we could. A few people, and uncounted thousands of animals, actually have.

Louis Pasteur can be thanked for bringing about our modern understanding of the microbial world. Our ability to understand and partially control the spread of disease, as well as our ability to stock fresh milk in any grocery store, we owe to Pasteur. And for most of us, his is a household name, at least due to the adoption of the word "pasteurization," the process of killing all microbes in a medium. However, he didn't support the idea that life could or should try to live free of microbes entirely. He just wanted to win a victory over the ones that made us sick.

If you frame the War on Bacteria in terms Pasteur may have agreed with, we have basically already won. The war on infectious disease in Western countries is remarkably entrenched in our favor. Sure, every few years the cable news networks terrify us all with reports of some blooming epidemic (more often viral rather than bacterial), but that such outbreaks are so infrequent and so jolting is a testament to how far removed most of us are from such dangers in our lives.

Consider the top ten causes of death in the United States in 2010, according to the US Centers for Disease Control and Prevention. What sort of diseases haunt us today? Of everything ranking in the top ten, only two causes of death are dealt to us by infectious disease: influenza (i.e., the "flu," spread by a virus, not bacteria), and pneumonia (which can be triggered by both virus and bacteria). Other diseases take the bulk of us, but they are not infectious: heart disease, cancer, stroke, diabetes, chronic lower respiratory diseases, and Alzheimer's.

Looking at a chart comparing causes of death in 1900 and 2010, the first, glaring shift is the massive decline in overall mortality, which was essentially halved in the last hundred years. A giant chunk of things that were killing us are now not. The second standout is the causes of death. Other ratios and causes have shifted around, but that missing half of deaths is largely due, you guessed it, to the decline in infectious diseases. As in, people in the United States in 1900 were dying from them with devastating frequency, and today, they're hardly a blip on the chart.

It should come as no huge surprise that we achieved such exceptional victory in such a short amount of time. The human species has proven remarkably adept at dominating competitors, at least once it has developed the proper tools to shift the playing field to its advantage. It is the very story of our species: struggle, adapt, invent, and conquer. We're so good at killing that we've wiped out numerous other species accidently, almost without noticing.

If this sounds like I'm painting us in a hyperbolically violent light, remember that it is only within these last few years that anyone has bothered to step back and wonder what the microbes we evolved with are doing *for* us. Only within the last few years has a concept like "probiotic" entered into the dialogue, where even now it sounds buzz-wordy, trendy—a gimmicky marketing tactic for yogurt.

Consider that, long before most of us began to consider how to ally ourselves with friendly, living bacteria via probiotic yogurts, we first dove into the pursuit of finding out whether we could live without them at all. Whether we could, in fact, destroy all microbes both friendly and foe, and still keep on living as we were.

Pasteur's keen intuition could not have come at a better moment in history; modern civilization would almost certainly not exist in its current form had someone not made the discoveries that he made. But even he believed we needed the cooperation of some microbes to survive, that our relationship was ultimately a partnership.

Not all agreed. Society's viewpoint that microbes are a scourge and best avoided altogether was certainly understandable. Only in the small bubble of place and time that is modern Western civilization can we horrify ourselves with the fear of disease outbreak mostly via our television screens and rarely through any firsthand experience. For all of previous human history, and still ongoing in many parts of the modern world, death by infectious disease was a constant threat. It was, for most of us, almost an inevitability. We had invented the tools to take out our bigger competitors, the largest predators. In fact, the bigger the animal, the easier for humans to kill with our deadly, unprecedented weapons. But for every one of us dragged off in the night by a wolf or bear, many more succumbed to invisible microscopic predators and parasites. We were still hunted long after we could see what was hunting us.

Prior to the germ theory of disease, many believed in miasma theory, that disease was spread by "bad air." Epidemics, it was thought, were caused by particles of rotting organic matter wafting through the air, planting miniscule seeds of harm in anyone unlucky enough to breathe them in. Sickness could be easily traced back to its origin by following the foul smells.

Conceptually, miasma theory wasn't actually too far from the truth. Putrid rotting flesh was an unmistakable health risk; no degree in microbiology necessary to figure that out. Small particles floating through the air . . . well, as we cringe away from anyone caught coughing in winter, we're still trying to dodge invisible bullets. Just of a different nature.

But what we didn't understand was the way pathogens spread. As usual, it took us a while to accept that we could be part of the problem, if unwittingly and unintentionally. But through the germs we harbored in and on ourselves, we were, nonetheless, spreading disease to each other.

The miasma theory held that bad air was another force of nature, a wave of bad luck emanating from some fetid swamp we weren't meant to stumble through, an unlucky shift in the wind. Unbeknownst to us, and certainly against our will, microbial disease spreads from human to human, using our bodies as incubators for their own growth, reliant on our social nature to spread. Upon realizing this, it didn't take long for us to push back as hard as possible. Researchers immediately sought the chance to create life that existed in a previously unimaginable extreme: free of any microorganisms whatsoever.

Researchers in the early decades of the twentieth century argued fiercely whether microbes were entirely harmful or occasionally necessary to the health of higher organisms, and the debate spilled quickly into the public imagination, inspiring both dystopian science fiction novels and sensational newspaper headlines. Countless chickens and guinea pigs were born and bred (and died) in attempted microbe-free environments, all in the name of science.

Two researchers at the Institut Pasteur in Paris finally achieved some success in studying the development of microbe-free animals through a sort of sterilization process. While the method was imperfect, the window of microbelessness was still enough to bear results. The surprising results were easily spun in a positive light. *"THRIVE WITHOUT MICROBES; Sterilized Guinea Pigs Grow 30 Per Cent. Faster Than Others,"* the *New York Times* announced in June 1914. The article goes on to explain, "Dr. Roux, the director of the Pasteur Institute, presented this week before the Academy of Science the report of the experiments of his pupil, Dr. Michel Cohendy, directed to prove that life without microbes is not only a practical possibility, but highly beneficial to children during the period of growth." The news seemed to confirm our species' worst fears: these invisible germs were not only making us sick, but potentially hindering our children!

Some devoted entire careers to this study and the lure of the elimination of random ailments; a future controlled with utter precision by the mastery of science. Perhaps none was more determined to explore the shiny promise of this sterile future than James Arthur Reyniers, a bacteriologist working at the University of Notre Dame.

To be fair, Reyniers was motivated by curiosity, not by fear. In his mind, our relationship with microbes must either be good, bad, or neutral. Children gaining weight more quickly could be seen as a possible benefit, but one that remained an unexplored reality, tested only on small animals. This wasn't good enough; it wasn't a complete answer to the root nature of our relationship. If we truly didn't need microbes at all, there was nothing to be lost by obliterating them all with antibiotics and moving forward into our sterile glistening new world. To Reyniers, it was yes or no.

Previous researchers had achieved various levels of success, gleaning interesting results, by simply removing existing microbes from an animal. Many of us take their approach in our everyday lives: scrubbing the microbes away with powerful sanitizers. Such methods were as imperfect then as now. Reyniers understood that we probably could never completely remove anything as abundant and adaptable as microbes, not when they pervaded us so thoroughly from the moments of our own birth. He wanted to start from a blank slate. Thus, Reyniers envisioned birthing animals— and eventually humans—that had never known microbes at all.

Reyniers was the rare person able to decide on a single project to consume his entire life. His was an effort meant to take fifty years, to study animals not simply in isolation but from generation to generation. He was only nineteen when he began.

The plan went like this: fabricate sterile chambers accessible through holes permanently fitted with gloves. Reyniers came from a family of machinists, with two brothers in the trade, yet the engineering of these airtight, germ-free chambers took years to perfect. Creating even a small vacuum of microbial life was an unprecedented challenge, requiring far more engineering prowess than previous researchers' attempts to merely sterilize a small animal. These chambers had to be fortresses impregnable by microbial invasion, for the entire lives of the kicking, birthing, growing, terrified animals inside. Cats were abandoned as test subjects, as they clawed at the invading gloves of researchers. Even the smallest tear was breach enough to sabotage months of experimentation. After all, it took only one microbe. From one came many; that was the point.

Eventually, determined and unrelenting, Reyniers managed this critical engineering feat with the help of fellow researcher Philip Trexler. But that was only phase one. With the chamber functioning, Reyniers and Trexler then had to find a way to get a germ-free baby inside it. The mother animal would herself have to be shaved of fur and sterilized with a dip in antiseptic fluid, then covered in an antibiotic envelope to maintain the sterilization. With the animal inside the chamber, the birth was performed by C-section, which negated a passage through the microbial-rich environment of the mother's birth canal. But even with the relative control offered by a C-section, birth is a messy affair. The process was dangerous to the animals and exhausting to the researchers. Any leak or faulty seal at any time would compromise the entire experiment.

It took years to produce the first germ-free animal. Reyniers did not succeed until 1935, but at the age of twenty-seven, he had his first test subjects. Having brought them to life in a germ-free world—or a small sterile bubble, at least—Reyniers then waited to see how they would die.

The process, once perfected, opened up more than one avenue of experimentation. Not every animal was meant to live perfectly germ-free for its entire life; indeed, the purpose of the experiment was to isolate and control, analyzing how different microbes reacted to us, and us to them. Once all microbes were gone, Reyniers could add them back one by one and observe what happened.

It took some reconfiguring of the diet to get nutrient levels right (we know now, as Reyniers did not, that the microbiome inside us unlocks many nutrients from our food that our own bodies can't process), but once everything was dialed in, Reyniers's animals showed results. As earlier researchers had also found with their sterilized animals, the creatures missing microbes seemed to be hungrier and faster-growing. They were free from tooth decay and, on average, longer living. The initial answers seemed self-evident: small rodents, at the very least, could survive without the interference of microbes. And not just survive, but thrive. Pasteur's insistence that we were mutually dependent on each other for survival seemed to have been debunked.

We could be free. At least, free to roam inside a perfectly sealed, perfectly controlled bubble.

Reyniers' research, much like Pasteur's, undoubtedly has helped to save millions of lives. Germ-free chambers are now widely used research tools, implemented since the time of Reyniers' initial success to study microbes of all sorts in isolation. There is much to be learned by gaining this much control over the world, and the impact of Reyniers' creations, both the chambers and the unnatural lives of the creatures within them, on our modern understanding of medicine and the spread of disease is far-reaching.

The chambers had proven that animals could survive without microbes in total isolation. But for all the hard work of Reyniers to create it, the goal of living in total isolation, free of microbes, is a fiction. Perhaps it could be achieved in the vacuum of space— though even that is dubious. In the sage words of Jeff Goldblum's character in *Jurassic Park*, "Life finds a way."

Reyniers once lost a decade's worth of research to a bacterial infection that stole into his lab and infiltrated his germ-free chambers. It wasn't simply that a breach contaminated the purity of the study: it killed the subjects. When a germ-free chamber becomes not that, the creatures inside cannot adapt. The sanctuary becomes a death trap.

Reyniers's tests did, eventually, extend to humans. While there was great faith at the time for our future life in germ-free colonies, testing children in these small and isolated chambers was, fortunately, more than a callous exercise in isolation. The infant human subjects raised in germ-free chambers already lacked an immune system, dooming them should they have any experience with the outside world. Living life inside of a protected bubble, isolated from both microbes and their fellow humans, these children at least stood a chance. The children could never leave, or they would die.

The animals, too, were prisoners. Not free of microbes, really, because their lives were now dictated by this absence. Foregoing microbes was a one-way passage. The dreams of whole cities, free from disease, were never to be a reality. Such a society would exist always at the brink of collapse. Should a benign bacteria like *Lactobacillus* find its way inside, the bodies of the germ-ignorant humans might be okay with the invisible alien intruder. But if a harmful microbe breached the bubble, it would find a colony of victims with no immunity, no defenses, no native population of microbes to buffer and thwart invaders.

We think we want to live inside the bubble, but we don't. Few of us would ever agree to undergo isolation in such a chamber, and yet we have tricked ourselves into hiding in a different way, trying to extend the bubble to encompass the entire world around us. Raising the animals we mean to consume on a steady diet of antibiotics, dousing our children and ourselves, furiously scrubbing sanitizer over every surface. As we allow this war on germs to pervade our lives, the bubble is inside us, rather than surrounding us.

WE NEED OUR MICROBES, AND YET SO MANY OF US FEAR THEM. FERmented foods need a champion to show us how to love them. A representative.

The champion they've found today would probably come as a bit of a surprise to anyone shopping for groceries even twenty years ago. As pasteurized, industrialized food first swept through our grocery stores and fermented traditions died out, no one could have guessed that, in the early twenty-first century, the most popular live-culture food in America would be yogurt.

And yet the yogurt craze is in full force, turning the stuff from a relatively obscure cousin of cream cheese into a massive multi-billion-dollar industry. An industry that, strangest of all, is not afraid of its microbes. Examine almost any yogurt brand on the shelf, and you will see a curious, even unprecedented thing: the scientific names of bacteria happily advertised on the plastic packaging of a food.

Why yogurt? And why *just* yogurt?

Yogurt is a relative newcomer to American grocery stores, until recently a specialty food that would have been impossible to find in most markets even a few decades ago. Given its late but dramatic appearance, its ascribed status as a health food, its exotic (to Westerners) origin, perhaps it's just that yogurt was able to slip in at the exact right window of time, late enough to retain much of its identity. We found it and pounced on it specifically because we were looking for something that had escaped industrialization, something with the semblance of a health food and the decadence of a dessert.

It is so easy to buy yogurt that, as I found my footing with my fermented diet, my motivation to make it at home flagged considerably. Unlike the cultured butter on my toast, my time and resources were spread very thin. The food in my diet was broken into three rough camps: that which I could easily buy at the store (butter, bread, cheese, yogurt, cured meat, tempeh), that which I pretty much had to make on my own (most veggies), and the few meals I could actually order on occasions when I found myself on the go or at a restaurant (Reubens, some Italian sandwiches, sauce-less pizza). The time it would take to make every single one of those foods from scratch would add up to a number of full-time jobs. Even making just the bread and cheese for my necessary daily allotment of sandwiches would have taken up much of my time.

At this point, I had fully committed to the leap in my career that this experiment had convinced me to explore. For months, I kept my day job as a magazine editor while working nights and weekends to help manage a local homebrew shop, through which I led workshops and fermentation classes. I would never in a million years have expected to be comfortable speaking in front of eighty people about anything, but apparently, sauerkraut is just so engrossing that the nervousness doesn't even register. I was eyeing ways to ferment things full-time, talking to a local farm/brewery about consulting on a wild fermentation program. But the great irony in trying to make a go of a fermentation-based career, of trying to learn everything you can about every fermentation you can find, is that it leaves less and less time in your schedule to actually make the stuff. My free time was as thin as my coffee intake was high.

It's not a complicated process to get good at something. All you have to do is devote every moment of your time to it. But it's very hard to get good at very many things. And that's both the wonder and challenge of fermentation: it's very, very many things.

Even yogurt is itself many things. Did I want to dabble in traditional yogurt first, or maybe kefir? Kefir seemed easier to make and, in many ways, more versatile. You can grab a bottle of it and drink it anywhere. No spoon required. But my first few milk kefir attempts came out dissatisfying: whether it was neglect or lack of skill or a weak, fledgling culture of microbes, I wasn't sure what I was supposed to be doing to make daily kefir production worth the effort compared to just buying the stuff.

Conventional wisdom seems to be that just about any food you make at home is better than the store-bought version. I'm not sure I'm entirely on -board with that assessment, considering that many delicious specialty foods are made by trained professionals, and I am an easily distracted amateur who has a tremendously difficult time following instructions.

I knew that basic yogurt was easy to make, but I put it off for months. What was wrong with the ludicrously vast selection at the store, anyway? That was always going to be there for me, anytime, anywhere.

And yogurt, I found, was quite versatile in my diet. An early staple of my mornings demonstrated how easy it is to inspire fermentation: quick oats, otherwise destined for oatmeal, can be soaked for a day or two to create a sort of fermented porridge of whatever consistency you like. Whatever microbes are on the oats is all it takes to get them going, plus time. I used just a handful of oats in coconut water and some whey to get a smoothie base going, then blended with yogurt and drank. Soon I was throwing fruit in, letting it froth for a day, and enjoying creamy, mildly tart and sweet fermented smoothies of just about any flavor I wanted. The brief fermentation strips away some of the sugar and makes for a bubblier concoction. The yogurt, creamy and smooth already, provides the perfect foundation.

Yogurt has been mostly relegated to breakfast meals in America. I wonder if this is because our instinct is to sweeten up anything sour, and yogurt just makes so much more sense for us when we're dumping fruit in it. That versatility does open up all sorts of breakfast options: no one can deny that the stuff goes wonderfully with fruit, the balance of tangy and creamy and juicy and ripe making for a pairing that is healthy, filling, and flavorful. Take a look at the staggering number of options available for yogurt flavors in the grocery store and it would be hard to call our selection limited. But amidst all the dozens of kinds of fruit blended in, or the vanilla and chocolate and dessert-like descriptions, almost every one of these varieties is trying to sweeten up and turn what is by nature a savory, versatile snack into a rich treat that still feels like a health food.

Plenty of us recognize the convenience of yogurt. Most of it comes in portable, single-serving containers. Much of it, more and more, seems to take advantage of the powerful versatility with which yogurt can be marketed, with kid-friendly varieties in all sorts of clever packaging. Kefir has a history almost as long and rich, but from just scanning the packaging, you'd hardly know it wasn't just another clever idea thought up by some sales guy.

While yogurt may be the standard-bearer of microbes in Western supermarkets, often the sole live-culture food in a typical store, it is only one of many fermented foods with historical associations to health and longevity. Yogurt has been in the health aisle for a long, long time: the Biblical patriarch Abraham was said to owe his long life to yogurt consumption; French kings cured bowel disorders with the food; and researchers studying the lives of Bulgarians, famous for both their yogurt and their longevity, concluded the two went hand in hand.

Fittingly, yogurt was first introduced in America, not all that long ago, in tablet form. Not as a supplement to strawberries and cereal, but for those with digestive intolerance. Later, to really cement its destination as a delicious breakfast accessory, it was administered to patients, both orally and in enemas, at Battle Creek Sanitarium, a health resort advocating the principles of the Seventh-Day Adventist Church. As hard as yogurt tries to sell itself to us these days, let's be very thankful it got through the enema phase quickly.

Only as recently as the 1960s was yogurt upgraded from a weird supplement to a food touted for its health benefits, though that unshakeable health angle remained. In more recent years, the swift rise in popularity of Greek yogurt has been driven largely by latching on to fresh health angles, with packages keeping the focus on nutritional buzzwords, protein and fat content, and, to a lesser extent, that decadent creamy texture. For all the hype you hear about it, all the touted health benefits, you'd think Greek yogurt was entirely unrelated to the regular stuff, made of magic rather than milk. But the actual difference between the two? Some of the liquid whey is strained out, so Greek yogurt is thicker. That's it. And yet Greek yogurt has been a blockbuster hit.

The size of the industry in the present shouldn't surprise anyone that has been in the dairy aisle lately: about $7 billion dollars are spent on yogurt each year in the United States, with that figure climbing steadily over the past decade. And that still pales compared to yogurt consumption in other countries. The yogurt business, pushing a food once so obscure you might have opted to put it in your body through something other than your mouth, is now doing quite well for itself.

Some foods sit on the shelf and sell themselves. Cheese and milk rarely look as heavily marketed as yogurt. They are commodities. You're going to buy them when you need them. But yogurt makes the hard sell. Yogurt grabs your attention. Yogurt is a closer. Glancing at the bright and busy packages, you might be forgiven for thinking it's still sold as a dietary supplement rather than a food.

For many it is, given that yogurt remains the one place where probiotic cultures are safe, however else the stuff is adjusted to our tastes. If the probiotic angle wasn't enough to grab you, most yogurt also boasts that it's low fat. What else do you need to know? It must be healthy. But this type of marketing obscures a crucial point: all those yogurts are loudly boasting of their low fat content as a distraction from the fact that they're loaded with sugar.

This strikes me as a bit odd, given that the signature feature of yogurt is its fermentation, in which bacteria consume the lactose sugar from milk, creating a tangy, distinct flavor prized over the centuries. Some of us, those many of us in America with a sweet tooth, preferred that we add sugar back in. Sometimes more than we started with.

Fruit and yogurt are a natural pairing. And so our store shelves are lined with just about every combination imaginable, though many of them do not contain any actual fruit. Fake or real, the sugar content often rivals that of a candy bar. Unless you pick your yogurt carefully, your kids may not be much better off than with that bowl of cereal. I don't think I was premature to deem yogurt as the reigning champion and best face of fermented foods in America today, but as the purity of its biggest brands grows more questionable, it's looking like a Trojan Horse: a secret gateway for bacteria into the modern grocery store, shuttling sugar into a historic, important health food.

In many grocery stores, it can be challenging to find a brand of yogurt that hasn't been adulterated in some way—a yogurt that was made simply, with only basic ingredients, the way it would have been made a hundred or two hundred years ago. But they're out there, especially in smaller stores with a focus on local products. I became a fan of Bulgarian yogurt especially, as well as a few local brands. When you're as reliant on quality yogurt as I was in my diet, you learn where to find the good stuff.

As it happens, a supply of the good stuff makes it quite a bit easier to make your own yogurt at home, too. Most store-bought yogurt, at least as long as it contains live active cultures, can serve as a starter for a homemade batch. Adding a small portion of yogurt from an old batch into a new is called "backslopping." It's a simple equation: fermentation requires just a small dose of microbes to begin. Ready-made yogurt contains plenty of microbes. This is how yogurt would have been made throughout history, before online stores and culture banks: you simply backslopped a bit from the last batch.

Fermentation is easy. Yogurt, though, is slightly more complicated, at least if you expect to obtain a yogurtlike consistency. One reason for this is that yogurt is the rare ferment that has to be heated first in order to turn out properly, and that heat also pasteurizes it. Heat changes the protein structure in the milk, allowing it to set as a solid instead of separating, and presumably, we want our yogurt in its standard solidish state. (This step isn't necessary with kefir, which is fermented with a different blend of microbes and comes out more liquid in consistency.)

Yogurt can be made with any high-quality whole milk, raw or pasteurized. Since even raw milk will be a blank microbial slate after the initial heating stage, cultures have to be reintroduced to make your yogurt, regardless of what milk you use at the start.

The process of yogurt making can seem like a bipolar bounce between temperatures compared to more introductory ferments. Cucumbers will happily transform into pickles with no fussy swings between various temperatures, though they do prefer the same temperature we humans do, the general range of "room temp." Yogurt is a bit pickier. First hot, but then you have to cool it down from those pasteurizing temps. Cool it down, but not too much, and then find a way to lock the temperature in without it dropping any further. Your yogurt will want to ferment overnight at around 110–120°F, the high-end range of what *Lactobacillus* prefers before the heat starts to kill it off. Add in your yogurt starter and find a way to keep it all warm for the next twelve hours. You don't want the temp to drop below 90°F, if possible. Keep your bacteria cozy.

By the next day, *Lactobacillus* has transformed ordinary milk into a tangy, low-sugar treat. This simple process is the start for countless yogurtlike products enjoyed in all manner of ways around the world.

But the relative complexity of the process still raised another fermentation mystery, at least in my mind: why is yogurt so much pickier than pickles? It's not some exotically different preparation, like my lusted-after koji pickles, that calls upon an entirely different realm of fermentation microbes. It's the same microbes. Why the fuss? It's odd that, given a slightly different meal, the same critters seem to enjoy a totally different habitat. It's like if we ate pizza sitting down at a table but could only enjoy tacos if reclined on our backs by a fireplace.

Then again, *Lactobacillus* is a diverse genus of bacteria. Species of *Lactobacillus* include, but are not limited to: *L. acetotolerans, L. acidifarinae, L. acidipiscis, L. acidophilus, L. agilis, L. algidus, L. alimentarius, L. amylolyticus, L. amylophilus, L. amylotrophicus, L. amylovorus, L. animalis, L. antri, L. apodemi, L. aviarius, L. bifermentans, L. brevis, L. buchneri, L. camelliae, L. casei, L. catenaformis, L. ceti, L. coleohominis, L. collinoides, L. composti, L. concavus, L. coryniformis, L. crispatus, L. crustorum, L. curvatus, L. delbrueckii subsp. bulgaricus, L. delbrueckii subsp. delbrueckii, L. delbrueckii subsp. lactis, L. dextrinicus, L. diolivorans* . . . In the interest of not giving over the whole chapter to this list, I'm going to cut it off after the first four letters of the alphabet. *L. et cetera.*

Okay, there's a lot of species of *Lactobacilli* and obviously a lot of diversity between those species. Maybe different *Lactobacilli* want to be warmer than others, and those are the ones we've relegated to our milk, while their chiller cousins have latched on to veggies and claimed them as their own. Let us not forget that even among the narrower realm of fermenting microbes, they're still competing with each other.

Maybe it is just the medium itself. Once you get a decent protective environment around them, veggies can last for a shockingly long time without changing much. Milk is far more perishable. That yogurt fermentation has to progress rather quickly to both keep the bacteria happy and to keep us safe. Even once fermented, yogurt won't survive outside the fridge for very long before mold finds a foothold. It's just too welcoming of an environment.

Maybe we still don't really know what makes the little guys tick. Simple as they are, bacteria retain plenty of mystery. There's a lot we don't understand.

For example: outside of the ups-and-downs of temperature required for the yogurt to set into the proper consistency, you'll probably be happy for the convenience of commercial yogurt to act as a starter. Not just because it's cheaper than ordering an heirloom yogurt culture online and having it shipped, but because you can find yogurt pretty much anywhere.

One problem with this: a homemade yogurt batch launched with most brands of commercial yogurt as the inoculate will fizzle out after reusing your creation over a few batches. This doesn't make much sense on the face of it: if your microbes are still alive and being fed, why should they stop working? And yet after the fourth, maybe fifth batch, you will find yourself experiencing yogurt failure. What should be yogurt will become something only partially resembling yogurt. Like a bread loaf that just won't rise, you will have a puddle of partially fermented milk that just won't be yogurt.

No big deal. You just start over.

Given a moment's thought, however, there is definitely something suspicious about this. While yogurt falls into the realm of unnatural ferments—there is just no pathway in nature by which Greek yogurt could come to exist without human intervention—it makes no sense that the cultures that make yogurt into yogurt would simply collapse after a few attempts. If that was universally the case, we probably wouldn't have yogurt anymore. Our ancestors didn't have the option of going to the store to buy more yogurt to start their next batch.

Heirloom cultures of yogurt exist that have been passed down through generations for decades, for maybe hundreds of years. One could argue that there must be yogurt cultures out there, precious and cherished by some tight-knit family in a small community, dating back to an era when Genghis Kahn might have theoretically stopped by for breakfast and sampled them. Many unique cultures have survived this way, passed down between the human hands that cared for them, fed them regularly, gave them a clean home, and spared them from extremes of temperature.

But this is not how modern commercial yogurt is made, at least not most of it. There are exceptions, small-batch yogurt-makers using cultures much like the cultures their grandparents and grandparents' grandparents might have relied upon. If you can find such a yogurt in the store, it might ferment again and again just as it always has, able to be passed down to your own ancestors.

But most commercial cultures will fizzle, because most commercial yogurt is not made by backslopping old yogurt into fresh dairy. Modern yogurt, like much of the large-scale food industry, is surprisingly high-tech, with its ample revenues poured into extensive research. When backslopping yogurt, you're simply adding again what's already there, with no real conscious selection on the part of the human. You can't skim off some of the yogurt and remove part of the culture—it's the whole ecosystem or none. A food producer's lab does not favor this level of mystery; we want to control not just the ship, but all its moving parts.

And so commercial yogurt makers select the exact strains they want and add only those. Today's yogurt is not made so much as it is engineered. And it's not engineered to continue—there's no reason for it to be able to continue, as the next batch will simply use freshly grown, eager young cultures from the lab once again.

All that is required of this pared-down, human-selected union of bacteria is to do their thing quickly, in the artificial environment of the yogurt plant. They don't need to form an ecosystem that will endure for centuries.

Without that ecosystem in place, they will soon collapse. For us, the yogurt makers, it hardly matters anymore. Why keep a thing running smoothly with maintenance when it's easier to simply scrap the last and start over new? Our yogurt can live and grow in the bubble we make for it. We're able to accept that this one particular food on our grocery-store shelves is laden with bacteria. They're safe, after all; they came from a lab. More tools than living things.

Again and again, we choose control over natural equilibrium.

# CHAPTER 7

# How Wild Ales Got Squashed

CAMPS ROAD FARM, IN KENT, CONNECTICUT, HAS GONE THROUGH many incarnations, dating back, so far as its current owners can estimate, over 150 years. A dairy farm in its past life, it's now host to a number of agricultural endeavors. It is small, as farms go, and does not come with the picturesque horizons of fields that I generally associate with farms from a childhood spent in the sprawling monocrop landscapes of rural Pennsylvania. The cornfields of my early years seemed to stretch from horizon to horizon, but in much of the northeast, the modern farm is more concentrated, more integrated into the landscape around it. Camps Road Farm is of a very different sort than those large-scale, commodity corn operations. Looking around—the potential harvests fenced in on all sides by a neat perimeter of hills and trees—one can fairly quickly deduce what the farm yields: chickens and hops. Assuming you are familiar with *Humulus lupulus* and could pick out a row of hop plants, that is.

Early in the season, you might mistake the rows of trellises for grapevines, unless you happen to be a brewer or a well-versed horticulturist. Reaching some twenty feet high at the peak of the season, these bines look like thin, tall bushes from a distance, but up close, you'd notice they are heavy with plump, pale green hop cones.

Walking through the rows of bines one late summer day, I pulled off a handful. Hops take a long time to fully develop, and these wouldn't be mature for another year or two. When Camps Road began the project, it was the first commercial hop farm in the state of Connecticut. Early as it was for these cones, they smelled wonderful regardless. Rub them between your fingers and a strong fragrance emerges: citrusy and floral, in this case, but the aroma differs widely between hop varieties. The yellow powder in between the folds of the cone sticks to fingers. Fortunately, it's a good smell to carry around with you.

I tossed a few cones into a glass jug. They joined a pile of odd harvests from the rest of the farm: flowers of all shapes and colors, squash blossoms, some undersized berries, a few lumpy crab apples, and scraps of tree bark. It was an arrangement both weirdly pretty and slightly grotesque, especially as I poured sugary liquid over it all later, until most of the contents of the jar were submerged. I gave everything a good shake and screwed the lid on halfway, so that no fruit flies could get in but gas could still escape.

The jar came home from the farm with me, strapped into the passenger seat of my car.

I gave it a good shake every few hours, swirling the contents around so that mold never had a chance to gain a foothold on some patch of dry surface. A few of the apples refused to stay fully submerged. The hops I threw in mostly for fun, to collect a sampling of as many farm products as possible, but they are also a natural preservative and theoretically would help to stave off mold.

This probably would have been the oddest ferment I assembled during the year if I had actually intended to eat it. Who knew what sort of soggy sugar bog the stuff would devolve into over the next few days? Fortunately, for once, I wasn't concerned about texture. I didn't even care how all this stuff tasted, together, in its stew. I was only interested in the yeast living on it.

Camps Road Farm was putting in a brewery: Kent Falls Brewing Co. I was helping to develop its wild ale program by culturing yeast native to the farm to make beer.

That night, as I was sitting at the kitchen table working on some kraut, I kept the jar close at hand so I could keep up with its prescription of regular agitation. The more often I shook it before it began to ferment, the less chance for anything nasty to take hold. After a long quiet period, something inside caught my attention. I noticed some turmoil in the liquid, a few hop cones at the top shaking as if caught in a violent current of bubbles. For a moment, I was baffled. This wild yeast harvesting project should have taken a week or so, if it even worked at all. I didn't expect to see signs of life for days, and yet I was staring at the liquid frothing before me—a most unusual fermentation too, as it all seemed to be concentrated in one small jetty.

Had I somehow managed to capture the most aggressive native yeast strain in the world? Nope, there was no action from the yeast just yet—I'd captured a bee. Having somehow survived being submerged in the sugar liquid for this long, it'd finally won its long climb to the surface of the fruit and flower swamp. Honey itself is full of microbes, and while I wasn't entirely sure what a bee would be carrying on its body, I hoped that maybe I'd picked up something interesting off this interloper.

HAVING BEEN IMMERSED IN THE VIBRANT, PASSIONATE COMMUNITY of modern brewers for some years now, I have encountered a great many opinions regarding the process of making beer. Through my writing and brewery exploring, I have met passionate fermenters from all over the world. We are an incredibly open bunch, eager to share recipes, swap pics of pellicles, and philosophize upon the nature of wild yeast. Talking to the average person whose interest is primarily in drinking the stuff, the general consensus seems to be that beer making is complicated. And yes, the vast majority of it is made in massive, warehouse-size factories crammed with building-size steel tanks, the floor a mess of hoses and chemicals, all of it controlled by some incomprehensible panel of switches. The average person might as well try to build their own car at home, if that's what it takes to make beer.

This is, I notice, what fills the cartoon thought bubble that pops up over someone's head when you utter the phrase "make beer at home." After hanging out in a homebrew shop on a busy main street with a lot of curious window shoppers, I've noticed that there is often a visceral display of shock at the thought that someone could do this. It's a possibility they had never considered.

I like to remind people that humans have been making beer for a very long time. It is one of the very first things we learned how to do as a species. People were likely making beer before they figured out a written language, and for most of that time, they weren't making it in large industrial factories. Most of us like to imagine we are smarter than the average person ten thousand years ago. If not actually smarter, we certainly have better tools and resources at our disposal, and a staggeringly vast base of knowledge. There's always someone—or some book or blog or forum—you can turn to for help. And judging by the many conversations about homebrewing I've had with strangers over the last few years, you almost certainly have a friend or family member who brews beer at home—if you don't do so yourself. It's gotten that popular.

I have more than once witnessed someone walking into a homebrew shop, scanning the buckets of grain and various tools that line the shelves, walking up to the counter, and ordering a decaf coffee. There are many for whom the concept of making a fermented beverage at home is so flabbergasting that it doesn't even cross their minds that such a store might exist. The only sort of brewing they can conceive of is something done in a percolator. But beer brewing, almost certainly the most popular fermenting hobby right now, is growing exponentially year by year.

According to the 2013 survey taken by the American Homebrewers Association, there are 1.2 million homebrewers in the country, brewing 65 million gallons of beer per year. That's an average of about 55 gallons per year, per homebrewer. If that sounds like a lot, consider that many of your friends, upon learning of your new hobby, will begin to view your home as an open bar. You will move through beer quite quickly.

When I lead workshops on brewing and fermenting, the questions I get asked about sauerkraut are typically related to health and diet, as well as how to pack the stuff into the jar until a brine emerges (it always requires more effort than you'd think). With beer, the comments are typically about how complicated it all seems and how much easier it is to just drink the stuff.

Why brew beer at home? Well, complicated though it may be, it's the most rewarding hobby I've ever taken up and easily one of the most creative. Brewing is fascinatingly, endlessly multifaceted. As a brewer, you are a little bit of a chef, an artist, an engineer, a biologist, a chemist, and (most fun of all) a janitor. If you are so inclined to build some elaborate new equipment setup in the garage, you can throw the role of a mechanic in there too. If you enjoy gardening, you'll get to that too—go ahead and grow some of your own ingredients. Hops are particularly rewarding and relatively easy for the amateur horticulturist to tend to.

If nothing else, at the end you get to drink a beverage that you made yourself. The value of making something so complicated and intricate and alive at home, and then being able to enjoy the fruits of your labor, cannot be overstated. Of course, try any moderately challenging ferment at home and you will know the feeling.

How complicated is beer to make? In all honesty, I think it's easier than baking, as it's much more forgiving. Yes, the overall process is detailed, requiring the juggling of a number of ingredients and unique pieces of equipment, all at various stages. On the face of it, it seems far more involved than producing a jar of sauerkraut, which requires nothing more than cabbage and some salt. But most of the nitty gritty is entirely optional for a beginner. Homebrew vendors are eager to bring new hobbyists into the fold and have made an otherwise intricate process quite simple.

These are the ten basic steps in making beer:

1. Grow grain, typically barley. [You personally do not have to worry about this step unless you are a barley farmer.]
2. Malt grain, typically barley. The malting process—sprouting and germinating grain kernels, sometimes followed by various degrees of kilning or roasting to create new flavors—allows raw grains to convert their sugars enzymatically in the brewing process that follows. [You personally do not have to worry about this step unless you are a maltster.]
3. Sugar can now be extracted from your malted grain kernels

by soaking in warm water for about an hour. The process of doing so is called a mash. Grains must be mashed within a certain temperature range in order for the proper conversion to happen, generally between 146°F and 158°F. [You don't have to worry about this step unless you are an advanced brewer or a professional brewer.]

4. If you are a novice, hobbyist homebrewer, your homebrew kit (or selection of ingredients from a local homebrew shop) will likely be based on an ingredient called malt extract, which comes in the form of either a thick syrup or powder. Malt extract is simply Step 3, reduced. In other words, the sugars needed for the fermentation have already been extracted for you.

5. Whether starting with malt extract or all-grain, now all that you, the brewer, have to do is boil the barley-sugar water. The boil helps to drive off undesirable flavor compounds that can be found in certain types of malted barley. Boiling also helps to concentrate the liquid into the desired volume. Finally, the boil pasteurizes the liquid, resulting in a blank slate into which any desired yeast culture can be introduced.

6. Add hops at various stages during the boil. Boiling extracts bitterness from hops when added early, flavor and aroma when added late.

7. The barley-sugar liquid (called "wort") is cooled to room temperature, at which time the yeast culture desired for fermentation is added to the stew. (Adding yeast to boiling-hot liquid would kill it). Within a day or so, fermentation begins.

8. Fermentation proceeds for a few weeks. At a certain point, the yeast will have fermented all of the available sugar that it is biologically capable of digesting and will retire ("flocculate") by clumping together and falling to the bottom of the fermenter.

9. Beer is packaged, generally either in kegs or bottles. Carbonation is created either through a controlled amount of additional sugar for refermentation or through injected $CO_2$.

10. Beer is consumed and enjoyed by all. Now you are a hero and everyone loves and respects you and will look up to you forever.

By reading those ten steps, you have probably now realized two things: one, you know all there is to know about making your own finely crafted beer at home, and two, it sure does seem like we humans, as brewers, are called to task for a great deal of work in the manufacturing of this delightful liquid. To make sauerkraut, all you need is a knife, a jar, and a flat surface!

Unlike brewers of the past, modern homebrewers even have the advantage of numerous shortcuts, like malt extract, which greatly simplifies the first half of the whole process. Brewing with malt extract is as easy as making soup: all you have to do is toss a few ingredients into a pot and boil them for a while. Then add yeast and make sure that the yeast remains happy and healthy during fermentation. Not all that different from making good sauerkraut after all.

Another of the more frequent questions I'm asked: what makes different beer styles different? Beer is remarkable in that it can taste like almost anything you might imagine. Partly, this is because it's quite easy to add unconventional ingredients to boost certain flavor profiles: spices, herbs, coffee, chocolate, vanilla, and fruit are common. But most of beer's potential variety comes from the sheer complexity inherent in its standard ingredients. Many hundreds of varieties of hops exist, with new varieties being bred all the time, and each bears a unique personality. That malting process, which you likely will never have to worry about, is capable of producing hundreds of types of malt, ranging from neutral base malts to toasty, bready malts, sweet caramel malts, and roasty black chocolate malts. Add a small percentage of dark malts to a beer and you'll have a stout or a porter. Select aromatic, fruity hop varieties, and add enough of them at the right stages, and you'll have an American IPA. Leave out the hops and use a blend of spices for a traditional gruit. Perform a more complicated version of the mash procedure, let the hot sugar liquid cool to ambient temperatures overnight, transfer into barrels to ferment with resident microbes, and finally age for one to three years for a Belgian lambic. Easy!

Of course, the great irony of homebrewing is that those super light, mostly flavorless lagers that once dominated America's beer scene (if you can even call what we had at the time a "scene") are actually among the more tedious beers to make at home. Much of their appeal is aesthetic: amber waves of grain represented through the clearest, purest straw color, totally free of sediment or yeast, with a perfect white foam atop. Beginners' extract brews tend to caramelize a bit in the boil, making that color hard to achieve, while very few homebrewers wish to invest in the equipment necessary to filter beer to the point of total clarity (doing so would also necessitate an additional investment in kegging equipment, since after filtering, there shouldn't be any yeast left in the beer to carbonate it naturally). Even in terms of brewing process, lagers pose new challenges and additional steps: lager yeast, different from ale yeast, prefers to ferment at cooler temperatures, meaning a brewer must devise some sort of temperature-controlled fermentation chamber, then monitor and adjust the temperature therein for a full two-month lagering period. After all is said and done, it would be much cheaper, and far easier, just to buy that cheap stuff by the thirty-pack anyway.

This might explain why homebrewing is so synonymous with the modern craft beer movement and the recent explosion in styles and flavors it has helped to restore. It might also explain why people who take the time necessary to make something themselves, something they could just as easily buy at the store, tend to have a deeper appreciation for that thing. The passion for beer in America today is practically unrivaled. Half a century ago, beer was the most basic of commodities, the most forgotten of complex foods, bastardized by industrialization like nothing else, with few complaints. Today, people from all over the world are willing to drive for hours to reach a dirt road in rural northeast Vermont, where, at one man's family-farm-turned-brewery, they will patiently stand in a long, slow-moving line for two or three hours, all to fill a couple of growlers of beer to bring home. Craft beer has inspired the greatest craze in collectibles since Pogs or Pokémon.

Why go to all that trouble? Why the sudden fascination with the stuff?

Clearly a lot has changed, not just in the public's perception of beer, but the very foundation of the business behind making it. In only a few decades, beer culture in America went from nonexistent to inescapable.

I'll go further: for those who really enjoy beer, there has never been a better time to be alive than the first couple decades of the twenty-first century. And when I say "those who really enjoy beer," I am not referring to those who simply enjoy getting hammered on a Friday night over a game of beer pong. We are finally in an era when those who appreciate beer have beer worthy of appreciation, not for the merits of its alcohol alone, but for the flavor, variety, and complexities of the stuff; the sort of deep appreciation that has been socially acceptable for wine drinkers and cheese aficionados for some time now.

Thirty years ago, it was common to hear a non-American remark, "American beer is terrible." This was true, though missing the sad irony that beer everywhere had gotten pretty homogenous and bland. There were a few wobbly holdouts, mostly Britain and Belgium, but beer culture in every country had been on the decline for decades. Even the most devoted countries struggled to maintain their identity. Americans simply made bad beer more loudly and proudly than everyone else, and due to our enthusiastic embrace of industrialization, made much more of it.

Today, America has the most diverse beer culture in the world. What happened? The path that led us to this sudden obsession with the flavorful, well-crafted beer we see today was rather complicated. It starts over a hundred years ago.

There were over four thousand breweries in the United States around the time of the Civil War, serving a country with a population of about 40 million. Most breweries were quite small: their ranks produced only around 4 million barrels of beer annually, or only about twice the amount that our 1.2 million homebrewers now make in kitchen-sized five-gallon batches. That's not all that much beer. These great many small producers resulted in a respectable diversity of beer styles across the country, as the melting pot of America had yet to really melt together. Just as with cuisine, the inhabitants of each region held on to the flavors and traditions of wherever they'd come from, keeping the Old World alive in the New, but also warping, tweaking, and experimenting with whatever local ingredients they now had to work with. Early American beers were brewed with pumpkin, corn, molasses, birch sap—anything capable of contributing sugar, particularly if barley was scarce in the area.

Prohibition began to rear its silly head early; few now remember how long the movement actually held influence before inspiring national law. While the Constitutional ban was dropped on us in 1920, Maine became the first state to enact its own prohibition—all the way back in 1846.

But something else was coming, something bigger, longer lasting, and far more powerful than a brief and highly misguided national alcohol ban. As was quickly realized, Prohibition in America was doomed to fail on the national level. When alcohol became illegal, what suffered was not our level of inebriation. Folks were getting plenty drunk one way or another. What suffered were our options and traditions. Prohibition made it harder to brew decent beer for a long time; any sort of operation had to be under the table and run by criminals. Drinking made you complicit in the crime too, and criminals couldn't be picky. And so Prohibition might have wiped the slate clean, reducing us to a nation willing to party with any sort of swill that would do the job. Eventually, our tastes would have rebounded regardless, yearning for something brewed with competency. But looming in the background, waiting, were the forces of industrialization.

To be fair, there is no secretive  industrialist cabal meeting in an underground bunker beneath the Coors headquarters to decide the mass-manufactured fate of the world, at least that I know of (I made some phone calls). Just boring old shareholder meetings on how to best maximize profit. And maximizing profit is most effective if you're selling a product that people, at least most of them, actually want.

The quick and near-total triumph of industrialization in America isn't actually that insidious or hard to understand, in retrospect. Consider the context: that melting pot of immigrants, with no real national identity or traditions, no "American" food. In the early twentieth century, we were ripe for fast food chains, national department stores, national brands, and beers that tasted basically the same no matter where you went. Coming out on the winning side in two brutal World Wars, on top of a long slog through a Great Depression, had made us proud, patriotic, and hungry for a unified national identity to latch onto. And we were soon presented with a vision of an America made up of uniform white picket fences, picture-perfect houses, and new cars cruising our new interstate highway system from sea to shining sea.

What did we want to see when we were out traveling, exploring this great land? Some beautiful horizons, certainly; a desert or an ocean or redwood trees; and the local tourist draws in each town. But something to remind us of home, too. A burger and fries. Coca-Cola (perhaps the first truly American national cuisine, if you can consider a beverage such). And sparkling, crystal-clear beer that tasted like we expected, every time, everywhere.

The technology had arrived just in time to deliver.

Refrigeration and a national transportation system made the expansion of regional brewers into national brands an inevitability. But shipping still took time, and it doesn't make sense to send beer to Kansas from Wisconsin unless you can already make more than enough for Wisconsin. Stainless steel, among other new technologies, enabled that huge growth in volume to actually become a safe and efficient reality. From an engineering standpoint, steel was sturdier and longer lasting than the great wooden vats brewers had previously relied on. Wood is easily damaged or broken. In England, there is the famous incident of an oversized wooden tank of beer at the Horse Shoe Brewery bursting, knocking out a number of other tanks in a domino effect, and swiftly flooding an entire city block with 1,470,000 liters (388,000 US gallons) of beer.*

A literal wave of beer may sound like a sight-gag from a college-set comedy, but the sheer volume proved extremely deadly: the deluge destroyed two buildings and killed eight bystanders.

Beer floods may have been a rare fluke (after a lawsuit was filed, the court determined the incident an act of God), but there's another important benefit of stainless steel: it's easy to clean and keep sanitary. Thanks to the efforts of one French scientist, sanitation was suddenly understood to be of the utmost importance. It allowed control. It allowed precision. Single yeast strains could be introduced ("pitched," in brewing terms) into a beer, and thanks to this newfound understanding of fermentation and a fresh world of easily cleaned brewing tanks, exact control was suddenly within the grasp of beer makers everywhere.

Beer makers, cheese makers, bread makers, you name it. A worldwide revolution was at hand, and America was ready and eager for it.

Allow me to introduce a theory of mine. I call it the "Triangle of Simple Complex Foods." There may be a few examples of foods that work within my theory, depending what part of the world you hail from, but as a Westerner, the three items best representing the points of the triangle for me are beer, bread, and cheese.

These three products share a great many similarities in the way they come to us. Yes, they are all fermented, but more so, each enjoys an unlikely existence, a degree of complication in their production beyond other fermented or cooked substances. Cider is simply fermented apple juice, you might say, and no real extrapo-

---

*For the brewers in the house, the original ruptured vat alone contained 610,000 liters of beer. That's equivalent to a 5,000 bbl tank! For nonbrewers in the house, most tanks that craft brewers ferment in today are measured in the hundreds of barrels at most; most breweries never grow to the scale that even a 100 bbl tank would be of practical concern. A majority of craft breweries can't even produce 5,000 bbls of beer over the course of a year, making this a staggering volume in a single tank.

lation is needed to explain how it comes to exist beyond that. It is what it is: itself, in a slightly altered form.

Bread, beer, and cheese require multiple stages in their production. They are far more than *what* they are. The cleverness of mankind, warping a series of natural occurrences and manipulating pliable ingredients to bring about an end product far more complex than the sum of its parts.

But human beings are, by nature, enamored with ourselves. It's true, we are certainly impressive; another unlikely occurrence in the natural world. If you held up the contents of Earth to some alien child playing the "which of these things is not like the others?" game, well, that'd be us. So, generally, we are proud of our accomplishments. We are proud of the things we do.

But sometimes we are a little too focused on the aspects of a thing we do.

Take beer brewing, bread baking, and cheese making, for instance. That whole series of events leading up to a vessel of sugary liquid to be fermented by yeast requires a great deal of effort, ingenuity, and gumption on the part of mankind. So no wonder that, as soon as we were able to do so, we built massive production factories to do all that and more—cathedrals to our cleverness in turning fields of mere grass into the greatest beverage in the world. We fashioned great complexes to churn out bread and massive, high-tech vats of cheese. We've poured vast, incomprehensible sums of money into the technology and equipment to further do what we do. Yet this escalation in funds and technology and knowledge had the unfortunate side effect of marginalizing what may actually be the most important part of the whole process: the part we don't do.

In my Triangle of Simple Complex Foods, the complicated and difficult technical engineering necessary for their existence is only half of the equation, the precursor to what, in each case, is a fascinatingly weird fermentation process.

Part of my theory is that these particular fermentations are as complex and wonderful as they are because they are so unnatural. Bacteria might get a taste of grain soup if some grain-water pools in a rut on occasion, but not in the carefully maneuvered environment that a barrel-aged lambic invites. And that same grain soup would rarely, if ever, be accidentally kneaded and prodded into a ball of dough by non-human forces. Cheese, existing briefly in a sort of nascent form inside the stomachs of a few animals, would never be exposed to the long slog of metabolic attrition that molds and bacteria play upon great wheels of the stuff in caves.

What I believe is this: microbes are much more honest in giving credit where credit is due than we are. Recognizing that we've engineered an exciting new party for them to join, they respond in turn with a dazzlingly complex fermentation. They reward us for our effort with even more of theirs.

And do we thank them for this? Do we recognize their own remarkable contributions to the foods we cherish?

Haha, no. Of course not. We've tried to rob them of their agency altogether, minimizing their achievements to whatever extent is possible. Reduce their diverse ecosystem to a single isolated, controllable culture. Train that remaining culture to function exactly as we desire. Turn their work into another knob on our control panel, an invisible occurrence to be quietly carried out somewhere in a stainless-steel tank.

Louis Pasteur is commonly credited with the discovery of yeast, and thus, the role of yeast in making beer. This is not entirely accurate. Many clever brewers throughout the ages no doubt grasped the importance of yeast in the success of their fermentations. They didn't know *what* it was, but they knew it was something. If they had been completely oblivious, the beer would not have come out at all; many of the old beer-making traditions are, incidentally, techniques for transferring yeast into subsequent batches. Often, actively fermenting beer from a previous batch was simply transferred into a new. Wood was relied upon for its ability to give yeast a perch; spoons that regularly led to good beer (because their pores were host to healthy colonies of microbes) were considered sacred. Historic brewers may not have been able to culture yeast in isolation, but they had a good idea that there was something going on in there, chemical or magical, sent by nature or gods, to make fermentation happen.

Brew beer at all and you can hardly miss it—yeast roars to the top of the liquid during fermentation, capping it with thick foam. While individual yeast cells are much too small for the human eye to see, they have a tendency to cluster together by the millions. You'll spot them at the bottom of a bottle-conditioned beer. Brew at home, and you'll have a great sludge of yeast after you empty out your fermenter. Brew a great vat of beer for your whole village and you'll have gallons of gooey grayish tan-colored yeast goop.

Seriously, you can't miss the stuff. Historic brewers knew it was there; they just couldn't say exactly what it was.

And it was evident as well that, whatever the mystical element was, it created alcohol and $CO_2$ where previously there had been only sugar and water. As scientists and thinkers turned their attention to the matter, debate ensued over whether the process was chemical or biological (presumably magic had been scratched off the list). In the 1800s, Pasteur settled the debate once and for all. Yeast were living microbes, and the fermentation, the alcohol, was a result of their metabolism. These living things made beer. Or sauerkraut. Or yogurt.

And sometimes, other similar living things also made us sick.

Louis Pasteur bettered the world in a great many ways. His work saved countless lives. Ultimately, Pasteur's work was beneficial to the diversity and creativity of brewers. Without the knowledge that yeast exists, we would not have banks of hundreds to thousands of individual strains, a vast library of fermentation potential at our disposal. Modern brewers can brew with practically any yeast in the world, thanks to Pasteur's efforts. Both the diversity of modern craft brewing as well as the homogeneity of industrial lager conglomerates are in debt to this Frenchman's work.

Lager brewing offered an appealing added layer of protection against bacterial contamination. Lager yeast have evolved a unique trick in the world of fermenting microbes, as most yeast and bacteria alike are comfortable working around the same temperatures we humans are. Almost all microbes will shut down if it gets too cold. Lager yeast, on the other hand, doesn't mind a little chill, and the mere temperature alone adds up to a new layer of protection against invaders. Add to that brewers' newfound ability to pitch pure, hardy cultures of yeast to their beer in the early twentieth century, and suddenly, a revolution was born.

Lager yeast—and the clean, crisp beers they produce—quickly swept the planet, fulfilling our desire for consistency. But we lost something spectacular in the bargain.

Humans have evolved a number of defense mechanisms to protect us against food we aren't meant to eat. While it's still not fully understood how different taste perceptions may have acted as warnings against poisonous foods, it's clear that bitterness and sourness are acquired tastes for most humans. How much of this is ingrained within us and how much of this is cultural is hard to say: flavors that most children cringe at as infants will be quickly accepted if the culture they're born into is heavily reliant on foods with such flavors. With our extensively sugar-saturated Western diets, many of us have a hard time enjoying foods that aren't on the rich end of the spectrum, but a taste for sourness would have taken much less getting used to in past eras, when soured foods and drinks were a feature of everyday life.

We haven't entirely lost our taste for sour. For whatever reason, the flavor combo of sweet and sour together sneaks in through some loophole. Take lemonade, a beverage that would be incredibly acidic if we didn't balance out its natural flavors with a heap of sugar. The world's most popular soda, Coca-Cola, would taste extremely sour with its vinegar-like pH level of 2.5 without its added sugar. We enjoy the contrast. Some of us even seem to instinctively crave raw sour flavors. I'm pretty sure I have never had an aversion to sour anything. A few years ago, I began adding lemon juice and a dash of apple cider vinegar to all of my water. More refreshing, more flavorful, and more sour.

So naturally, I remember the first sour beer that left an indelible mark on me and that would shape my tastes from that point on.

My tastes shifted from enjoying sour things to craving them, the way they make you salivate and thirst for more. I began to enjoy kombucha and started making it at home. When reading labels, I perked up at any mention of *Lactobacillus*. Sour cabbage held new appeal. Sour was my jam. (No actual jam please, that stuff is too sweet.)

A few years ago, at a Manhattan bar called the Blind Tiger, I went to a mid-October tap takeover featuring a number of specialty beers from Allagash Brewery, in Portland, ME. The first beer I tried for the night was a novel sour beer called Ghoulschip. My friend, who'd read up a bit more on the event than I had, told me I might never see this particular beer again. They'd only ever made the beer once thus far, four years ago. Even freshly released, it would automatically be one of the oldest beers I'd ever tried.

For many, four years might sound like a ludicrous amount of time to let a beer sit before getting around to drinking it. New brewers frequently ask me how many months they have before their beer will go bad, and it's hard for me to give a succinct answer to this question. Beer shouldn't ever spoil if it's handled properly, but not all beers will improve over time, either. Some will oxidize or stale, particularly hoppy beers. Many beers taste best fresh. Others will age as gracefully as any wine. But Ghoulschip was a special beer—it took a couple of years just to make it.

Throughout history, sour beer was not simply a unique style, but an inevitability of almost all beer. The patient forces of entropy are always waiting quietly on the threshold, and for beer, fermentation with pure cultures of isolated yeast is a modern novelty, not the norm. Consumers had to drink their beer fresh if they wanted to enjoy those clean flavors. Given time to age, the wild strains of yeast and bacteria that stubbornly persisted in almost all barrels and tanks would rework the flavors into something funkier. Beers dried out through the extended fermentation, backed by a new foundation of lactic acid.

Beer invites a complex ecosystem. Most fermentations happen in stages, with successive waves of bacteria achieving dominance over their predecessors, but in the simpler world of a jar of vegetables, these kingdoms rise and fall in a matter of days or weeks. Sour beer, on the other hand, begs for months or years to complete its life cycle. Our longtime friend *Saccharomyces*—fermenter of beer, wine, cider, and bread alike—consumes most of the sugars rather quickly, which is why beer can be ready to drink in only a few weeks. Our modern brews, generally fermented with only a single strain of *Saccharomyces*, are already done at this point. But as wild yeast like *Brettanomyces* and lactic-acid producing bacteria creep into the beverage, a new growth cycle begins. Some wild yeast strains are able to scavenge resources from the dead cells of yeast that came before them. Some work in cooperation with bacteria to break down longer-chain sugars, unlocking food that no *Saccharomyces* strain on its own would have been able to chew through. Some can even feed on sugars from the wooden barrels they're aged in.

The beer ages, sours, and grows funkier.

The result—a beer like Allagash's Ghoulschip—is as complex as anything you will ever taste. But many tasting such a beer for the first time will feel like they've hit a brick wall of sourness. It is the nature of nuanced, acquired flavors to seem impenetrable to uninitiated taste buds. Just as with music or other intricate arts, subtle nuances can be totally missed when there's a big glaring siren of something to first catch your attention, which is why mothers across the globe can be depended on to complain that, "All the songs by [new band in loud new genre of music] sound exactly the same!" Perhaps you would have tried that same beverage as me and registered nothing but SOUR! No way to know but to try a sour beer yourself and find out. Just keep in mind: do you want to be that person that complained loudly and belligerently about kids these days and their noisy punk music? It might take a few spins before you get what it's all about.

When foisting sour beer on people, I'll usually opt for something on the tame side so as not to scare them away, but I've heard people try what I consider to be a mild, barely acidic sour beer and proclaim, "This tastes like vinegar!" Well, to each his own. We all have to follow our own path in coming to realize that lambic-style beers are the most delicious of all possible liquids. Under that blanket of acidity—the big, overt guitar riff of sourness that's the first thing your senses notice—weirder, more nuanced and hard-to-describe flavors seep out. You'll hear adjectives like "barnyard" and "horse blanket" (creative ways to pin down the elusive nature of something that tastes funky and wild) in the same sentence and relating to the same beverage as "tropical fruit" and "citrus." Whatever they are, the flavors are memorable.

Where do these exotic flavors come from? A complex, living world of yeast and bacteria, of course. But where do those critters come from? You may recall that we boil the sugar-water from the grains to pasteurize the liquid and start with a blank slate. Unlike making sauerkraut, we can't just dice up some barley, stuff it in a jar, and let the native residents have at it.

Most sour beers rely on *Lactobacillus* for the bulk of their acidity, as the succulent flavors of lactic acid simply seem to be the most appealing to humans. Acetic acid (vinegar) is harsh and pungent, but a lactic sourness can be as refreshing as a glass of lemonade on a hot day. How brewers inspire *Lactobacillus* to create that acidity can vary greatly depending on the specific beer style, however.

Long-aged sour beers, hibernating through season after season in their barrels as ecosystems of microbes work at dismantling every last one of their sugars, tend to ferment through cooler temperatures, similar to what we'd prefer for a batch of sauerkraut or cucumber pickles. As with the veggies, the cooler temps mean the microbes work slower, allowing each successive wave of species to take over at its own pace, with its own rhythm. Layers of flavor are created by layers of microbes. Patience rewards complexity.

But what about yogurt, which also relies on *Lactobacillus*, but is fermented only overnight? What about those fast-working bugs? Couldn't they sour beer too?

While brewers may not use the same strains as their dairy-making counterparts, a few German styles of beer—Berliner weisse and gose being the most popular among modern drinkers—are given, in a manner of speaking, the "yogurt treatment." Patience is abandoned in favor of getting a big wallop of sourness in a short amount of time with some fast-acting bacteria. The process of making a quick sour beer and a bowl of yogurt is fairly similar: after initially heating the liquid past temperatures where bacteria could survive, we cool it down to about 100°F, where *Lactobacillus* thrives. While the trick for most of us is holding the temperature within that range over time, the principal is simple: at temperatures that push the bacteria to their most active state, the fermentation rips along quickly, creating maximum sourness.

Given the similarities to making yogurt, you may be wondering where one obtains the *Lactobacillus* cultures necessary to make this particular kind of beer. Might one actually use yogurt? I'm all for experimentation, but that sounds as if it might be weird. Dairy and beer don't often mix well.

One option would be to backslop with finished beer, repitching a portion of a previous beer's trub, if you had made a Berliner weisse or gose recently. But for most homebrewers, this wouldn't be an option, not unless you're regularly making such beers. Maintaining a healthy sourdough culture or yogurt culture requires dedicated feeding and maintenance, and keeping a sour beer culture in this way would be no different. It's very much like having a pet. Except it's millions of pets.

With other ferments, part of the magic is that they're able to ferment themselves. Self-inoculating, self-consuming, a little ouroboros in the circle of life. But how could you do that with beer, with so many steps involved in its making? Especially when hops, an integral ingredient in most modern beer styles, excel at inhibiting bacterial activity?

It's a bit more roundabout than stuffing cabbage into a jar, but beer can, indeed, ferment itself. Berliner weisse and gose often begin their fermentation with what's called a sour mash. This is exactly what it sounds like: the mash is allowed to sour overnight with the same steps for yogurt making outlined above. The bacteria themselves actually come from the grain: both *Lactobacillus* and yeast seem to fancy chilling on the hulls of grain kernels, even though the grain, in that form, is immune to their powers of fermentation. So all a brewer has to do is introduce unheated grain kernels to the sugary wort liquid. Not the *same* grain that was used in the mash to extract fermentable sugars, mind you, as that was already stewed too hot to allow most bacteria to survive. Instead, most brewers will add more grain back into the mash once it's reached a cool-enough temperature, or even add a pure *Lactobacillus* culture that was plucked off of grain previously, either from previous batches or a test jar (the method I favor, for purposes of repeatability). Either way, it's really no harder than making yogurt.

Of course, *Lactobacillus* is only one of the microbes capable of creating succulent sourness in wild beers, and just one guest to the party in the complicated, multiyear lifespan of a really complex aged sour. But the rest of the microbes involved in that dance don't seem to be present on grain. So from whence do the rest come? Seemingly out of thin air.

The Allagash Ghoulschip that won the heart and mind of the young Fermented Man was an American re-creation of a traditional Belgian style of spontaneously fermented beer. No sour mash, no *Lactobacillus*-harboring grain in the kettle, no additional yeast or bacteria added by the brewer at all. Spontaneous fermentation. An embrace of the fact that microbes can arrive seemingly out of nowhere, because they are everywhere, all around us, waiting to tumble into our beer.

Beer is typically fermented in some kind of closed vessel, a vessel specifically designed to not let outside microbes float in. An airlock acts as a moat against outside invaders while providing a vent for $CO_2$ from the fermentation. Spontaneously fermented beers begin their lifespan in a very different sort of vessel, which is specifically designed with the opposite goal: expose the liquid to as much outside air as possible. The more air, the more microbes.

And so, after wort is boiled, it is pumped to a large shallow trough called a coolship. As the name suggests, this vessel, with the massive amount of surface area it provides to the liquid, allows the steaming-hot wort a place to cool down in the embrace of the chill night air (don't forget to leave the windows open). As the liquid cools, it contracts, drawing in air and microbes from outside. After the liquid cools to room temperature over the next twenty-four hours, the beer is transferred into barrels downstairs, where fermentation begins.

The beer resides in barrels for a long time to come. Lambics are eventually released as they are, aged and fully sour, more complex in flavor than perhaps any other beverage in the world. Sometimes fruit is added, and additional fermentation is carried out for a few more months as the microbes digest the fresh feast of sugar. For a really dazzling display of the complexity possible through fermentation, there's gueuze: a careful blend of one-, two-, and three-year-old lambics by a master blender.

Any properly made sour ale birthed through a spontaneous coolship inoculation is truly a beautiful thing, and unsurprisingly, there are only a handful of them being made around the world today. Though experimental brewers are trying their hands at the technique in increasingly novel ways. The brewers at Prairie Artisan Ales, in Oklahoma, rigged up a makeshift coolship in the bed of their pickup truck. Gabe Fletcher, brewmaster at Anchorage Brewing, simply filled a few barrels with wort and drove them out to a field north of his brewery in Alaska, cut holes in the tops of the barrels, and let them sit overnight. At Kent Falls, we've modified an old milk mixer left from the farm that preceded us into an open-top coolship vessel. We use a tractor to move this vessel weighing thousands of pounds, full of precious liquid cargo, in and out of the brewery, letting the beer cool off overnight in the chilly early-spring air, before bringing it back inside the brewery to enjoy temperatures warm enough for fermentation to occur. Brewing often requires creativity in more than recipe development.

Trying that rare release of Allagash Ghoulschip when I did was an incredible stroke of luck. It was a special beer in a few ways: the Halloween-themed spontaneous sour was not only one of the first things run through an American coolship, ever, but a decidedly American spin on the traditional style that included a whole lot of pumpkin tossed into the mash for added complexity. (Hopefully by now you've put together the inspiration for the name Ghoulschip.)

Sour beer has fascinated me for years, in particular the weird trajectory of aged sour beer, a fermentation full of pellicles and mysticism. But ever the curious fermenter, I wasn't quite satisfied with the knowledge that this weird, unique cocktail of microbes came from the air. Microbes can't ferment air, so clearly they are mere passengers in that space, waiting to float down upon their next feast. Yet lambic beer is no explanation for their existence either: the exact environment that allows these successive waves of yeast and bacteria to work their magic hasn't been around all that long. If one follows any other form of fermentation, you'll notice that everything seems to have its natural state, a host environment to which it's perfectly suited. Sour beer is not a natural state: it's manufactured. These cultures must have their own place in the natural world too.

Then I remembered my attempts at fermented sweet potato fries. And later, fermented butternut squash. All starchy vegetables, all with the same result: the gnarliest, most outlandish pellicles I'd ever witnessed. Just like the pellicle on a good sour beer.

Allagash used squash in their Ghoulschip beer to keep with a Halloween theme, by flavoring the mash with it. While pumpkins aren't particularly flavorful on their own, some of the starches and sugars would have made their way into the beer along with the grain sugars and been fermented. But any microbes from the squash were boiled to death.

I had a slightly different idea. A very unique take on pumpkin beer.

It began just like any veggie ferment: in a jar, with some vegetables and salt brine. In this case, red kuri squash from Camps Road Farm.

I let the extra-large jar of squash ferment as I normally would, and sure enough, it had soon formed a bodacious pellicle, a real spectacle of filmy white otherworldliness. I let the fermentation creep along for a week, cozy beneath its bacterial bubbles.

I probably could have brewed the beer sooner than I did. A week and change out, I had grown up every microbe that was going to grow on those orange cubes of squash. In fact, it smelled like I'd grown some that I maybe hadn't wanted to grow. Over a couple of days, I noticed that the smell coming out of the jar took a shift away from bright, tangy veggie aromas toward vegetables that you forgot in the back of your fridge until they began to rot. The differences between fermentation and rot may be arbitrary, but the smells associated with either are pretty distinct, at least to my nose. There was a definite back-of-fridge-vegetables thing going on here.

Some of the squash cubes, I noticed, weren't quite beneath the level of the brine. Their stubborn buoyancy was too much even for the protective power of the pellicle. It wasn't like the whole jar was ruined—fermentation had occurred and completed. But a few strips, a few wedges here and there, were touched by rot, too.

Barry, my partner at the brewery, smelled it and recoiled. "That's horrifying. That's absolutely something rotten."

He thought we should toss it and try again, but I wasn't so sure it was doomed. The squash itself was what had rotted, and only a few pieces at the top. They'd already delivered what I needed them for: their microbes and sugars. So I skimmed out the nasty and used the rich liquid underneath, which was teeming with fermentation agents, and pitched it into a bucket of unfermented wort.

The airlock on the bucket of squash beer was bubbling steadily by the next day. It hadn't taken long: whatever critters had converted the squash to mush were more than happy to switch over to beer, it seemed. A good first sign. Of course, a healthy fermentation doesn't necessarily mean a beer that tastes good. We could still be dealing with something frightful in the end.

The first samples I pulled didn't taste like beer brewed with squash, exactly, but maybe like a beer brewed with something from the earth. A bit spicy, herbal, earthy, and vegetative, this wasn't the cleanest or smoothest beer I'd ever made, but it was certainly interesting for something that was very young in the lifespan of something that could age to be very old. If the squash had delivered similar microbes as those used to ferment a beer like the four-year-old Ghoulschip, then I could be letting this one sit to do its thing for a very long time. *Saccharomyces*, *Brettanomyces*, *Lactobacillus*, and *Pediococcus* would all dance around one another for months, acting in concert to reduce even the most complex sugars to nothing.

I'd picked up some hungry microbes. The sugars were all gone, and the rot hadn't stood a chance. As funky and different as this beer will likely end up, whenever I'm ready to package it, it will also be its own self-made fortress of fermentation, untouchable to the decay that briefly gained a foothold in that jar.

Right now, if you squint hard, you could maybe guess there was some squash involved in making the beer. But fermentation flavors tend to go off in unprecedented directions. Through fermentation, a beer will rarely taste like what it is, no matter how you try to reduce it to its separate parts for analysis. The best fermentations can be described in nothing but grasping metaphors. The sommelier's notes on a vintage wine may sound like they're reaching, a tyranny of intangible flavors you'll never be sophisticated enough to zero in on yourself, but it's a lot more fun if you believe that such descriptions of any complex fermented product are merely impressions, subjective, rather than affixed and concrete landmarks.

Most complex fermented creations cannot be said to taste like anything with certainty, because they have no fixed analogue.

There is nothing like them but those things themselves. We can share with others the impressions we took out of this shifting, living world.

There is sometimes failure and rot, but also mystery to be found in letting go of our control.

# CHAPTER 8
# The More It Smells Like a Goat, the Better

THE WEATHER BREEZY AND MERCIFULLY FREE OF HUMIDITY, THE CALendar slogging toward the final third of the year, it was the perfect evening to sit outside and share some ferments. Bottles of beverages were ferried in and out of the fridge.

If you aren't friends with any devoted beer nerds, you should understand that even in a casual, impromptu gathering like this one, these tastings are taken as seriously as those hosted by any wine connoisseur. There's no hasty splitting of six packs. Each bottle is brought out one at a time, momentarily examined, and then shared in carefully poured equal portions.

Yes, this is devoted nerd behavior. But beer is no less deserving of the attention than wine. Whether saddled with flowery adjectives or aiming for sheer simple drinkability, beer can be just about anything. And many of us have now realized how satisfying it is to explore a new bottle and see what beer can be next.

As it was my turn to retrieve a new bottle, I explored my friend's fridge. It took only a second of scanning the shelves before I noticed a powerful aroma wafting out at me. This friend of mine, Max, is extremely handy in the kitchen, has worked in the restaurant industry for years, and is one of the most fastidious apartment-keepers I know. For such a stench to be left unattended in his fridge was a bit odd.

There were a few vegetables sitting around, waiting to become salads, but none of them looked particularly rotten. A large mason jar of milk in one of the door shelves looked fairly questionable, so I assumed it must be the culprit. Back outside, I alerted him to the fact.

"It's not the milk," he sighed. "I'm pretty sure you're just smelling this cheese I got."

"I don't know, man." I was slightly offended he thought I might fail to recognize a weird cheese smell. Me, of all people, failing to recognize weird cheese. "I've had a lot of cheese in my life, and I've never had a cheese smell like that. Something is doing the wrong kind of fermenting in your fridge."

I first thought it smelled like vegetables that have been thoughtlessly thrown into the trash just after you've replaced the bag, dooming them to a few days of open-air decomposition before the trash would be emptied again. Or no, that wasn't quite right: there were powerful notes of something animal in there. Something that has been dead and vanquished and shit itself in the process.

Definite notes of fecal matter. Something that no vegetable is capable of.

From back outside: "It's the cheese, I'm telling you." Max sounded certain. Obviously, he'd had more experience with the contents of his fridge than my brief, ten-second expedition to grab a beer. I guess he'd know. "It smelled like that when I got it. I think that's how it's supposed to smell."

"Did you actually try any of it?"

"I tried a piece. I survived."

"Seriously?"

"I'm not eating any more of it, but yeah. I think that's how it's supposed to smell."

I looked to my other friend, Dan, whom I knew to be a game consumer of weird foods. "So, clearly we have to try this."

"Indeed we do."

I brought forth the cheese. Through the plastic bag in which our host had stored it, that same aroma filling the fridge escaped its loose plastic boundaries. There was no containing an odor like that: it was as clear a metaphor of the downward spiral toward entropy as I have encountered in any food. And yet, bless the magic of fermentation, it looked normal enough. It wasn't a soft cheese, like many of the stinky cheeses I've encountered. It wasn't a blue cheese, nor did it show any visible signs of mold. Just an innocent, semifirm cheese with a thin, hard dam of rind sheltering it from the outside world that happened to smell on par with the manure pit I grew up next to.

"What kind of cheese is it?" I asked.

"It's from Holland. Or no, Germany, I think."

That was hardly specific, but I trusted that I could track down the name of it later, if I wanted. All I'd need to do was stop by the cheese section and sniff.

We started with thin slices. Max elected not to participate, having already had his fill of the stuff. I figured the small portion I was about to consume couldn't possibly be a match for the legions of microbes I had already invited into my digestive system, even if this stuff tasted like it smelled. Surely, I would survive.

Dan and I chewed, looked around in confusion, and exchanged glances.

"It doesn't taste at all like how it smells," Dan said.

I tried another slice, to be sure. "Not at all. I'm not gonna lie, I kind of like this."

Dan too. "No, it's actually . . . really good."

We had more. The flavor was shockingly mild, nothing like the pungent decay hinted at by the odor it cast off. It was like that aromatic outside rind was a literal fortress against the forces of decay, close enough to touch the food we were eating, but not enough to rot its soft, tangy insides. Like a good beer or wine, an eccentric cheese like this is nearly impossible to describe in equivalencies and adjectives. Its flavor has become too far removed from its base ingredients.

Dan and I chewed happily, trading slivers of the stuff. It paired perfectly with the beer we were drinking at the time, an equally complex farmhouse ale with enough lactic tang to cut through the meaty, buttery cheese.

Max sat back from the table through it all, remaining resolute in his disgust.

"Man, you guys can have all of that shit if you want," he said. "You're crazy."

I split the remaining cheese evenly with Dan. The next week, I bought another wedge for myself. My roommate is vegan. Considerate to the end, I made sure to wrap the cheese in about fourteen pieces of cling wrap, plus stuffing it in a thick sandwich bag and burying it in the back of the bottom-most drawer so I wouldn't be asked why our fridge smelled like actual shit.

QUICK, THINK OF A PRODUCT THAT'S PASTEURIZED.

When you think of our old buddy Louis and the process he's famous for, what first enters your mind?

Was it milk?

Milk products are more closely associated with pasteurization than probably any other food. And not without good reason. In the early twentieth century, unpasteurized milk was something of a scourge, spreading illnesses like tuberculosis, brucellosis, diphtheria, scarlet fever, and Q-fever, in addition to harmful bacteria like *Salmonella*, *Listeria*, *Yersinia*, *Campylobacter*, *Staphylococcus aureus*, and *Escherichia coli*. That's quite the nightmarish roster for one of the most commonly consumed foods in Western culture. According to the CDC, improperly handled raw milk is responsible for nearly three times more hospitalizations than any other food-borne disease outbreak.

There's much about milk we take for granted, frankly. Dairy, and the many products derived from it, comprise one of the most complicated and interesting categories of food out there. Milk is in itself something of an artificial food. It exists for most of us through technology rather than transportation. Nature never really intended for us to be drinking milk year-round or for the duration our lives. It is a stolen food; nutrients specifically set aside for other mouths that we have figured out how to commandeer through our cleverness. And it only gets weirder from there.

I must admit that I have a slight inclination to love milk. Maybe that, too, I can pin on my upbringing in central Pennsylvania. Lebanon and Lancaster Counties, where I was raised, are in the heart of dairy country. It's the reason Hershey chose the area for his chocolate plant: he needed access to a lot of milk.

According to several reliable family sources, I drank over a gallon of whole milk per week as a kid. Several times a day, whenever I was thirsty, I drank milk. Never water. Not soda. Maybe, sometimes, chocolate milk with Hershey's chocolate syrup. But usually just tasty plain whole milk.

Milk is without a doubt one of the most ubiquitous beverages in modern America, after soda. Can you imagine walking into a gas station, a bodega, or a small grocery store that doesn't sell milk?

Milk may now be universal in America, but it's highly unprecedented in the scope of history for us to have access to dairy the way we do. In order to enjoy milk historically, one pretty much had to have a cow. Or a generous neighbor with a cow. Milk, in liquid form, does not travel or stay fresh for long. And what happens after that short window can go in two very different ways.

Way one: fermentation. Fermented forms of dairy were, for most people throughout history, the only forms of dairy that could be practically consumed on a semiregular basis. Without investing in a personal cow, that is.

Way two: all those nasty bacteria listed above beat the friendly fermenting bacteria to it. One or more of those diseases from a few paragraphs back strikes.

It sounds like this course could play out with almost any food. Maybe less quickly but just as surely. Yet milk, throughout history, has spread disease far more often than sauerkraut or beer has. Why is milk so especially deadly?

First, consider its origin. Though one gender of our species is capable of producing milk from their own bodies, that's not the milk we drink (assuming you are not an infant child with unusually advanced literary comprehension reading this). No, we steal milk from the teats of animals. The very production of milk, milk that we enjoy drinking, is a bit of a cheat on the natural world.

Due to its intended function, milk is extremely nutrient rich, packed with lactose and casein. It's specifically designed to deliver that which is needed for growth, for life. And therein lies a potential problem. Milk also is an excellent medium for microbial growth. It's liquid, and liquids are ideal habitats for microbes. Worse still for us, the type of sugar found in milk, lactose, isn't fermentable by most strains of yeast, so our closest ally in other liquid ferments can't touch the stuff. Plenty of other microbial critters can, though.

In the late nineteenth and early twentieth centuries, the population density of cities grew exponentially. Sometimes cows were themselves brought into the city to supply milk to the masses. The lives of many poor urbanites in that era were quite miserable, and if human living conditions were bleak, those of mere cows were worse. Relegated to squalid, cramped quarters in dark and musty cellars, they certainly had no green pasture to roam. Rations were waste food products from other industries, and those assigned to care for and milk the cows were often diseased themselves.

To meet demand, many farmers attempted to ship milk from the countryside to city vendors. This meant that shipping times went way up, while quality and sanitary practices went down. Questionable from the start, the milk was diluted with water to make it go further; molasses was added to return the expected creaminess, and chalk was added to make sure it was actually white. And you were lucky if the worst you were getting was some diluted milk—I mean, hey, that's basically just skim milk. And while we can all agree that skim milk is a disgusting abomination, it still beats tuberculosis.

For a while, if you lived in a city, there was no particularly good way to drink milk, yet people continued to do so. Milk fulfilled its potential as a microbial breeding ground, and people got sick. Lots of people. Tens of thousands would die in near-constant disease outbreaks.

Raw milk became a thing of the past with Pasteur's new methods for food preservation and storage. As bad as things were with the dairy industry, it was a no brainer. Tainted milk was a killer.

But it wasn't necessarily the concept of raw milk itself that was the problem.

Raw milk is currently undergoing a renaissance in popularity for the first time since that era, though a great deal of controversy surrounds the consumption and legalization of it, at least in America. In many states, small black markets to obtain the raw white stuff exist, usually conducted at farmers markets. More than once, I've been told, "You have to be introduced by someone." Presumably you have to be checked for a wire too; it really is almost that contentious. Raw milk cheesemakers have been subject to law-enforcement raids and FDA crackdowns. We are entering a future America where it is easier to obtain marijuana than the raw milk our species consumed up until a hundred years ago.

Yet people rave about raw milk, and clearly there must be something to the stuff for so many people to risk their lives (presumably) consuming it. In all the world of microbial foods, after all the bacteria I've happily thrown past the barriers of my body and into my welcoming gut, raw milk at first made even me a touch nervous. There is no record of diseased sauerkraut acting as a killing engine, let alone spreading tuberculosis and typhoid to tens of thousands of humans in a short window of time. Bad wine or bad beer might just taste off, but no fear of death looms in those bottles.

What makes it different this time around? There are plenty of instances of regulation and government intervention gumming up perfectly safe traditional food practices. But raw milk, and by extension raw milk cheese, is a bit more complicated.

When making cheese and yogurt and kefir for my fermented experiments, I could certainly just buy a high-quality pasteurized milk at the store. There are plenty available in the Hudson Valley—a number of local farms are clearly passionate about turning out good milk from healthy, well-treated cows, and it shows in the quality of their product. Would raw milk really be much better? I'm probably a bit on the snob-spectrum about plenty of things, but even as someone who practically lived off of milk for the early part of his life, it struck me as a bit of a stretch. After all, the milk itself is theoretically the same. All that's happened is that pasteurization killed off the microbes therein. Why should that affect the taste so dramatically?

My childhood love of the stuff led me to another, deeper question: as the Fermented Man, could I drink raw milk without violating the rules? It's an academic query, as there could be many other ways to put my raw-milk supply to use, but it raises a very interesting point, one I haven't seen discussed much in either fermentation or food-science circles. Can a food be live-culture and probiotic but *not* fermented? Or just barely fermented? If the milk is on the verge of fermenting any minute, is already teeming with microbial life but hasn't yet received that final nudge toward fermentation, does it count for my diet?

Still mulling those questions over, I knew I had to obtain some of the raw white through the black market, either way. I spoke to my friend [redacted], who I knew had been buying raw milk through [redacted] at a small [redacted] in the [redacted]. He got me on the List; I was told pickup was on Sundays.

The purchase was an undramatic affair. With no security cameras at the farmer's market, no SWAT team members loitering nearby, I didn't even feel as if I were doing anything illicit. The vendor had her milk stashed away in a cooler, unadvertised, but not exactly hidden. I guess the half-gallon jar I walked away with could have been full of just any old milk, to the casual observer. Raw, whole, 2%, maybe even that water with white food coloring they call "skim milk": who could tell? Still, I made sure to not break the speed limit while I was driving back home.

Raw milk does taste good. At least, the raw milk I've tasted tastes quite good. Half the appeal is the *terroir*, the character theoretically imbued by each cow's pasture's particular grass, the grass particular to each region and soil and climate and longitude and latitude. Wine, beer, dairy: there are few fermented products that don't gain in some way as a raw manifestation of the land that produced them. So this milk was rich, unique, layered: the sort of adjectives you'd expect to hear from some fancy milk connoisseur wiping the mustache from his lip, but at the same time, not *that* drastically different from good pasteurized milk from a good farm. Until it'd begun to ferment a little bit, I was hard-pressed to describe an exact way in which it tasted different. Most of it, honestly, went into smoothies and a few cheese experiments. Some of it got left in my fridge a bit too long and began to smell like Parmesan cheese. I thought about making some sort of dressing with that, then reconsidered.

A few weeks later, I would discover that you can buy raw milk quite easily in Connecticut, just a short drive away. Not secretively at farmer's markets: it's on grocery store shelves there. It's perpetually strange to me—and for once, I don't mean to be glib about this—how difficult it is for us to collectively decide what's healthy and what's not.

Neither side of the raw dairy debate is wrong, per se, though many are beginning to feel (and I'll include myself in this camp) that overregulation of the raw-cheese realm is pushing too far, getting overzealous, without a particularly good reason. Maybe even to the detriment of the product that it's supposedly keeping safe. And it seems, once again, the root of the problem is a basic misunderstanding of fermentation, a confusion over the alliances we've forged with the microbes around us.

Healthy animals in a nurturing, natural environment produce safe milk. As with other ferments, the naturally occurring lactic acid bacteria that have adapted with us to the existence of milk will entrench themselves in this new territory and ward off pathogenic competitors by creating an acidic environment. If all milk-producing animals were treated well, and their milk handled diligently, concerns over raw milk would be significantly fewer.

But as things stand now, making pasteurization the default failsafe for the milk we drink is the right decision. The industry could not be switched over to raw milk as it currently runs without disaster and death following close behind. Not because raw milk is inherently unsafe, but because it matters a great deal how it is produced. The way we produce milk today, in the conditions that we keep our cows, is not conducive to safe production of all-raw milk.

On the other hand, maybe we should be taking it as a very bad sign that this is the case. It says a great deal about our food system that raw milk remains under suspicion after so many decades of advancement in technology and health codes and general living conditions. It boils down to this, in essence: our economy, our demand for reasonably priced milk, cannot sustain healthy animals. Better to utilize compromised animals without adequate land to graze, better to give them artificial growth hormones and boost milk production. We can always sterilize the milk to eliminate the risk to us humans, after all.

While milk may be, to some extent, a product conjured through human machinations, it makes for an incredible example to illustrate the many further transformations capable through fermentation. It is perhaps through its unusual status as an engineered food, and the ability of bacteria to adapt and thrive in any new environment to which they're introduced, that so many interesting and odd food creations have come of the dairy world. Few other basic foods transform their physical state in so many ways, with so many distinct results. From milk to kefir to yogurts of all textures, heavy creams and tangy buttermilk to rich cultured butter, to string cheese, gooey cheese, incredibly dense and dry cheese, and all the bricks and wheels of cheese somewhere in the middle, milk can be everything from beverage to solid meal.

Nutrient- and calorie-rich liquids rarely occur in volume in the natural world, at least that hang around for long. Milk would exist without humans, sure, but not whole liters of it, sitting outside, collected yet undrunk. Without us, milk isn't really given the chance to sit around and ferment. But raw milk from healthy animals, when left sitting out at room temperature, will very soon begin to change. The first stage in the weird and wonderful pyramid of transformations that make up the dairy world is called clabber. Clabbered milk is sort of the wild form of yogurt. Yogurt is cultured—we add microbes to initiate the fermentation—where clabbering happens naturally, with whatever microbes exist in the raw milk. Since yogurt is pasteurized through heat before it's cultured, we're able to control the consistency of it. Clabber is more unpredictable, but also more effortless, since it will just happen. Milk will naturally take the path of clabber. We can steer it further when we want to make something else of it.

Like cheese. But to become more than clabber or runny yogurt, the milk needs a few triggers. Fresh cheeses like mozzarella can cheat a bit, avoiding any microbial influence at all by adding vinegar as the acid necessary to curdle the milk. But to go beyond a soured cream of partially separated solids and murky whey brings us to the second of the greatly weird quirks in this unlikely food's existence.

Cheese—gloriously weird cheese—is a product that we would not know or enjoy but for two thefts from other animals. Our first theft is the milk itself, the liquid from the mother, meant for a child. But then, bringing a whole new level of weirdness to the cheese table, the crucial next step transforms the dairy from soured cream into the aged, portable wheels of flavor we know. This step requires something called rennet.

Cheese without rennet could be no more than fragile curds or stretchy mozzarella. In simple, technical terms, rennet is the delivery vessel for some humble enzymes like chymosin that cause coagulation, allowing the milk to set into a rubbery solid with some tensile strength, binding together what we will soon know as cheese. And that's just great, because if we couldn't get the stuff to turn solid, well, cheese would never get much further than strained yogurt. And who ever heard of a grilled yogurt sandwich?

Cheese, like many ferments, almost certainly predates recorded history, so it does seem a bit weird that we're relying on such a complicated process involving fancy obscure enzymes to make the stuff, no? How did early cheese makers know what they were doing? I mean, where does rennet even come from?

Ah, yes, now we arrive at that incredible second level of weirdness I had mentioned. For most of history, the only way to make cheese was to extract rennet from the inner mucosa of the fourth stomach of a young, slaughtered, unweaned calf. (But honestly, the inner mucosa of the fourth stomach of a young, unweaned ruminant animal of your choice will do just fine.) While Inner Mucosa of the Fourth Stomach of the Ruminant Calf gives me a great name for my cheese-themed metal band, that all seems *very* specific to me for such an ancient process.

Fortunately, in case you aren't totally on board with killing small animals and ripping out their stomachs (and make sure it isn't the first through third stomach) to complete your sandwich, modern food technology has, mercifully, figured out how to manufacture rennet from other sources, mostly from genetically modified microorganisms like the mold *Mucor miehei*. Some plant sources for rennet can be found as well, like fig tree sap and the juice from lady's bedstraw (which sounds like a euphemism, but is, I swear, the colloquial name for a real herb: *Galium verum*), and were employed by societies that couldn't spare too many young ruminants, or were just totally not-metal about getting their hands dirty.

Today, most rennet used in cheesemaking is produced recombinantly. (Remember when you thought that making beer sounded complicated?) What does "recombinantly" mean, you may wonder, as I wondered? After researching this for a good deal of time, I frankly still have no idea. It's got one of those definitions that just circles back on itself, getting you nowhere: "of, relating to, or denoting an organism, cell, or genetic material formed by recombination" (New Oxford America Dictionary). Yes, very helpful. Fortunately you don't need to learn the definition of "recombinantly" in order to understand the rest of the cheese-making process.

If this is still sounding awfully complicated for something that has been around since before recorded history, and technically involved enough to intimidate even a dedicated, obsessive fermentation enthusiast, well, it is. And it makes the ingenuity of our ancestors all the more impressive—people who you have to figure must have been really, really hungry when they first tried some of these things.

Given that cheese, like almost every fermented food, predates mankind's ability to write about it, we aren't sure where cheese came from or which culture may have figured it out first. But in spite of the complexity behind the process, there are a couple of ways we can guess at for how some traveler or herder might have made the discovery. Whether naturally occurring or intentionally placed, milk was left in a young animal's (fourth) stomach. Once removed, the lucky herder found that it had transformed into something different. And weird. No longer milk, but curds.

From there, we can suppose, it was only a matter of experimentation to develop new varieties and uses for these curds through different tricks of processing and storage. All cheese has a major advantage over milk: it's solid, it's portable, and it lasts longer. When you're traveling and hungry, that's a game changer.

It's no great mystery why we crave the stuff, meant for our species' consumption or not: to some extent, dairy is one of the only foods inherent to all of us, the only food promised to us from birth. Burp a baby (if you happen to have one handy, or if you yourself are one) until it spits on you and you will see the action of chymosin firsthand. In the baby's stomach, the chymosin is naturally present to curdle the milk, which slows its absorption, improving digestion. We may not be aware of the cheese inherent in all of us, but inherent it is. No wonder at our enthusiasm for the stuff, upon discovering, against all odds, we could re-create it and enjoy it at will, devoid of the context of birth. (Devoid of the Context of Birth: I think I just found a name for my metal band's first album.)

As talented as I am at thinking of names for metal bands that I do not have the talent to play in personally, I am definitely not an expert on the making of cheese. There are hundreds of types of cheese, dozens of different pathways to turn milk into some weird and varied reincarnation of itself. My cheese making experiences are extremely limited; I've never attempted to make more complex aged cheeses at home. You may rightly wonder: how could I, a brewmaster obviously so learned in the arcane magicks of fermentation, be intimidated by a block of cheddar?

Cheese is messier. The fermentation is less visible, less predictable, more fraught with potential pathogens and molds both good and bad. Personally, I've come to accept that I only have the time and energy to master a few complicated, labor-intensive, ritualistic hobbies at this point in my life, and I suspect that becoming a master cheese maneuverer is not going to be in the cards for me.

The existence of cheese in its many varied forms and flavors throughout the world is a credit to the inventiveness of mankind, a great conjuring of flavor and portability that dwarfs our clever theft of milk in the first place. Talking to a professional cheese maker is a glimpse into this world, its staggering complexity, well beyond that of many other culinary pursuits, even other ferments. Talking to a professional cheese maker about their process and their craft, with the thought in mind that this is something you could attempt to learn at home, is like standing at the base of a mountain and trying to map out a path to climb it. It certainly can be done, but there's no denying the significant commitment it would take.

But just as beer brewing can be boiled down to a short list of deceptively simple-sounding steps, so too can cheese. Once again, you can even make a neat list of ten basic steps: you take the milk, heat it, add culture, let it ripen, add rennet, let it coagulate, cut it, cook it, drain it, and then put it into molds. And yet, of course, it's so much more complicated than that.

"The variation that you're doing within those steps depends upon the cheese that you're making. And depending on the cheese you're going for, you'll get that cheese based on how you change, really, just the slightest factors," Colin McGrath, head cheese maker at Sprout Creek Farms, in Poughkeepsie, NY, told me. "It could be the size of the cut, or the acidity that you're achieving, or the level of cooking, or the amount of the whey you drain, the size of the wheel, how long you drain it on the table, how you're salting it, how you're drying it, how you're aging it. You're still following those same steps. But it's always the slightest little change that you're looking for, that ultimately significant tweak, whatever it may be."

Sprout Creek had caught my attention years before I spoke with Colin, first based simply on the flavor and uniqueness of their cheese, and later for reasons both in and outside the rind. Sprout Creek is itself a fascinating place, a 200-acre dairy farm producing very distinct, hard-to-categorize hybrid cheeses from its own animals, functioning simultaneously as an education center that works to improve knowledge, agriculture, and way of life in the region. All things near and dear to my heart, and led by a cheese maker clearly unafraid to stray from convention for the sake of something his gut told him might be interesting. Colin McGrath seemed like the exact person I should be asking about raw, about safety, about tradition—all about the arduous and unpredictable process of turning milk into cheese through the power of microbes.

A cheese called Margie was out on the ripening table when I visited. Margie is a bloomy rind cheese with a creamy paste inside. Almost buttery in its delicacy, the flavor is surprisingly clean. But that's the point—Colin wants Margie to function almost as a showcase for the quality and natural intricacies of their milk.

"If you were to watch, the process that we use for Margie is really simple and very basic," he said. "But to have gotten to that level, it took us countless amounts of trial and error to get it to all come together. I've been working on that cheese for the last ten years."

That's because the basic cheese-making steps, the many potential multitudes of variation each step may represent, are still not the only variations that need to be accounted for. Before humans and microbes together even work to begin the cheese-making process, there's the milk itself, the cows it comes from, the pastures they feed off of, the season of the year—the whole world seems to conspire over a wheel of cheese.

The milk coming into the creamery can be handled in a few different ways: it can be pasteurized, it can be thermalized (a sort of quick, less intense pasteurization that leaves some of the native microflora alive), and it can be left totally raw. The government is slightly more lenient toward raw cheese than raw milk—slightly. There are a multitude of strict enforcements placed on cheese makers too; dozens of safety checks, some more logical than others. And according to some in the industry that I've talked to, it's getting harder, more strict, more frustrating—worse for the cheese maker, and likely worse for the consumer, who may soon see less diversity in their local gourmet cheese selection. But at least raw milk cheese can be sold to the public, without scouring secret black markets, so long as it's been aged a minimum of sixty days. Those sixty days, the thinking behind the regulation goes, are enough time to ensure sufficient fermentation, fermentation which will give benign, healthy bacteria sufficient time to set up their camp and ward off pathogens. Thus fermented, a raw cheese is therefore a very different product than a glass of raw milk.

Even to me, the government's thinking here seemed fairly sound. One can always assume a little extra buffer of paranoia built in when it comes to anything related to public health, but sixty days of fermentation, two solid months, I didn't think that sounded unreasonable. It's actually in tune with the general tenets of fermentation. At that point, any fermented product is going to be quite different from its original form. Cheese, like beer and bread, undergoes a particularly severe transformation. It looks different, smells different, tastes different, and our bodies even handle it differently.

While cheese may be no more than concentrated milk in one sense, nutritionally, it is quite changed from its original form. What's the difference between eating a brick of cheese per week and drinking a gallon of milk per week? This was a real question I had begun to debate, because it was my reality. I grew up drinking a gallon of milk a week. Eating a lot of dairy is clearly something that my body is adapted for. Not everyone's would be, of course. But I had to take that question literally: what is the difference?

The answer highlights another benefit of the predigestion powers of fermentation: the lactose in dairy that some of us cannot process is processed out (literally consumed) by the bacteria in dairy ferments. Knowing the basic process of fermentation and having a modest grasp of linguistics, it's not hard to guess at the connection between *Lactobacillus* bacteria, lactose sugar, and lactic acid. And if you have trouble digesting lactose but could eat a form of dairy in which most of the dairy has been predigested for you . . . well, you can imagine the benefit.

Various dairy products will have varying levels of lactose depending on their specific fermentation. A ripened cheese like cheddar generally contains only about 5 percent of the lactose that would be found in whole milk, while an aged cheese might be entirely lactose-free due to its long fermentation. We have fed the microbes all they can eat.

Which microbes are eating what, and when, is a far more complicated question. The potential complexities and diversions grow almost exponentially through the different life cycles of different styles of cheese. The life of a cheese wheel goes something like this: first there are simply the curds. Curds can be ripened. Ripened cheese can be aged. Salt can be added, and the amount will affect the flavor as well as the speed of fermentation. Salt will also draw out moisture and will alter the cheese's proteins, affecting texture by making the cheese firmer. Curds can be stretched, as in the case of mozzarella and provolone. Curds can be cheddared, in which the pieces are repeatedly piled on top of one another to draw out moisture, or washed, in which warm water is used to rinse the cheese and soften its final flavor.

And those are just a few of the techniques used. The process will determine the shape and moisture content of the cheese. Aging and fermentation affect just about everything. The terroir of the milk may make a huge difference on its own from cheese to cheese, but a mild Monterey Jack and a stinky weird Camembert can both come from the same milk. It's the microbes that bring the funk.

Given the government regulation and interference that can make cheese makers' lives a headache, one might expect all small artisanal cheese makers to be ardent, uncompromising devotees of raw cheese production. It just seems the most punk rock; the opposite of what The Man wants. But as an outsider from this world, I hadn't taken into account the many challenges that go into cheese production. A process that makes a logical pathway for one cheese might be a disaster waiting to happen with another style, and I found Colin's opinions on the matter more complicated than expected. His reasons were entirely logical, not emotional. Just as it wouldn't make sense to ferment all beers spontaneously, with wild microbes floating through the air, so it goes too with cheese, where different styles also vary enormously in their desired qualities.

Colin speaks of these matters, the choices a cheese maker has to make and justify, with nuanced deliberation. He is not the laissez-faire, care-free fermenter you often find in other realms of the craft, so prone to grabbing a jar and winging it. You can sense a precision behind his philosophy. Every cheese contains a long history of evolution, and within every step, a dozen carefully weighed decisions.

"I've definitely changed a lot in my experience here . . . I actually personally enjoy working with pasteurized milk," he told me. "It is way more consistent, way more predictable, way more manageable, and it's that small ounce of predictability that brings me that satisfaction. Because my feeling on cheese is, even pasteurized, it's still so unpredictable." Colin has gestured at the smallness of our confines more than once—the space is not large, and all the cheese must therefore share the same air. Milk vats and aging trays and maturing chambers are all within feet of one another. "Its life is only beginning in this vat here. It's taking off and you're trying to control it to do whatever you want it to do. Being an environment that is absolutely not standard, ever-changing, it always brings variance. My feeling is, even when I'm using pasteurized milk, I'm still achieving and picking up some of our native profiles, but retaining a bit more control."

As with Margie, a cheese that ages only for a short time and is meant to retain the nuanced flavor of Sprout Creek's milk. It is pasteurization, Colin says, that allows him to keep the cheese like this, clear and direct. "You can really taste the purity of it, the freshness of it, the grassiness of it. It's exactly what I love about it; it really exemplifies our milk."

The proximity Sprout Creek cheeses share with one another has benefits, adding native microbes and complexity back to even a pasteurized milk. And as Colin describes, it's not that any method of handling the milk is the correct and best way of doing so: each is a technique, a tool, with a time and place. This makes perfect sense to me: you do whatever is best for that particular cheese.

"I definitely go totally raw and totally wild when it's a cheese that I feel it's suitable to do that for. The ones that I like to run wild are the ones that can handle it, whether it's in terms of their acidity, their moisture content, or the age that I'll get them to." He points out a cheese called Toussaint, a raw cow's milk cheese, which is typically aged for five to seven months. "I just let that baby run. Once we put it in the rooms, it's very free game for all. A lot of different things move into that rind and change over time."

I'm beginning to get a better sense of a cheese maker's whole game as I talk to Colin, and I'm realizing their task is not to push the fermentation, to set it up and keep it going in the way that we steer so many other ferments. The cheese maker's task is to keep the fermentation manageable, safe, and tasty. And hopefully consistent. Not necessarily to drive the fermentation, but maybe, strange as it feels for me to write this, to restrain it. More riding a bull than herding cattle.

"Consistency does not exist 100 percent in the way that we make cheese," Colin said, explaining that, the way they operate, their wholesalers and customers know to expect this, and appreciate it. "Even with a pasteurized cheese, the composition of my milk is changing drastically season to season, and less significantly day to day, and you see that from batch to batch. So even though the milk may be pasteurized, I will definitely see variation in terms of texture, in terms of flavor, in terms of hole formation, that will still be passed through."

Colin said something that at first puzzled me in its phrasing.

"That definitely satisfies me in that realm." Then I took his meaning: there are so many variables lending complexity to the cheese ecosystem, he's all right with partially relinquishing that one factor with certain cheeses if it means more consistency and predictability. Not every cheese, after all, would benefit from a wild and mad fermentation that might overshadow some of the other flavors he'd like to leave at the forefront.

"Over the last ten years I've found some degree of a balance," said Colin. "Every cheese maker you talk to, they're probably going to be speaking like its gospel what they're doing. But at the end of the day, it's really all about what works for your operation, for your milk, your animals, your creamery, your skill."

Wild fermentation in cheese is far less predictable than in other ferments, because so much more diversity exists in the microbes wishing to call milk home—and in those able to exist alongside and one after the other. Despite its nomenclature and association with knocking out the lactose in dairy, many cheeses contain a far broader culture of microbes than just our old friend *Lactobacillus*. Heat-tolerant thermophilic bacteria like *Streptococci* are also frequent guests at the cheese party, and the colorful veins in blue cheese are a welcome, useful colony of molds. The colonies of bacteria and mold that may form in or on an aging raw-milk cheese are almost too numerous to name; too numerous to have all been discovered and named in the first place. There are more microorganisms living in one gram of cheese rind than there are human beings on Earth. Every factor of technique, in turn, may influence which microbes come to proliferate and shape the resulting cheese. Some may succeed, others fall out—a natural ecosystem, shaped by environment, temperature, natural selection, available nutrients, and the quirks of the cheese maker.

And it's not just one burst of complicated activity, either. Multiple fermenting agents thread aromatic byproducts down the line like runners passing off a baton. Each stage of development represents a potential new stage of fermentation, and a potential new realm of complexity.

Depending how you want to define those successions of microbial activity, yes, the process is not much more than a staged form of decay, microbial competition for ever-dwindling resources, removed from the workings of a landfill mostly in content and texture. All manner of species may get involved. The initial waves of familiar *Lactobacillus* may be followed by *Streptococci*, which can play a role in the initial ripening of the cheese, yet don't pose a risk of making us sick. And in cheeses like Emmental (and a few obscure others), bacteria like *Propionibacterium freudenreichii* and *Staphylococcus epidermidis* get involved to contribute acids not usually encountered in any other foods, but whose smell you may already be fully acquainted with. If you've ever had a cheese that smelled like body odor, that was likely a gift of propionic or isovaleric acid.

Getting into washed rind cheeses—a class of particularly pungent cheese in which the rind is bathed, skewing the pathways taken in its microbial development—opens up further opportunities for diversification. A rind can be washed in all sorts of liquid. Water works, but wine and beer are common choices for the particular characteristics they add. Beyond a simple direct addition of flavor, they alter factors like pH and salinity and steer the subsequent fermentation in often unpredictable ways.

"I see a lot of varying rind formation and rind diversity when it comes to what types of molds, yeasts, and bacteria will hop onto that environment after you've treated that rind with whatever it may have been," Colin told me. "Whether it's blue mold, or *B. linens*, or *mucor*, something will tend to favor that kind of environment after you've raised the pH, lowered it, added that alcohol, so on. Whatever change it brought, it's killed off something and brought something else on."

Most ferments follow a fairly predictable path once they get going. Cheese, not so much. It can't be an easy thing for a business. Working at Kent Falls Brewing Company, I can say from experience that brewing beer with a consistent profile and fermentation character is an incredibly anxiety-inducing endeavor. Efforts like harvesting yeast from around the farm or spontaneously fermenting a beer in our old converted dairy chiller "coolship" are certainly risky, highly likely to fail, but they're also small efforts, more whimsy than anything. The bulk of (most) beer production is (at least mostly) predictable (most of the time). The stress of cheese making seems as if it will never end. "Absolute certainty" is a feeling you never feel.

"There aren't too many rules, that's for sure." Colin sighed. And then, with a smile, added, "But that's America, right?"

Cheese may be chief among our elite food pleasures because it reminds us of us. For our sweat itself does not smell: it's the high moisture content of the sweat on our skin fostering an environment friendly to bacteria, feeding them with our dead skin and other delicious treats, allowing them to churn out their flavorful compounds. Have you ever noticed that our sweatiest regions are also our smelliest? Have you ever noticed that certain regions of our bodies maintain certain distinct aromas? The more you learn about cheese, the more questions seem to arise, and the stranger it seems that we enjoy something that evokes our dampest parts on our worst days.

*Brevibacterium* live all over human skin, while a member of their genus, *Brevibacterium linens*, brings us room-clearingly aromatic cheeses like Münster, Limburger, and the notorious Epoisses. These bacteria, known as "smear bacteria" for both their method of application and the reddish-orange tinge that heralds their appearance a few weeks in, can't survive in overly acidic or aerobic environments, so they thrive instead on the outside rind of the cheese. The differential in pH creates a gradient between the inside and outside of the cheese, furthering the complexity in a way few other ferments could match. Washed-rind cheeses commonly promote *B. linens* growth. Ironic, perhaps, that the best way to get *brevibacter* to be its most pungent self on a cheese is to wash it regularly, while failing to wash ourselves will bring a proliferation of the same happy bacteria. *Brevibacterium* are known, in particular, to enjoy spending time in the human armpit and between our toes.

Fed by milk from birth to death, reminded of the very human scents that give us our sensory identity, we savor some sort of strange, familiar comfort through the odiferous pleasures of fermented dairy. It must explain something in a way that mere flavor preference cannot. Of course we love cheese. It is an edible Oedipal ouroboros.

The complexities and difficulties of making a fine aged cheese have always been an intimidation to amateurs like myself, and even to lifelong professionals. Making cheese employs more mystery and seemingly-magic than perhaps any other fermentation — those waves of bacteria and mold, preying one on the other, the very unnatural birth of the stuff, propped up through our machinations and a few lucky alliances with just the right teams of cooperative microbes. Temperature, humidity, time, the very material of the chamber in which the cheese is being made and aged all play a huge role and might spell doom in the form of a failed, crumbly, or rotten cheese.

While cheesemakers like Colin would probably put up a good fight, I am fairly certain that I must hold the World Record for Most Cheese Eaten in One Year. Many times, I've had to ask myself that age-old question, "How much cheese is too much cheese?" My body became fairly accustomed to this deal and at a certain point, you just really don't feel like eating more cheese. Cheese is filling, as food should be.

In my readings, I am always delighted and amused to find some tale of a person following something like my Fermented Man diet but narrower. You'd be surprised how many people have been even crazier (or more desperate) than me.

It turns out that I may be but an amateur when it comes to the consumption of cheese. A philosopher named Zarathustra living in Persia in the fifth century B.C. decided to become a hermit and retire to the desert. While living in the wilderness for twenty years, meditating on moral philosophy, Zarathustra is said to have consumed nothing more than water and cheese, sliced off of one giant wheel he took with him at the beginning of his journey. Granted, this sounds far more feasible a lifestyle for twenty weeks than twenty full years, but either way, I personally feel like I get what Zarathustra was all about.

But for all the passion this weird and wonderful product has inspired over the years, as integral as it has been to so many civilizations, it is still caught up in our War on Bacteria, and for a brief time in America, was a cold fatality of our war of convenience. Taken from its traditional site of creation in the farmstead, the task of dairymaids throughout the English countryside, cheese appeared in a sterile new twenty-first-century incarnation: American processed cheese. This new "cheese" was unadulterated by bacteria, consistent, versatile, conveniently packaged, accessible to all, and lasted nearly forever. How many Americans in the second half of the 1900s never tasted a cheese crafted meticulously by hand, subject to the whims of battling microbes?

Our threatened cheese economy came at great cost not just to us. So removed from our past of weird local farmhouse cheeses, American troops landing in Normandy in 1944 destroyed several French complexes that reeked of corpses. Yet inside, no bodies were found, just incinerated Camembert cheese, lost to the world on account of its stench. Sure, I may have had a similar reaction upon exploring my friend's fridge, but at least I checked to see if there was something edible behind it. How many wonderful cheeses might be lost to history if we fail to familiarize ourselves with their bizarre nuances?

Please, make the world a better place: eat weird cheese.

# CHAPTER 9

# Differences Between White Bread & Cotton Candy

WHAT DO YOU DO WITH A LOAF OF STALE BREAD?
About the best idea most of us ever come up with is making bread crumbs or maybe croutons for a salad. So what does one do with a village bakery producing excess stale, unsold bread every day?

That's a whole lot of bread crumbs. Mankind can only be expected to consume so many croutons on a weekly basis. Let's be reasonable here.

However, if you happen to be a clever and resourceful Slav living in Siberia during the Middle Ages (in which case, apparently. you were clever and resourceful enough to invent a time machine allowing you to read this book), you might have come up with a very-clever-indeed way to use up all the stale bread your local bakers could hope to produce: a beverage called kvass. (Let's face it, the average Slav in tenth-century Siberia was likely far more resourceful than most of us are today.) Kvass made use of old rye bread well past its prime by soaking the hard loaves in water until they were mush, then straining the bready soup to obtain the golden liquid. The beverage is then spiced with a mixture of herbs and allowed to ferment for a few days. It's consumed fresh, while effervescent and only lightly sour.

As kvass starts with a relatively low amount of sugar extracted from the old bread, it's not a very alcoholic drink. Most kvass tops off at no more than 1% ABV, so it's generally consumed in place of soda. Soda makers in Eastern Europe, of course, didn't like the competition and made great efforts to co-opt a traditional old food in order to steer it in a more industrialized, profitable direction. Much of the kvass on the market today is made by those soda makers in a form more closely resembling Western colas than the traditional stuff, but there's been a push back, and the traditional stuff is hanging in there. You can even buy plastic bottles of kvass in Russian markets, like those at Brooklyn's Brighton Beach, although you won't see the traditional kvass carts that are staples on city streets in Eastern Europe.

My friend Dmitri, whose family moved to the United States from the Soviet Union when he was young, can remember the childhood experience of going up to a kvass vendor on the street corner and filling a mug with the golden, thirst-quenching beverage. Full of yeast and vitamin B, kvass is considered a restorative drink, and these mobile tanks dispensing kvass can still be found in Russia, Ukraine, Poland, and Lithuania. For those of us elsewhere, kvass can be made at home and remains an extremely clever use for old bread—nutritious, refreshing, flavorful. And, in an interesting twist on the cycle of life and decay, it returns baked bread to its live-culture soup state.

I needed plenty of refreshment to wash down all the salty food I was eating, and kvass offered a promising new option, less sour than kombucha and lacking the inebriating effects of beer. I mean, sure, I could still drink water . . . but what was the fun in that?

I turned to Dmitri for advice in making my own kvass at home. There were plenty of blogs and Web sites with helpful guides, but I was curious to hear his take on the most authentic approach. He told me that even those making kvass at home nowadays take many shortcuts. Rye extract for kvass is available in Russian markets; he gave me a few pouches to experiment with, though I set them aside to start. There's nothing like kvass made with good stale bread—what extract could hope to replicate that natural freshly stale taste? To ferment, Dmitri suggested simply using bread yeast. The manufacturing process for those packets of bread yeast isn't as sanitary and exacting as pure cultures packaged for other forms of brewing, and *Lactobacillus* bacteria take a ride along with the bread yeast. Many other sources recommended using a bit of sourdough starter. I decided to split the difference and try both together.

There was only one thing I was missing to make my kvass: the bread. Not only did I not have enough stale bread sitting around to make kvass, I didn't really have enough bread in general. I mean, I needed to eat the stuff. And frankly, I was finding good bread to be one of the hardest things to both make and buy. The sourdough culture I'd started never seemed to get the love it deserved, and as a result . . . well, I was buying most of my bread. And eating it quickly, not letting it sit around and go stale. At least here was an opportunity to put my sourdough starter to some good use even when it wasn't advancing to its final form. Maybe it wouldn't even notice that I was uniting it with old bread instead of nascent dough and take more of a liking to me?

As I brainstormed, I knew my kvass wasn't going to be all that authentic anyway. I just didn't have access to that much stale rye bread. And buying extra bread just for the purpose of letting it sit around and go hard seemed, well, cruel to the bread. But I had another idea, anyway.

OF ALL THE SPECIALTY FOODS NEW YORK MAY STAKE A CLAIM OF mastery on, perhaps its most unassailable triumph is the bagel. And any bagel shop offers pumpernickel—rye. I'm all about embracing local flavors. This one seemed like it was meant to be: sour bagel bread juice.

While I live an hour train ride from New York City, I'm only a five-minute walk from Beacon Bagel, where bagel master Art has brought some excellent boiled bread rings to the Hudson Valley. Prefacing our conversation with a mention of how grateful I was for good bagels within walking distance of my home, I told Art what I intended to do with his creations.

He laughed, but he was game for his bagels to be subjected to this unusual experiment. I went home with a paper bag stuffed full of day-old pumpernickel bagels.

The bagels weren't *quite* as stale as I wanted them to be, so I toasted them in the oven for a bit. After that, it was time for the hot water bath. I'd let them soak overnight to make sure adequate levels of bagelyness were established for my bagel juice, and so that any rogue microbes that happened to be along for the ride could get a head start. For a boost of flavor, I threw in a bit of lemon juice and some mint leaves, as well as a tablespoon of salt to ensure the fermentation went down the right track. Everything could stay in the stainless-steel pot I'd heated the water in; I covered it with cheesecloth and left it for the night.

The next afternoon, it was time to strain the mess. I had not accounted for how fun this particular stage of the process would be. Or, to be more specific, how not fun.

The bagels had swelled to multiple times their original size; each was now more of a soggy inner tube than bagel. And their sogginess was . . . visceral. Few sights are as unappetizing as soggy bread, but the pumpernickel bagels, being darker and denser, formed a determined mass in my pot, overextending themselves to greedily suck up as much liquid as possible.

I grabbed my largest funnel and a glass jug. My colander fit into the wide opening of the funnel, and for extra straining power, I lined it with a thin layer of cheesecloth. This way I could ball up the cheesecloth once most of the liquid had dripped out and still wring a bit more from my bagels. They had soaked up so much liquid, I figured it'd take some serious straining to get it back out. Little did I know.

I let the soggy bagel lumps sit in the funnel/strainer setup for a long time, draining. The bagels seemed to enjoy their rebirth as sponges and were not eager to move on. Adding to the tediousness of the venture, I could only fit so many of them in the funnel-colander reception area at a time. Attempting to squeeze more liquid prematurely from the pot with a heavy wooden spoon proved a futile, mess-making decision. At this point, most of my surroundings, and much of myself, has been christened with bagel juice.

Perhaps, I considered, this could have been planned out a bit better. Some setup with more bagel capacity than my funnel. Few household tools, it turns out, are engineered to accommodate a swollen soggy circle of dense bread.

For lunch: grilled cheese. A few hours dripped by. For dinner: bologna and cheese sandwich. I wish I had saved a bagel to make the sandwich with, but no matter.

Finally, the jug was full. A swamp of damp bagels remained. I gifted it to the woods behind my house.

After I'd added the cultures of yeast and bacteria that would ensure some fermentation kicked off, as well as a cup of sugar to feed them, I put a stopper and airlock on the jug. As with beer, a ferment like kvass has the potential to pump out a decent amount of $CO_2$; more than I'd want to trust to the care of a mason jar with a loose lid. Sure enough, by the next morning, there was a thin crown of foam on the liquid, a sure sign that the critters inside the jug were doing their thing.

But the kvass still wasn't quite ready. In a few days, when the bagel juice was almost done fermenting, I would pour it into bottles and add a bit more sugar to feed the yeast so they would produce the extra $CO_2$ necessary to carbonate the drink. And I'd have to wait a few more days after that for carbonation to happen before I could finally pop the stuff in my fridge and have the cold, refreshing bagel juice I desired.

All worth it.

I love kvass. Slightly bready, slightly lemony, it's unexpectedly stripped of almost all the pungent character of the pumpernickel bread it's made from—even its dark color. It really is like drinking liquid sourdough bread, if slightly weirder in flavor than most bread usually tastes. Additions like mint or lemon or raisins can be increased in order to steer the flavor in bold new directions, or to cover up the flavor of the kvass itself. The level of sourness, too, will depend on both how much extra sugar you add and how long you let it sit to ferment.

In some ways, I was happier drinking my bread than I was eating it. While my kvass came out great, bread projects were a bit hit or miss. The limited time I could dedicate to each of my various pursuits prevented me from really focusing on any one of them. With good sourdough bread, it's a bit harder to be part-time than with other ferments. One can ferment pickles any time they please, but one does not simply walk casually into sourdough bread baking. I had no real plans to live off of kvass, but bread, by necessity, formed a large portion of my diet. Nothing would have made me happier than producing a perfect rustic loaf of sourdough every few days, but it wasn't in the cards. I knew I wanted sourdough, but I also had enough experience with bread making to know what such a lengthy fermentation entailed: making a starter, feeding a starter, discarding portions of a starter, feeding a leaven with your starter, testing the leaven, using the leaven to make dough, proofing the dough, baking the dough, and, last but not least, burning your mouth on the moist crumb of the bread because you'd waited so long for the damn thing to be ready and weren't going to wait any longer.

Of course sourdough bread (or as people used to call it: bread) would be the most complicated type of loaf one can make. The longer a fermentation, in general, the more complex the flavors it will produce. The steps involved in sourdough-bread making might be on par with making beer, but I was already making beer, and fermenting barley is demanding enough just doing it one way.

Plus, something bothered me about sourdough-bread making that I don't see too many bakers mention: I felt guilty about the amount of flour wasted in just feeding a sourdough starter. This culture, regularly fed, would be used to ferment the sourdough bread that theoretically I would be making five steps down the line, but as a food there was nothing wrong with it—it was just too premature to become bread. The conundrum was this: to keep the culture healthy, it needed to be fed on a regular basis. To feed it on a regular basis, one needs to either toss out some portion of the existing culture and replace that with new flour and water or end up with a swimming-pool-sized sourdough culture.

Rather than toss it, I devised other uses for the excess of funky living-flour goo. It could become sourdough pancakes. (Why not? Pancakes don't need to rise much.) It could even become sourdough kimchi pancakes with fermented gochujang spicy chili soybean sauce: fermentation trifecta. Same with sourdough pizza crust: another perfect application for sourdough bread that wasn't quite prepared to take the shape of a loaf. And of course, discarded sourdough starter could go into my tasty fermented bagel juice. Not that the kvass was any less work to make, or that it required a whole lot of sourdough culture to begin the bagel fermentation, but still, any overlap between my fermentation projects felt harmonious and useful.

I enjoyed my alternate uses of discarded sourdough starter, and as time went on, I took the time to actually advance the starter into the form of bread less and less. I'll admit, I was not confident. I'd made some upgrades to my baking repertoire from previous years. Bread had always emerged pale and uninspired from my oven, lacking the epic lunar-surface crust of a rugged artisanal loaf. So I picked up what I had heard to be the secret for a great crust at home: a Dutch oven pan, which traps moisture, thus emulating the conditions inside a commercial oven. Even with this neat trick, the loaves I made turned out only acceptable, and that didn't seem quite good enough.

Acceptable bread is easy to find. There's acceptable, average, mediocre bread all over the place. Americans are drowning in flour. I wanted exceptional bread. Healthy, filling, flavorful bread.

The guidelines for bread making laid out by world-class bakers only made me all the more concerned that incorporating the perfect loaf of bread into my life was going to be harder than I'd anticipated, even as someone who'd dabbled (failed) at bread making off and on now for years. Fermented veggies require basically only one stage of effort: the initial brining and packing. Even beer making falls mostly within two stages of effort: the brew day and—separated by a few weeks of patience—the packaging day.

Sourdough, like any other ferment, is alive. And it is hungry for attention. Simply maintaining the sourdough culture is far more involved, commitment-wise, than producing a beer. There are no isolated incidents of effort; the culture will ask a daily routine of you. To me, at least, making pancakes from discarded starter never felt like a cheat, never felt like I was shirking my bread-baking responsibilities, because I had already spent a perfectly substantial amount of time keeping the thing alive. But when you want to make bread with it . . . well, now it's time for a few more exercises. And not just, "Roll the bread up into something resembling the shape of a loaf, preheat oven to 500°F, and plop it in your Dutch oven," but an entirely new series of activities.

After the continual fermentation of the starter, but before you begin on the bread itself, an intermediary fermentation of the leaven is required—you're sort of halfway to having dough here. Following this new growth phase for the culture, you mix the rest of the dough up and let it ferment some more, much like the first of two steps involved in making beer. This is called the "bulk ferment." After this stage of fermentation, you can finally shape. Some bakers do multiple shapings, but after the first, regardless, you'll need to let the dough rest. If you do a second shaping, you'll then need to do another rest. All of these stages can eat up hours quickly, and some bakers will *also* leave their dough to mature in a fridge overnight between the bulk fermentation and the first shaping, so by this point, you may well be on day two or three of your hands-on bread-related efforts, not to mention weeks into your sourdough starter nurturing. But at long last, after all this shaping and rest, you can finally preheat your oven and bake that needy dough.

I'm far from the first to see the significance of the sourdough culture as its own distinct entity. As the primary means of making bread throughout history—before packets of yeast were available to buy in a grocery market, before anyone knew what yeast was to even think of putting it in a packet—a sourdough culture was cherished within families, by bakers, as the semimystical stew that it is. Some of the mysteries of sourdough remain stubbornly unsolved even today: some of the microbes that perform sourdough bread fermentation have never been found outside of a sourdough starter, begging the question: where do they come from in the first place? Just how adaptive are bacteria that they can seem to appear in these unlikely environments anywhere in the world, apparently spontaneously? And what did historic people imagine was really happening in that weird bubbly flour soup in the jar?

Sourdough starter is basically bread porridge that has not yet become bread in the way we think of bread but without which bread as we think of it cannot be made. Stories abound of someone's distant relative smuggling their family sourdough culture along for the ride from the Old World to the New, among their very few other possessions. Rugged prospectors in Alaska and western Canada who spent an entire winter north of the Arctic Circle were nicknamed "sourdoughs" for their habit of keeping a sourdough culture warm against their body to ensure it would live.

A fitting parallel, because without discovering the process with which to ferment grains into bread and alcohol, human society would look quite a bit different than it does now. In fact, it might not have existed at all.

AMONG FOODS NEARLY LOST TO THE MAW OF INDUSTRIALIZATION, those most neglected in our darkest decades are often now those shining the brightest, subject to the most innovation and fanfare. Good and possibly even great beer can be found in just about any corner of America these days. Good and often even great cheese can be found almost anywhere—if not in the town where you live, then at least in a market the next town over. We have come so far since our days of swilling light lagers and melting uniform squares of semisolid orange "processed cheese product."

And then, of course, there's bread, the third point in my Triangle of Simple Foods. But bread is still in a sad state.

Going into the year, I knew bread would be one of the easiest sources of calories for me; my practical fallback food. While I didn't want to underestimate the amount of cheese I could consume, bread is even more readily available, is more portable, more easily eaten while traveling or walking, and is already the foundation of a great many meals. Part of my thinking when agreeing to this mad project was this: well, if I get really desperate, I can just eat a loaf of bread every day. I haven't found any examples from history of anyone living entirely off of bread just yet, and there is that idiom about "bread alone" we're all familiar with.

But here is the thing about opinions, and the unfairly maligned art of snobbery: the more immersed in something you are, the more intimate and regular your experiences with it, the more intense, and very specific, your opinions on that subject become. Doesn't matter whether it's the discography of Led Zeppelin or the tenderness of a French baguette.

In other words, one (not entirely unexpected) repercussion of my year of fermentation: I have developed extremely strong and highly specific opinions about bread.

And I have concluded that American bread has a long way to go, at least in catching up with the resurgence that beer and cheese have enjoyed. Personally, I believe this is because we have mostly failed to actually realize what went wrong in the first place. With beer, this was fairly easily diagnosed. Hundreds of years of innovation and regional diversity were obliterated by a culture obsessed with a newly invented, more aesthetically pleasing and easier-to-consume-in-volume beer style, as well as the gleaming sanitary practices that gave rise to it. Essentially the same for cheese: diversity died as a selling point, old-world styles were forgotten, and cheese became a commodity. Bread, beer, and cheese: why complicate the world by having more than one option for each?

At last, we've redeveloped some of the variety that we were missing, stolen at least some portion of these foods back from the mass-production factories and begun to put them back into the hands of artists. So why hasn't this same movement fixed bread?

The first sign of trouble struck me as I hunted for bread throughout the early months of the year. Eating such large quantities of it, I was determined to track down the best bread anywhere

I went and learn from it. Bread was one of those things I had always enjoyed, occasionally tried to make at home, and didn't think about terribly much otherwise. I could tell when it was bad, when it was good, and had already figured out that most of it was just okay. But I wanted to become, if not a master baker myself, then at least someone who understood the basic tenets of a brilliant loaf of bread.

The first warning sign that Americans as a whole do not particularly respect bread, even still, clicked for me as I entered bakery after bakery. I had always had it in my mind, naively, that a bakery was where one might go to find good bread. Generally, this is not really the whole story. It seems to me now that a bakery has become a place where desserts are made. I have visited a number of bakeries that do not make bread at all. The business of a bakery seems to have evolved into a more general range of flour-based concoctions. Most bakeries that I've been in since I started paying attention to this have a few generic-looking loaves in four or five varieties, and then a huge assortment of baked goods like pastries, rolls, muffins, cupcakes, all variations of dessert or its sugary breakfast equivalent. The business has shifted. Loaves of fermented dough are perhaps no longer the bread and butter of a bakery.

Maybe, I thought, it was just New York. I've found great bread elsewhere. It's not too difficult to track down in NYC, but upstate, there were only a handful of bakeries to begin with, few of them focusing on the type of bread I was looking for.

But unlike with beer and cheese, having a few decent bakeries in a nearby city wasn't going to be much help to me. Because here's one of the major problems with bread. Unlike many ferments, freshness is inescapably crucial. Sure, bread can sit around for a bit before it starts to get hard or moldy, especially if you aren't picky. But if you are picky? If you have this vision in your mind of the perfect loaf, moist and tender inside, weighty and substantial but not too heavy or dense, with a firm, dusty crust? Only possible if it's fresh. And thus probably not made in a large factory. There may be a few food items that are more effectively made on an industrial scale, but factories will inherently fail at bread, unless the goal is simply to load it with preservatives and see that its cotton-candy-like texture remains unchanged for days and weeks.

The average local bakery has both the advantage of proximity to its consumers and the disadvantage of competing with zombie bread and its illusion of freshness. Extend your distribution too far, and a solid loaf of bread out of the oven becomes a hard, crunchy brick of sadness by the time anyone actually eats it. Sure, one or two weirdos might still pick up your hard bricks of sadness to ferment into sadness-free kvass, and maybe a few others will realize they're out of bread crumbs, but the challenge of freshness remains the key to industrial bread's current victory.

Putting a bakery back in every town would help. But it wouldn't solve every one of our problems with bread. The hardships in the way of a perfect loaf are multifaceted and frustratingly misunderstood.

Another similarity between bread, beer, and cheese: they are a few steps removed from the world of natural, straight-forward fermentations. Each requires some steps of human engineering. A kraut requires only cabbage. Bread requires more work than simply plucking wheat from the ground. It must be milled, turned into dough, kneaded, let sit to rise, let rest, and baked. Even the most generic of fluffy white nonsourdough loaves necessitate a long, intricate series of steps.

And here, I think, is where we got tripped up. It is very easy to pick out just one of these steps and point to it as the part where what went wrong with bread went wrong, missing other steps that have, over time and thanks to industrialization, also gone equally wrong.

In talking about the state of modern food, many have a tendency to fall back on an argument known as the "Appeal to Nature": that something (food or otherwise) is inherently good because it is natural, and vice versa. The term "natural" as related to food has become so over- and misused that it's been rendered essentially meaningless these days, but we nonetheless feel fundamentally compelled to label our food in this way. And we assume, whether misguided or not, that the deeper into the past we look, the closer to nature we return. When talking about food and health, there also seems to be an inherent assumption that things were always better in the past: that the food our grandparents and their grandparents ate was more natural and, therefore, healthier.

It would be unwise to always fall back on this assumption for every single issue of food or health. There are many ways in which our great-grandparents were worse off than we are today. And there may be ways in which they lived more simply and perhaps ate better. Our ancestors did not die from heart disease as we do today, but paring out what change in our food or lifestyle caused this massive shift is tricky. Tracing an arc of "better" or "worse" from the present into the past is a treacherous task. What we can do is observe the instances in which food has unambiguously changed and diagnose whether that change was necessarily good for that specific food product, if not necessarily its direct, linear impact on our health. And with bread, that's actually pretty easy.

There are a couple of very apparent ways in which bread has changed drastically over the last century. We no longer rely on local bakers, for the most part, but on industrial bread production. Bread has gotten whiter and whiter over the years, which isn't a new phenomenon, but could not reach its final pale endgame without recent technological advances in milling. Flour is now as white as can be, and white flour is ubiquitous—so much so that most "whole wheat" flour is made by taking white flour and returning components from the original wheat that were removed to make the white flour in the first place. Bread, which once could not have been made without maintaining a culture of some kind (either a dedicated culture of sourdough microbes or sometimes yeast from beer) and a lengthy fermentation, can now be churned out in a matter of hours with lab-bred, quick-rising yeast.

Gluten, the magic that binds bread together, has fallen between the crosshairs of the modern American fad diet. While a small percentage of the population is indeed allergic to gluten—some seriously so, others mildly—millions are now cutting gluten out of their diets to dodge its supposedly toxic effects. This latest of our imagined dietary evils is a protein composite that gives bread its elasticity ("gluten" is Latin for "glue"). It allows the dough to stretch and therefore bread to take the consistency and shape we desire of it. Without gluten, we would never have had bread at all. And without bread, humans may never have had reason to abandon the hunter-gatherer stage of our existence and form society. Without society, we would never have evolved TV personalities to promote fad diets.

The importance of bread as sustenance to people throughout history cannot possibly be overstated. Were an advocate of the gluten-free diet to travel back in time and begin preaching his message to some European village, I imagine he would be laughed out of town within five minutes. Throughout various periods of history, it was not uncommon for over half the daily calories of a people to come from bread. And lest you think, "Well, poor people didn't really have a choice, maybe they had to choke down all this wildly unhealthy bread whether they liked it or not," bread's value and sanctity is encoded in even the language of our religions. The Bible tells of Jesus's famous declaration that he is the bread of life, a metaphor that has remained at the forefront of religious language for some two thousand years. How much of an impact did gluten make on human civilization? In order to convince his followers that he was kind of an important guy, Jesus had to vouch for his awesomeness as being on par with bread.

Partly, this paradox may be explained by the mere nature of diets. A positive change in diet for some may earn them significant health benefits, while at the same time remaining pointless or even harmful to the rest of us. But the percentage of the population with gluten sensitivity is rising. Some speculate that new breeds of wheat introduced in the last half century may be responsible, but studies have turned up no significant change in the amount of gluten between heritage and modern wheat. Maybe, if there is some new conflict between our bodies and wheat, it's not a fundamental difference in the stuff we're making our bread out of, but rather a difference in how we're making it.

Again and again, microbes display their value to us in prefermentation just as much as any probiotic benefits they may impart. As usual, nutrients become more accessible to us: iron, zinc, magnesium, antioxidants, and other B vitamins are rendered easier for our bodies to absorb by a long fermentation. So it shouldn't surprise you at this point to learn that a lengthy sourdough fermentation also partially breaks down gluten, even eliminating some of the peptides in the wheat thought to be responsible for gluten intolerance. Acids released by the fermentation also allow our bodies to process the calories from the bread more efficiently, by slowing down absorption of the sugars remaining from the flour. Indeed, sourdough bread will be less sweet and contain less sugar, once again due to the metabolic forces at work during fermentation. In a 2008 study published in *Acta Diabetologica,* subjects with impaired glucose tolerance were fed both sourdough and quick-rising bread: the sourdough bread produced a significantly lower glucose and insulin response. In another Italian study, published in the journal *Clinical Gastroenterology and Hepatology*, patients suffering from gluten intolerance were fed sourdough bread for sixty days with no clinical complaints.

It is only in recent years that any researchers have thought to connect our gluten concerns with the fermentation of bread and the possibility that a change in how we ferment bread may be tied to the small-but-growing percentage of the population that now has issues digesting it. But for large-scale bakers not entirely fixated on flavor, focused instead on making bread making easier, any chance to speed up the process was a massive improvement.

Let's be honest: sourdough bread fermentation is kind of a pain in the ass. And pain-in-the-ass pursuits are best left to the artisan weirdos who specifically demand such things. Considering my struggles to find the time to hone my bread-making skills, who am I to blame bakers for battling these same concerns? Reducing a process that once took days down to something that requires only an afternoon makes bread both more accessible to the average person and more productive and profitable for bakers. If the change in flavor from a new process doesn't inspire boycotts, what could possibly be the worth of a harder and longer sort of fermentation?

Consumers, after all, were leading the charge on the switch, embracing white flour just as they embraced this new, easier method of production. Pristine white bread. It is what we have always wanted, from the beginning of history. Bread that was airy and fluffy as a cloud.

White flour can be easier to work with in many ways, too. When a loaf of bread comes out heavy, thick, its density is felt not just by us, but by the microbes fermenting it too. White flour makes for a manageable bread. To early bakers, I'm sure, it must have seemed a magical bread.

The breakthrough came not in a bakery, but in a mill. Wheat kernels are seeds comprised of a germ (the embryo of the grain) surrounded by its endosperm (the stuff that becomes white flour) and the bran (the hard outer layer). Stone mills throughout history simply crushed the tiny germ, releasing oils that would go rancid within days. But a new type of mill brought control to this process, the ability to isolate the germ and the bran and the endosperm. The endosperm could be processed into pristine, shelf-stable white flour, able to be shipped across the country without going bad. The rest could be fed to cattle, or tossed.

In certain parts of the country, it's interesting to pay attention to the names of small back roads. You can learn a great deal about an area's past simply by realizing that street names were at one time quite literal. It's easy to let these inconsequential names bubble out of memory the moment you've driven by, but pay attention, and you'll see just how many names repeat across towns, across counties. In the northeastern United States, "Grist Mill" is an incredibly popular road name. These buildings once dotted the landscape, but when industrial milling operations took off, wiping out their small, locally focused competition, the ghosts of these small old mills are felt today only in the avenues that bear testament to their presence.

White flour exploded the industry, but all this efficiency had its costs. In fully removing the germ and bran, these new roller mills likewise removed nearly all of the nutrition from a kernel of wheat. This isn't some hippie-dippy fetishizing of the past: this is a quite literal transition in the content of the bread we eat today compared to the bread we ate some generations ago. The bran and germ may be only 20 percent of a wheat kernel's total weight, but together they comprise 80 percent of its fiber and other nutrients. What's left is essentially just sugar, as far as our bodies are concerned. Think about how many things we consume on a daily basis that are made out of white flour, and then consider that white flour is not significantly different, nutritionally, from cotton candy. One of the great ironies of the modern industrial food system is what we do with all the nutritionally dense waste we strip out to make white flour. That which isn't fed to factory farm animals is sold to the pharmaceutical industry, which extracts the vitamins and puts them into, well, vitamins. You know, the pill kind that we're advised to take to help make up for nutritional deficiencies.

I hate to sound so down on one of my favorite foods, but there are a lot of things wrong with bread today. The more they stack up, the more obstacles in the path of a perfect daily loaf, the more exhausting and frustrating and hopeless the problem seems. Or maybe I'm just a curmudgeon too lazy to make my own loaf once a week.

Bread is arguably the most important food in human history. We look to bread as a metaphor for life itself. So why is it so hard to find good bread these days?

CAMPING IN NORTHERN VERMONT IN THE FALL, WITH NO METHOD OF cooking or refrigerating food, part of me savored the detachment that this cabin retreat offered from typical everyday conveniences. Any other year, this trip would have been just standard lakeside camping, a few days of roughing it, but my diet superimposed limitations that suddenly, then, no longer felt like limitations. Eating simply, without giving thought to having to prepare food, was immensely satisfying within this relaxed rustic context. Thinking about food was no longer stressful, I realized, at least for those few days. I could concentrate on other things, on just relaxing and enjoying myself, and bite into some bread and cheese whenever I was hungry. No planning. No preparation. No real thought toward the next looming meal. Of course, it helped that there's very good food of all kinds to be found all over in Vermont.

A few days into my monkish cabin retreat, I was out running errands, picking up supplies, and tracking down elusive Vermont beers. While wandering around a large natural food market killing time before a delivery of Heady Topper came in (see also: ways that totally normal people pass an afternoon), I cruised this new bread selection. I'm always on the lookout for better bread, and I figured Vermont wouldn't fail to deliver. Vermonters, God bless them, take great pride in the basic necessities of life: beer, butter, cheese, maple syrup, and bread.

A bakery called Elmore Mountain had a nice display of eye-catching loaves at this particular market. Not eye-catching as in fancy or intricate: the shelves that composed it were just simple, rustic wood. The bread itself was what caught my attention: there was a solid variety, but all of them looked expertly crafted, hearty and meaty and yet aesthetically appealing. They looked surprisingly fresh, too. So far as I could tell, this bakery seemed to shun generic white flour, always a good sign. A little placard made sure you knew which days of the week the loaves from the different bakeries were delivered.

I selected one that looked closest to my ideal loaf of bread. It was an incredibly attractive loaf, though with bread, I've realized sometimes appearances can be highly deceiving.

An hour or so later, hungry from running errands, I tore off a hunk and went for it. Tender but dense, meaty, flavorful, obviously crafted from genuine ingredients and well fermented for more than a couple of hours, this was some of the best bread I'd had in a while.

By the end of my trip it had dried out some, but the small quarter left of the loaf was not yet stale. A good sourdough made with good grain, I find, stays good for longer than your typical quick-rising artisanal loaf. Maybe not entirely fresh, but not quite a brick of sadness, either. The powers of fermentation may be limited in this realm, but still: fermentation preserves. And short of loading the bread up with preservatives, sourdough will hold out the longest.

I examined the crumpled bag that my bread had come wrapped in. Elmore Mountain seemed to be hitting a lot of points of differentiation from your average bakery. Under their name, a tagline of sorts: "Wood Fired | Micro Bakery | Stone Ground | Flour Mill." Of all the things a bakery might try to capture the consumer's attention, I couldn't recall hearing of a tiny bakery with its own stone mill before. A baker taking the time and effort (which I assumed was considerable) to process its own flour, placing the milling on equal importance with the flour and fermentation, was certainly worth further investigation. This bread was apparently focused on hyperlocal, too: called Vermont Redeemer, it was named after the variety of wheat that it's made with, grown twenty miles from the bakery itself. "Stone milled and baked in Elmore, VT. Redeeming tradition," the bag read, before detailing its refreshingly short list of ingredients. Wheat, salt, and a sourdough fermentation. This was practically the Holy Grail of specialty artisanal breads—it seemed to cover everything you could ask for, all in one loaf.

How does a society save its beer? More small brewers, focused on the traditional craft of brewing. How does a society restore diversity to its cheese? More cheese makers, focused on the traditional craft of cheese making. How do we salvage our dismal, industrial-made bread? Maybe, in this case, the answer was a little more involved. But as someone starved for good bread—for the stuff that made such an easy meal for me, this year and any other—I needed to find out. I needed to go right to the source, to one of the few bakeries I knew of that had apparently cracked this riddle. I needed to know: why isn't it easier to find better bread?

Elmore Mountain Bakery, as it stands today, did not emerge fully formed with its oven and its mill and its rustic whole wheat loaves as the realization of some grand master plan. Like a good sourdough loaf, it has evolved, the product of a series of circumstances and adaptations. After stints in the restaurant business elsewhere in the country, Blair Marvin and Andrew Heyn moved to Vermont in 2004 and bought a small commercial bakery attached to a house in Elmore. It is not a large operation: from the unassuming driveway entrance, it would be almost impossible to guess that there was any sort of business at work off this scenic residential backroad. They started off, as most bakers do, focused on one task: baking bread. A variety of breads: creative breads, artisanal breads, and breads that their small local community desired.

For the first seven years of their operation, Blair and Andrew made Elmore Mountain's breads with high-quality organic flour ground by large roller mills, purchased from their distributors. The division of flour would go something like: 100 bags of white flour, 6 bags of whole wheat flour, and 2 bags of rye. This was the sort of bread that people wanted. Blair and Andrew are skillful bakers, and proper fermentation, they would tell me, is equally as important as the flour that's being fermented. Each bread at Elmore Mountain is given a different fermentation schedule, but all are long fermented, with most getting a sixteen-hour overnight rest before baking.

"We try to bake for a variety of tastes and preferences in our small community," Andrew told me. And they were, making artisanal loaves using commercial white flour that their customers thoroughly enjoyed. Or, one might say, demanded: throughout history, the general consumer has held a clear preference for lighter, whiter breads. Soft, moist loaves that looked handcrafted, sure: as long as they were something very close to white in color.

As inevitably happens, the goals for the business changed over time, though not so drastically at first. Elmore Mountain's wood-fired oven is itself quite special: the oven bakes off of residual heat, meaning there's no fire left at the time of baking. When a new loader was worked into the routine, hours were shaved off the day. The bread came out better, faster. The fermentation itself evolved, and Andrew's sourdough culture grew stronger—he's never had to restart the culture in the many years since he first obtained it. First born sometime around the year 2000, over the decade of the culture's employment at the bakery, Andrew has learned its quirks. It performs best with twice daily feedings, and for certain breads, a fermentation followed by shaping and a long (fourteen–hour) retardation works best. Blair and Andrew had stumbled into baking with no training or background, but they found their footing quickly. They made the sort of consistent, quality product that allows a business to thrive and, if it wishes, to expand. It is the typical trajectory of capitalism—and of simply paying the bills and being able to sleep easy at night—to grow bigger and bigger. But the couple wasn't sure that they wanted that. Their little bakery, run out of an annex of their house, was sustainable and adaptable partly because it was so lean.

A few summers ago, an organic wheat crisis threw the industry into turmoil. Prices skyrocketed. Organic flour became practically unobtainable. Bakers and farmers alike questioned the sustainable growing practices of the industry. Business models shifted. Eventually, prices slunk back down a little, but Blair and Andrew kept a newly wary eye on where their flour was coming from.

Then, another change: they had a son, Phineas. The impossibly long hours demanded by the business had to be carefully weighed. And as Phineas grew older, he developed a real hunger for bread. At only a couple of years old, he was already eating a lot of the stuff. So Blair and Andrew made a decision that would once again improve the nutrition and flavor of their bread, as well as circumvent the looming long wheat crisis—and, whoops, double their workload. They would build their own stone mill.

"Without even realizing it we had completely created a second job for ourselves, on top of already working insane hours," Blair said. "But for us it couldn't be any other way. We want to be eating and feeding our kid and our community the best food that we can. That has to translate over directly to making the best food that I can."

The goal was to mill flour that still contained the full spectrum of nutrients—to retain what was lost in white flour—but that would produce breads of the same aesthetic that Elmore Mountain had previously been known for. Their breads would still manage to look appealing to the white flour–obsessed everyman, but through art and subterfuge, sneak all the nutrients and vitamins of whole wheat back into the loaf. And properly fermented, on top of that: the Holy Grail of breads.

The mill, Andrew's creation, comprises two pink granite millstones, each thirty-six inches in diameter and weighing seven hundred pounds. I was shocked to see it in person: there is no question that the thing is handmade and home-designed; it is simple and functional and unabashedly utilitarian. With the exception of the gigantic stone disks that make up the heart of the mill, it looks like something that might have been cobbled together with a weekend at the hardware store; the same sort of creative McGuyver'd engineering that any budget-conscious homebrewer relies on. Yet this simple mill is able to process two hundred pounds of grain per hour with a 75 to 80 percent yield, depending on how much of the bran is sifted out along the spectrum from whole wheat to white flour. The broken-down grain powder goes into a blower that blows it up into the sifter—what's known as an "eccentric" sifter, Blair explained. The sifter is a series of boxes with screens that shakes like a hula dancer; a way of sorting out as much of the bran as they desire.

Baguettes, the bread most classically dependent on its whiteness, receive the least amount of bran. Still, the flour retains the germ and the endosperm from the wheat berry, and thus inherently more nutrition than typical white flour. Other breads get a larger percentage of the bran added right back, ensuring the full nutritional spectrum.

Blair and Andrew always bake with freshly milled flour. I learned that flour, unlike bread, is generally thought to be best with some age on it, and thus Elmore Mountain's milling/baking schedule is a bit unusual, even controversial.

"A lot of people will say to us, you can't be using flour the day it's milled," Blair told me. "And we're like, well, clearly we can. Because it's awesome. It works great."

And, whatever is happening on a molecular level as the flour ages and oxidizes, the tests that Elmore Mountain has run on it for their own edification showed one major change in using the flour super fresh: more aroma. Much more aroma. But even so, taking the plunge was massively intimidating. Aside from the sheer increase in hours and skillsets that integrating the stone mill necessitated, there was the way the fresh flour changed the bread itself. They started with small experiments, trying to calibrate how and when they'd make the shift. Their test batches, a few loaves at a time, here and there, would be given away to friends for feedback.

"We'd been in the groove for so many years," Blair said. "All of a sudden there was this product that was performing so differently from what we were used to. It ferments differently. It's a lot thirstier, so all the hydration had to change.

"One evening I went in for our shaping shift and I got on the shaping bench and started preforming the dough. Immediately I thought, 'What's going on here? What's wrong with the dough?' And Andrew got this like ridiculous look on his face. 'I just went for it,' he said. 'I mixed all three hundred loaves of bread with the fresh flour.' I wasn't sure what to say. It was nerve racking. It was just a leap that he had to take. But the bake the next day, the bread came out of the oven and it was hands down the best bread I've ever baked. The color, the reaction to the oven, the way it handled the amount of steam that we were able to provide it with. It totally blew us away. And as soon as we tasted it, we were like, boom, done, sold, we're never going back. All the regular and organic flour that we had was just phased out and kept for dusting loaves. We never even looked back."

Andrew found that the stone-milled flour fermented much faster and absorbed more water than roller-milled aged flour did.

"There are so many more available enzymes and nutrients when it's fresh," he said. "I have seen autolyzed dough, just fresh flour and water, that rests for a few hours and starts to develop gas from wild yeasts in the flour. I have to use a much lower inocculation of starter when I refresh (feed) it because it ferments so vigorously. It gives a much younger, less acidic flavor to our naturally leavened breads that really complements the freshness of the grain."

The multitiered scale of this operation raised one obvious question for me. Was the solution to America's bread problem to install a small mill behind every bakery? And the common sense rebuttal: would that even be possible?

But maybe it wouldn't take an actual stone mill in every single bakery; maybe just a few for each region. Such endeavors are already under way, all over the country. In Ithaca, New York, where Cornell University serves as a sort of agricultural research hub for the region, a group called Farmer Ground Flour operates as a regional grain co-op with a test bakery. Other, similar projects are popping up all over. And interest from bakers and millers alike is skyrocketing, according to Blair. She thinks the movement of bakers working simultaneously as their own millers is going to be far more than a niche few. And Andrew, who strikes me as a constant tinkerer—apparently still bored, with only the casual pursuits of baker, miller, and father to chip away at his free time—is helping to build a number of these mills himself.

But still, what sounded like the voice of common sense in my head fired back: could the answer to saving an industry of difficult, exhausting, low-margin businesses possibly be to ask those entrepreneurs to also operate essentially a second business simultaneously, one that doesn't even generate any additional revenue?

"I think that's actually what's going to happen," Blair said. "That's what I'm seeing. The amount of bakers that come to visit us . . . it's almost a revolving door."

Yet such a transition for a baker and business owner must be a bit of a nightmare to contemplate. Such an undertaking changes almost every aspect of the business. The freshness, control, and precision that the mill brought helped to make up for some of the other challenging shifts that Elmore Mountain had embraced. As the bakers themselves were faced with dough of a different nature, their consumers were suddenly buying a different bread. Some would grumble that the new loaves were too "wheaty," but as small bakers in a small town, Blair and Andrew are offered the chance to engage with the people buying their product, and to put a great deal of energy into education. And likewise, to hear feedback. They realized, for the most part, people who had been buying their bread for years mostly just wanted the new bread to look the same. Or at least not look too dark. Whatever first triggered the bias against dark bread, it seems to be ingrained in many. But if the texture and flavor are right and the color passes, that's okay. And to some degree, the new mill allowed Elmore Mountain to achieve this.

"The whole idea is to kind of educate someone on why they should eat this over white flour that is void of nutrition and minerals," Blair said. "We do have an advantage in Vermont. People pay attention to the food scene here."

After a number of trips to Vermont in recent years, the thing that strikes me about its food culture is its simplicity, its relative lack of frills. Vermont is known for being a state of foodies, and more than that—or perhaps as the root cause of that—maintains a fierce embrace of independence in its commerce. In Vermont, it seems the population as a whole has agreed to always favor small and local over corporate and industrial. Vermont is the perfect breeding ground for high-risk, high-effort small business; the exact state where the efforts of such entrepreneurs stand a good chance of being rewarded. The state's food scene has built a reputation not necessarily on a sophisticated, bohemian restaurant scene— though it undoubtedly exists—but on a mix of the essential and artistic, the refined with the rustic. It is an empire built on foods like maple syrup: an indulgence, certainly, but of the simplest, purest kind. It is a supernaturally beautiful state supporting foods close to the land, foods bearing an essential heritage for humanity, like beer, cheese, and bread.

Vermont may be my bucolic ideal, a place where the simplest foods are placed on the highest pedestal. After all, such ingrained interest may be the only way to support a lifestyle of eating simply, with widespread availability of the best of basics; a lifestyle that, the longer I entertained it, increasingly seemed to me the healthiest, richest approach. When eating simply, I've found that one will, almost by necessity, eat less, and eat more nutritionally substantial foods, regardless of their caloric scorecard. Eating simply, one essentially has to demand of food that it is wholesome and nutritional, and not some faux-food masquerading its worth with a veneer of hollow flavors. If we eat simply, we are forced to pay attention, forced to scrutinize those foods, to return them to what they are meant to be. Because we need those foods to matter.

Given our history with the stuff, few foods matter more than bread.

# CHAPTER 10
# Taking Cartman's Advice

I'M GOING TO TOSS OUT A FEW CONTROVERSIAL STATEMENTS IN THIS chapter, but this shouldn't be one: Trey Parker and Matt Stone are the greatest American satirists since Mark Twain and Kurt Vonnegut.

For two decades, Parker and Stone have skewered the extremes of political and societal nonsense through absurdist humor, way-better-than-they-have-any-right-to-be musical numbers, deft reliance on unashamedly vile characters as foils, and an almost supernatural ability to find the logical centrist viewpoint within nearly any controversy. Parker and Stone seem like not only some of the funniest, sharpest people around, but also the most reasonable.

Most of this, of course, is expressed through their phenomenally successful cartoon series, *South Park*. I had high hopes for episode two of season 18, titled "Gluten Free Ebola." If anyone could be counted on to properly skewer the extremes of the gluten-free diet fad, it was *South Park*.

The approach the show takes is, I suppose, predictable, but for good reason. Nothing shines a light on how absurd people's reactions can be than ratcheting up the behavior of their fictional representatives to just a notch or two past reality. In reality: people are freaking out about gluten, avoiding it like it's the plague. In *South Park* reality: people are freaking out about gluten, avoiding it like the plague . . . and then it actually turns out to be just as horrifying and plaguelike as everyone claims. In *South Park* reality, too much gluten causes some truly visceral symptoms. Certain, um, body parts fly off and explode.

In typical *South Park* fashion, the stakes are escalated and emergency plans hatched in the tone of a generic disaster movie: blaring sirens; computer techs frantically crunching numbers; scientists rushing frantically around the lab, using markers and whiteboards to sketch out an equation to save society.

"It's dinnertime on the East Coast in less than an hour," one scientist announces gravely. "People are going to die!"

Cartman, the comedic heel of the show, has a vision. In this dream, he receives one vague instruction: "Flip the pyramid. The pyramid is upside down." As usual, his idea sounds nonsensical at first. But with the plague of gluten running rampant and the government forced to quarantine the infected victims in a fortified pizza shop, the USDA has no choice but to jettison its existing dietary recommendations. Their computer simulations can't compute a stable nutritional platform to recommend, not with carbohydrates off the table.

When Cartman calls in, still shouting about the pyramid being upside down, a possible solution clicks into place. Skeptical, the USDA runs the computer simulation: flip the Food Pyramid.

It works. As the computer tech announces, "Nutrition is stabilizing!"

Shocked, relieved, and a bit dejected, USDA agriculture secretary Tom Vilsack turns to his aide. "Get the president on the phone. Tell him to have some steak with his butter."


I DON'T KNOW IF THE CONCLUSION TO "GLUTEN FREE EBOLA" MEANT anything in the minds of Trey Parker and Matt Stone. It's entirely likely that they were simply turning the tables on conventional wisdom for no reason other than to land the most absurd, left-field ending to their satire of the gluten uproar. From a comedic standpoint, the image of the children of South Park mingling at a big outdoor party eating butter popsicles is a home run.

Part of me, I will admit, was fairly weirded out by how much my own life mirrored an episode of *South Park*. Was the joke on me, or everyone else?

One thing I do know for sure: this year, this diet, was not easy. I definitely hadn't started it to prove any scientifically valid points about nutrition or health, and yet the deeper into the year I got, the more tangential health issues it raised. I fell down rabbit holes I could have never seen coming. I got stuck, often, on nutritional tangents. I hoped the way I was eating wouldn't kill me, as this particular project would be a pretty stupid way to do myself in. However I felt, whatever I ate, every element of my life this year seemed determined to raise new challenges. For a variety of reasons, personal and professional and cheese related, it may have been the hardest year of my life. While I brought most of these difficulties upon myself, those not strictly related to my project were then exacerbated by the fact that I couldn't just run out and take a break from the world with a bowl of guacamole. No, whatever I was doing, wherever my career and personal life took me, I always had to be contemplating my next meal.

I felt trapped, cornered, and buried in work. It was often maddening to think that I was stuck on this self-made mountain of cheese and butter and bread with no way down until January 1, 2015.

As I descended slowly but surely into madness, I became bitter at mealtimes, annoyed morning to evening at the grumbling in my stomach, constantly resentful that calories were no longer something I could tick off my daily requirements with barely a thought. So much effort was involved, and that was new. I never before could have imagined having to work so hard just to ensure I would have enough food—or at least a supply of food that wasn't comically redundant. This isn't how people eat anymore. In Western society, we have become the lucky humans so secure in our food supply that eating is now a recreational activity. A sport for some, artistry for others, a means of punishing or rewarding children ("If you don't eat your meat, you can't have any pudding. How can you have any pudding if you don't eat your meat?"), even a political statement. Few of us think of the ticking deadline on our next meal as a cruel necessity.

You'd think the year would have leveled out at some point; that the routine I fell into would equalize with the amount of effort it took to forage for dinner. At the beginning, at least, I figured this would be the case.

The first third of the year was a lot of work, yet mentally exhilarating, as I threw myself into a dozen different experiments. I tried all sorts of crazy concoctions; whipped up as many different meals from as many different ingredients as I could pull out of the jars in my fridge. Many of them were acceptable at best, and few were worth the amount of effort it took to conjure them. I tried numerous times over the first half of the year to make a dish out of fermented rice and beans that didn't have an oddly gummy texture once cooked. I tried my hand at fermented French fries again and again, and while this never led to a recipe that I felt would replace that old fast food staple in my future diet, it did lead to some interesting-tasting potatoes, and more excitingly, an interesting sour beer culture. All these challenges were a game worth playing. This was what I had signed up for. Something amazing would come of all this, with enough effort.

The second third of the year, I crashed hard. Distracted by all the bubbling jars around me, I suppose, I had somehow failed to notice as a long-term relationship imploded; the person who had grounded me, gave me a window of normality out of all this fermentation madness, suddenly gone. The resulting vacuum rotted me through mentally and emotionally for most of the summer. At just the same time, I switched careers—a risky move, on top of the risky move I made in signing up for this book project. I blamed my self-assigned workload for neglecting my relationship. I was a mess, and yet I had so much to do, I didn't have time to fall apart. I couldn't just hole myself away and take a mental vacation. Trying to pretend you can maintain peak productivity while slogging through a mental breakdown is like a Chinese finger trap: the harder you struggle, the worse it gets.

I can't even describe the pressure, the anxiety, I felt throughout most of the rest of the year. What the hell was I doing to myself?

How could this possibly be worth it? I told friends I was probably doomed to age into the male version of the cartoonish Crazy Cat Lady, hoarding jars of yeast rather than felines. All the same, I struggled to care about all that I was doing with the same intensity that had dominated me just months before.

All this anxiety, all this turmoil, this probable descent into madness as my stomach began to digest itself in earnest, for what? Just to learn how much cheese I could eat?

The final third of the year, I began to accept my fate. I needed calories. Calories are units of energy, and our bodies would like to have energy to continue doing useful and/or satisfying things, like walking to work, hanging out with friends, driving our cars to see the latest movie about a teenage girl saving the world from a dystopian future, or making more cheese. Every meal I had ever eaten in the past became a hazy memory, a mythical blur from a period of my life that seemed ever-so-distant. My schedule got busier and busier, the weather colder and more ominous, my bank account smaller, and my patience thinner and thinner. Elaborate, four-stage meal preparations that might or might not turn out passable were now, it seemed, not a very good expenditure of my resources.

I dabbled as much as I could, when I could: wild-caught salmon fermented in a vegetable brine came out exquisite, though that twenty-dollar meal was a bit too pricey to become a staple in my fridge. My mind, weary of the bullshit I had forced it into, chiseled itself into a grim economist of caloric accounting.

ME: "I could really go for some crazy sandwich and, like, what if we did marinated tempeh fried in miso and topped it with some pickled onions and lacto-fermented hot sauce on top of—"

STOMACH: "Why are you not eating guacamole or salads or burgers? This is insane. What is wrong with you? Please eat a salad, for the love of God. We'll even accept iceberg lettuce, just please—"

BRAIN: "MAXIMUM CALORIES AVAILABLE FROM CHEESE. EAT CHEESE EAT MORE CHEESE DO IT DO IT NOW."

It seemed to me that I had two main options for where I would obtain my calories: seemingly healthy stuff (sauerkraut, kimchi, miso, tempeh) that sadly offered very few calories to power me through the rest of the day, and conventionally unhealthy foods (cheese, butter, cured meat) that packed plenty of calories.

Inevitably, the latter category won out. I was hungry.

I couldn't imagine the turn this diet was taking was particularly healthy. I had never set out to prove that eating only fermented foods was in and of itself a worthy full-commitment lifestyle, but I also didn't set out to give myself a heart attack, either. I had begun thinking all these health topics would pile up around the most obvious subject—bacteria, harmful or healthy—and soon realized that I was finding myself up against a nutritional wall every bit as mysterious and controversial: fat.

Pop quiz: out of the three main types of calories (fat, carbohydrates, and proteins), which is the worst for you?

You don't have to answer me. (I can't hear you anyway, you're reading a book.) But the answer has been decided for you, in any case. Take a walk around your average American grocery store, and you'll see what we, as a society, have decided must be the answer. We've made it perfectly clear that fat is just the absolute worst.

It seems to be unanimous. Unquestioned. Actually, it seems obvious: fat must make you fat, right? Common sense, really: it's the same word. It's fat!

How odd, I began to think, that yogurt, a dairy product, brags of its low fat content almost across the board. I couldn't even find a yogurt that wasn't low-fat or nonfat in most stores, which seemed increasingly conspiratorial the more thought I gave it. Dairy inherently has fat, almost any other dairy product retains its fat, and yet with yogurt, we aren't even given the option to leave the fat in the stuff. Why? Perhaps because yogurt is so heavily positioned as a health-food, and no one is going to buy into something as a health food if it contains fat. Nevermind that we go in afterward and pack it full of added sugars—it must be the lack of fat that makes yogurt superior to, say, cream cheese.

Breakfast cereal, the highlight of Saturday mornings for children everywhere, now advertises in big letters that it is fat-free. Why in the world would there be fat in something that is composed almost entirely of sugar? Doesn't matter how illogically misplaced this healthy-sounding absence may be, fat-free is good! Never mind the calories from simple refined sugars, just make sure it's served in a bowl of skim milk.

Gummy bears? Fat-free. Dodged a bullet there. Ketchup? Yeah buddy, that's fat-free. Anthrax? Totally fat-free. Gluten-free too! Amazing.

While the gluten-free market is making a noble push to capitalize on our love of dogmatic exclusionary dieting, it'll be hard to take the crown from the great evil of fat. And nothing illustrates just how nonsensical this tendency is than the fact that companies can advertise fat-free sugar puffs for breakfast and actually get away with this strategy as a successful marketing tactic. Companies don't want us to care about context; they want us to believe we can be healthy with just one dietary trick.

Most of us have at least a small suspicion that sugar is not great for us. Yet whatever its ills, it's not demonized the way fat is. When was the last time you saw the packaging on a block of cheddar advertise "Sugar-Free Cheese!" or a steakhouse tout their "Low-Sugar Ribeye Steak!"

When we remove certain proteins from our bread products to theoretically improve their nutritional properties, we pay no attention to the composition of the resulting product. As long as there's no gluten in it, the stuff must be healthy. That's dogmatic exclusionary dieting for you: we care more about what we're not eating than what we are.

When we examine the questionable nutritional attributes of a hamburger, we point to the meat patty as the scourge of our arteries. That limp, processed mound of sugar and starch holding the whole thing together is barely given a second thought.

Now, I must once again interject and remind you that I'm not advocating for any particular diet in *The Fermented Man*. I will not be suggesting that we drop carbs from our meals, that one might never again enjoy a red velvet cupcake, that we avoid anything even vaguely resembling bread as a possible carrier of the plague. I love bread, after all, and while most of it is now a poorly made parody of the stuff, I will defend the virtues of a great, handcrafted loaf of whole wheat sourdough to my grave.

All I'm saying here is that we should probably give butter a second chance—and consider that it's actually a health food. Does that sound like the punchline to a joke? Something *South Park* might play upon for the absurdist gag at the end of a parody of nutritional fads?

It's not. I'm completely serious.

I HAVE ALWAYS ENJOYED EATING SIMPLY, AND I HAVE ALWAYS LOVED toast. I've eaten my fair share of it throughout life. During 2014, I ate at least several hundred people's fair shares of it.

Thank goodness for cultured butter. I had no idea that butter could even count as a fermented food before beginning the diet, but in retrospect, it seems obvious. Historically, you couldn't really stop the microbes in milk from doing their thing eventually, and by the time you made butter, well, it had to be a little bit cultured. Now you have to seek the stuff out—most grocery stores I've been in do not carry cultured butter. It's certainly worth hunting down. The probiotic nature of cultured butter is a nice bonus, but in my professional opinion, it simply tastes great. I don't know if that's actually a result of the culturing process or simply the fact that more effort is naturally going to be spent making the expensive cultured version a quality product compared to the cheap commodity stuff it shares a shelf with.

Before this adventure began, I used to skip breakfast most days. Yeah, yeah, I know breakfast is the most important meal of the day, claims science or whoever, but sleeping in until the last possible second used to be the most important meal of the day for me. But not anymore, not this year. My stomach would be a festering black hole threatening all around it with the gravitational pull of its hanger if I skimped on the calories for more than one meal in a row, and this was especially true at the beginning of the day, when I was already pretty hungry from whatever light dinner I had passed off on my gut early in the evening previous. As the year went on, the ratio of butter to bread on my toast gradually shifted more and more toward the high-calorie, high-fat portion of the breakfast. My brain saw this strategic alliance in purely mathematical terms. The more butter, the more calories.

It was a precious resource—more concentrated than yogurt, so I could scarf my toast down on the go, and smoother and less rich than cheese. Not that it mattered, I figured, outside of convenience. Wasn't I basically just eating a whole lot of concentrated milk?

At first, yes, this concerned me. Cheese and butter are essentially the same thing as far as their nutritional value, I figured. High fat. Dense in calories. My body ripped through them so eagerly that I couldn't imagine what could be left over to clog my arteries, but conventional wisdom nonetheless dictated that maybe I was setting myself up for a heart attack, or would be if I were any older.

"How do you stay so skinny for someone who eats so much cheese?" was a question that I was asked again and again.

My response seemed obvious to me, if to no one else: "I am hungry all the time. I'm definitely not consuming enough calories, or if I am, it's just barely at the threshold. High-fat foods don't just magically make you gain weight."

Maybe I was eating a lot of concentrated dairy, as far as the general ratio of cheese and butter to other elements of my diet, but I certainly wasn't eating many other high-calorie things. Even a gratuitous 800 calories of cheese per day isn't going to somehow crash the laws of thermodynamics to make me gain weight when I require 2,500 calories a day. And God knows sauerkraut isn't filling the rest of that void.

Given the state of affairs between myself, my stomach, and dairy products, I decided I should maybe do some research to see how many months I had left to live. Would I survive the year? While thus far I wasn't noticing any alarming weight fluctuation or heart attacks, the lack of certain obvious setbacks could always be an unfortunate red herring. Would my diet pose problems down the line? I didn't really know how to account for my general healthiness or unhealthiness so long as my body wasn't exhibiting any unusual signs, like exploding appendages or scurvy. I put the question to my doctor, and he told me much the same thing: I was in good shape to begin with, so if I felt healthy and normal, I probably was. When I went in for a checkup, my stats were all normal, even improved. My blood pressure had gone down, in spite of all the salt I was consuming.

Okay. The doctor seemed to think I passed for a normal human being. Vaguely comforting. But in order for my life expectancy to average out to whatever it had been before, would I have to follow this year up with a year of eating nothing but kale?

At least you hear nothing but how healthy sauerkraut is. And if I wasn't gaining weight, I just couldn't imagine what specific negative consequences a bit too much cheese or butter could really have. So no choice but to ride it through. I'm not a quitter. Dig myself into a hole, and I'll dig myself out through the cheese.

Earlier in the year, I had been brainstorming ways to add dairy back into my coffee without creamer. Yogurt in coffee, for some reason, just didn't sound too appealing, but I was willing to try anything once. So that happened once. Afterward, someone told me about a new trend of adding butter to coffee. That sounded more reasonable, so I looked into it.

All of a sudden, I was reading advice to put butter in your coffee for extra energy. To give yourself a boost in the morning and curb hunger pangs. Sounded fine to me, but where had this come from? While basically every food in the grocery store is still hung up on its antifat stance, all of a sudden the newest fad diet is telling us to add butter to our coffee, as if we've just skipped right over the fact that butter was considered an unhealthy menace in the first place? What'd I miss?

And why not just have your butter on toast, the old-fashioned way, with coffee separate?

I had to do some research. Something wasn't adding up—both in my own eating habits, and this whole butter-coffee business. The concept jived with my own experiences, sure. I felt satiated and satisfied with my butter decisions, like this was a food that was actually delivering what food is meant to deliver. I felt like I had a lot of energy, in spite of the fact that I probably was eating only the bare minimum day to day. So I could grasp where this butter-coffee thing was coming from, though it had the ring of a fad trend to it. But there was a missing link. Something breaking the chain of conventional wisdom that had demonized butter in the first place.

What was I missing? I started digging. I also started applying a thicker layer of butter to my toast in the morning. Might as well just go for it when you've come this far, you know?

I turned up more than I expected. That whole butter-coffee thing still has the framework of a fad, in my opinion, because it's not really getting to the heart of the matter. This thing goes much deeper than just butter.

Would it surprise you much, at this point, to hear that most of our conventional wisdom regarding fat and cholesterol and butter is a load of utter nonsense?

It wasn't always this way. Butter was once such a staple of our diets that it was considered an entire food group. Butter went down in a coup, but butter was framed.

You already know the story—it's just a rehash of the plot I outlined before, with beer, with bread, with cheese. A great deal of marketing dollars were spent on turning butter from a wholesome diet staple into a maligned, heart-murdering junk food. In its place: a creation of industry. A wonder of human engineering. A shiny, sterile, miracle of science. Margarine.

Took us a few decades after we spent all those marketing dollars convincing mom to replace the butter in the fridge before a bit more research revealed the polyunsaturated oils that make margarine the unnatural space-age foodlike product it is are also kind of terrible for us. Whoops.

And butter?

Well, just because margarine has largely been exposed for the fraud that it is doesn't mean that we've entirely welcomed butter back into our hearts. We fear the failure of this vital organ, perhaps more than any other. Our hearts—or, I should say, the failure of our hearts to work properly—still kill more of us than ever, decades after the uniquely modern scourge of heart disease first arose. And we think we know why. I mean, of course we know: the government has been telling us why for years. We know what our ancestors did not know, even though they strangely failed to die from the same causes in spite of their ignorance: there are good fats and bad fats. There's good cholesterol and bad cholesterol. Maybe sometimes we're getting a mix, maybe sometimes we're getting one or the other, but if we avoid fat and cholesterol altogether, we should, logically, be on the safe side.

Heart disease is terrifying, especially as modern ailments go. True, there's something brutal about a disease that takes its time, that wears you down and reduces you to someone you aren't. All diseases are horrifying and undignified in some way. But there's something especially alarming about a disease that can strike out of nowhere, ending your life within moments, with no warning. No one wants to die slowly, but wouldn't we at least appreciate if a disease could let us know it was coming? Give us a chance to fire back with some pills or an emergency room visit?

I mentioned before that a couple things happened in the first half of the year that really threw me off my game for a while. The end of a relationship left me feeling isolated in my stupid brine of self-imposed anxiety, and some ambitious leaps in my career felt like stumbling into a fog. Compounded together, I was suddenly left feeling adrift and uncertain about decisions I'd made. I don't want to sound overly dramatic here: these were normal life occurrences that everyone goes through at various points in our lives. I dealt the best I could, stumbling through the summer with a brick of cheddar in one hand and a bag full of research material, pens, and Post-It notes in the other.

A third thing happened that spring, though not to me. My mother's heart stopped.

She'd been fighting breast cancer from the year previous, though by that winter, the doctors told her she was in the clear. Huge relief. But for some reason, no one had warned her that some of the treatments, so helpful in allowing her to beat the cancer, had the side effect of weakening her heart.

My mother is a supremely healthy person, mind you. She's only in her fifties, and we've talked about nutrition and health many times over the years. We've discussed the nature of the American meat industry, and while we both seemed to reach slightly different conclusions, we could both agree that factory farmed stuff was an obvious problem. She began cutting out red meat in particular, and while not fully vegetarian, her diet is a perfect example of what the government recommends. She exercises more than almost anyone I know, of any age. She goes to spin class, doesn't touch alcohol or smoke or do drugs, takes our dog (a massive, bearlike, short-haired Akita) on regular hikes, goes to church every Sunday . . . you get the picture.

But as no one had warned her to watch out for heart troubles, and someone as healthy as her had no reason to suspect any imminent danger, she missed some warning signs. In April, she began to have a few weird episodes. One day, she passed out at work. My father arrived and took her to the hospital. Which, thankfully, meant she was already in the emergency room when her heart stopped.

She described the experience later as just like waking up after fainting. Having no real recollection of what had happened. Just: boom. Looking up from the floor to see everyone gathered around you, staring down at you.

It was some time before she seemed to be in the clear. She was careful, followed the doctor's advice, but the extent of her frustration was clear. Frustration and confusion bordering on bitterness. This shouldn't have happened to her. She followed the rules, did everything right. It didn't add up.

The more I read, the more I questioned conventional wisdom, the less I felt sure about pushing her to follow any particular nutritional advice. Everything seemed to contradict something else. At best, nothing was certain. At worst, any of it seemed like it might blow up in her face.

The world can be a deeply frustrating place when it just refuses to make sense. We may not all like to follow the rules, we may all hold a slight rebellious streak inside of us, but we do like having the answers available. We want at least to understand what the rules are meant to be, if only so that we can break them.

As far as nutrition goes, for a while it did seem as if we might have had that figured out. Over the last couple decades, the guidelines set by the Food Pyramid may have shifted slightly in the little details, and sure, we might have cornered the good cholesterol and bad cholesterol a bit more specifically, but we all grasp the general outline of a healthy diet, even if we choose to ignore it. As Michael Pollan famously puts it, "Eat food, not too much, mostly plants." And as Morgan Spurlock famously demonstrated, don't eat fast food for every meal, every day. These suggestions feel like common sense, and thus, they resonate.

Following a healthy diet may not be easy in practice, but we've been told for long enough how to do it in theory. And yet heart disease rates continue to climb. Diabetes marches on. Food allergies are popping up at unprecedented levels. Obesity is out of control, a plague spreading through developed countries around the world.

Between 1920 and 1960, the rise of heart disease in America seemed to be exponential. While it's true that many diseases we grapple with today may have been misdiagnosed in previous centuries— underreported rather than entirely nonexistent—heart disease was genuinely rare in turn-of-the-century America, by any reckoning. It's strange, on the face of it, that butter consumption plummeted at the same time heart disease skyrocketed. But nutrition seems full of weird contradictions like that. Due to the difficulty of creating a perfect control group with which to isolate and study specific dietary habits, there always seem to be these weird correlations popping up that may or may not hold significance. For instance: butter consumption dropped from 18 pounds per person in 1920 to just four around

1960, but maybe we took up a new source of fat and cholesterol that negated all that. Maybe the drop in butter consumption would have helped, were it not for a number of other factors that hurt us, worse. That's how nutrition often works: there's usually a lot more than one clear-cut thing happening to shape a whole nation's health. Parsing out the reasons one person may be healthy or unhealthy is hard enough. Figuring out the trends that turned a whole nation in or out of health becomes staggeringly difficult.

I estimate that I ate roughly a quarter pound of butter (one stick, if you're thinking in terms of crappy butter) per week for most of 2014. That adds up to roughly 13 pounds (just under 6 kg) for the year, or what an inhabitant of the United States a hundred years ago would call "Amateur Hour."

I won't even try to estimate my cheese consumption, but it's got to be at least two or three times my butter numbers, at a minimum. Hopefully that helped me catch up and balance out some.

On the other hand, our modern average American will down about 141 pounds of sweeteners per year, 42 of those pounds in the form of corn syrup. All told, we eat an average of just about 2,000 pounds of food by weight per year, a 2011 study estimates. So butter is but a very small percentage, even for me.

Here are some other interesting tidbits we've noticed since demonizing butter. It actually contains a lot of nutrients that help protect against heart disease, and were they not contained in butter, might sound suspiciously healthy. Butter is high in vitamin A, necessary for the health of the thyroid and adrenal glands, which play a role in maintaining the proper functioning of the heart and cardiovascular system. Butter contains lecithin, a fat that is essential to the cells in our body and helps us assimilate and metabolize cholesterol. (Lecithin is also taken as a medicine, as it's useful in treating memory disorders such as dementia and Alzheimer's.) The vitamins in butter also contain antioxidants that help protect against free radicals that damage our arteries. All good things.

But another way of looking at it: you could put arsenic in a tomato and it wouldn't mean the arsenic is good for you. The bad would still outweigh the good. So what's so awfully bad about butter?

Or cheese, for that matter? Or red meat?

Conventional wisdom and the last fifty years' worth of research from the nutritionist community would suggest it's the saturated fat and cholesterol. The stuff we go to great lengths to cut out of our yogurt just so we can safely consider it a health food.

But something about this has never added up. Presumably, we know more than we ever have about nutrition. We understand diet better than our ancestors. They just weren't educated to know that fat was bad for them, so they ate tons of butter. And yet they weren't dying from heart disease, and we are.

How did we decide that fat was so bad? Well, first we killed some rabbits.

RESEARCHERS IN THE EARLY 1900s WERE TRYING TO SOLVE THE RIDDLE of atherosclerosis, a waxy plaque buildup observed in the walls of arteries. Rabbits, at the time, were popular test subjects, and so we stuffed the little guys full of all sorts of things to try to figure out what was causing the ailment in humans. A Russian pathologist named Nikolay Anichkov figured out that a diet of meat and eggs, rather than the rabbit's usual vegetarian fare, caused the plaque to accumulate, but it took some sleuthing to find the exact component of the carnivorous diet that was responsible. Test after test, rabbit after rabbit, he broke the mystery open: it was cholesterol forming a murderous plaque throughout the bodies of the poor little bunnies.

To achieve this, Anichkov fed the rabbits a diet of 5 percent pure cholesterol by weight, or the equivalent of a human eating approximately a hundred eggs a day. Also, rabbits are strict herbivores, unlike humans. So you might say that stuffing them with cholesterol to prove a point about the diets of humans is about as helpful as stuffing humans with wood chips to prove a point about the diet of termites. But hey, again: nutrition is hard.

Researchers conducted the same experiment on other animals. Herbivores had problems. Dogs, on the other hand, are evolved to eat meat, like humans, and were able to regulate and excrete excess cholesterol fed to them. So we didn't learn that much about how human arteries get clogged, but we did learn, at least, that cholesterol was involved.

Unfortunately, many of these experiments on animals were flawed from the start, as the researchers did not know to prevent oxidation of the cholesterol in the animals. As cholesterol oxidizes, it builds up plaque much more easily, enhancing its negative effects. In retrospect, the experiment falls apart completely. But at the time, it seemed like a promising start. For us, the layered inefficiencies of this experiment are important to keep in mind through what followed. I've noticed this pattern in much of the nutrition research I've read: an experiment will feed X subjects Y food, to produce A result. And it can look as simple as XYZ, at first, until you step back and notice that Z was actually skipped over, and another twenty-three factors may have skewed the whole initial premise, but no one was paying attention to them, so who can really say for sure?

Decades after those rabbits died for nothing, a man named Ancel Keys came onto the scene. By then, the general assumption that more fat in our diet led to more fat on our body was, like a plaque of conventional wisdom in the arteries of science, already building. But it was low level. It needed something to rough out a surface in order for it to stick.

Keys was a bulldog. A pivotal figure in the history of nutritional science—perhaps one of the most influential men ever to have worked in the field. Few people in history have had as much influence on the health and lifestyle of entire populations as Ancel Keys. The habits of millions of us today are informed by a man whom most people have never heard of. Keys's biggest mark on the field came from his groundbreaking Seven Countries Study and his initial Six Countries Analysis. His research was the first to systematically examine the relationships between lifestyle, diet, and heart disease in different populations around different regions of the world.

In brief, the studies suggested that the risk and rates of heart attack and stroke could be tied to one's levels of total serum cholesterol. The cause seemed obvious, at least to Keys, who had already suspected fat as the culprit before he began. Put six countries on a chart—Australia, Canada, England, Italy, Japan, and the United States—and measure their population's fat intake, and one can plot a striking, distinct upward curve.

The significance of those six dots seemed pretty clear-cut to Keys, who campaigned on the damning ills of fat for the rest of his career, winning converts with his aggressive research tactics and dogmatic conviction. It certainly appeared that the more fat a country's people ate, the more they were dying from heart disease. But that is the trouble with such research: correlation is easy to find, causation not so much. How our bodies work (and fail to work) is extremely complicated, and everyone's body is a bit different. Recommending a diet universally, I think we can all agree, would be a bad move. In studying for what works and what doesn't, what hurts and what helps, it's very hard to control for variables. What may seem to damn one factor in lifestyle or diet may simply be the result of some totally unrelated secondary factor that was unknown or overlooked.

Worse, nutrition is an emotional subject and a political subject, hard to research at all without outside complications and biases. It's easy to cherry-pick research. It's easy to pick out conclusions based on how you already felt or what you already assumed.

Keys's Countries Studies laid the foundation for our conviction that saturated fat and cholesterol cause heart disease. Six dots on a chart is all it took. Of course, many more studies would follow. The Framingham Heart Study, the Nurses' Health Study, the Women's Health Initiative, the Guy Writing a Book Who Ate a Ton of Cheese and Butter in One Year Study.

As my year progressed, hunger and dietary aggravation occupied more of my daily mental space. I worried about my mother.

What she should be eating, or if diet even made a difference. The butter conundrum became vitally important to me. I started rambling to clearly alarmed friends about my newfound confusion over the supposed perils of saturated fat. Most shrugged me off. Most at least raised an eyebrow at my conspiratorial rants and at least conceded that I definitely hadn't gained weight eating all that cheese.

My friend Dan had born witness to some of the weirdest things I ate throughout the year. Cheese that smelled like a manure pit, green eggs with mucus yolks, stringy spider-webbed natto beans, and smelly old fermented fish. Watching me eat a piece of toast that was more butter than bread, he leaned back in his chair and told me, "That may be the most disgusting thing I've seen anyone eat. You put butter on bread like people put cream cheese on a bagel."

What's the difference, again?

Whatever I read, I wasn't about to change the amount of cheese and butter I was eating. But at the very least, I had to know if my monotonous lunches were killing me. If conventional wisdom was correct, they should be. But I read some thousand pages of research on the subject over the year, books dissecting and reinvestigating dietary studies on the effect of fat in diet, and I just wasn't seeing the evidence that butter was the thing that'd do me in.

Ancel Keys's critics pointed out that he'd chosen only those six dots that most strongly supported his hypothesis. Add in the other points of data that Keys had started with—a full twenty-one countries whose populations had been studied—and you had a chart that was much less of a clear pathway and more of a smattering of loose data points. Granted, on this updated chart, there does still seem to be some upward correlation (remember: correlation does not imply causation) between fat consumption and heart disease, an association that's enough to be deemed statistically significant. So we can infer that fat intake and heart disease are not totally unrelated to each other, but it all gets so much more confusing than the open-and-shut case Ancel Keys presented. Even in his own data, puzzling data points emerge: France and Finland share an equal intake of fat, and yet instances of heart disease in Finland are seven times higher. Why?

Fat consumption is of course only one part of a diet, and humans (unlike say, rabbit test subjects in some curious human's diet study) rarely eat pure substances. Few of us ever order a tube of pure cholesterol for dinner, as those unlucky rabbits were forced to consume. And certain habits and associations go along with one another, making it hard to pinpoint which bad habit is actually having the most impact. People who eat a lot of red meat have been shown in studies to exercise less and to smoke more, for instance. And a modern eater who consumes a lot of fat is likely to also eat a lot of sugar. But Keys from the start dismissed any possibility that sugar might be a culprit as laughable, not even worth examining. Saturated fat was so clearly the guilty party when it came to heart disease that any research not focused on its association was a waste of time.

But here's where it gets really weird: whatever the tenuous association between heart disease and fat intake one could draw from this population data, a far stranger picture emerged when looking at total morbidity. Deaths of any kind. After all, even with all the plagues modern medicine can shield us form, a heart attack isn't the only way to die.

Repopulate the graph with this version of the data—broadening cause of death beyond heart disease—and the result is stark. The more fat a population consumes, the longer, in general, it seems to live. That's right: the less fat you eat, the sooner you die.

Does this prove fat is good for you? Once again: no. Data of this sort simply can't be interpreted so simply, though it often is. Regardless, research continued to pile up on the possible perils of dietary cholesterol, but the type of long-term studies able to even draw a correlation between something like diet and disease are supremely difficult to manage. Because subjects must still live a normal life over the years of the study and can't all be observed at every moment, it's hard to establish an appropriate, reliable control group. Some studies have shown nothing. Some have shown a correlation between fat and heart disease and were touted as proof. Others showed the opposite of this, and were ignored as outliers or flukes. I would describe the scope of the results as "smattered" across possible conclusions. There's plenty of opportunity to cherry-pick and show evidence for almost any nutritional platform.

The data that was agreed upon as useful to the heart disease research continued to show a strange correlation between overall longevity and higher fat consumption. That, of course, wasn't the part that was fed into the public consciousness.

There were associations between fat and cholesterol and heart disease, after all, and that's what we were trying to resolve. Modifiers—good cholesterol, bad cholesterol, good and bad fats, poly and trans and mono and un—get thrown in when we talk about these things, blended together. Yet, it always seems to emerge out of the echo chamber repeating the basic message: fat is bad.

In another study, the Oslo study, the control group continued to eat saturated fats from animals, but also a large amount of hard margarine and hydrogenated fish oils amounting to half a cup of trans fats per day. The experimental low-fat, low-cholesterol diet contained no trans fat at all. And another kicker: the experimental group, who saw a significant drop in heart disease, reduced their use of tobacco by 45 percent compared to the control group.

So what are we really learning, in a study like this? That saturated fat provokes heart attacks? Or that trans fat is bad for you? That smoking causes heart attacks?

Nina Teicholz describes the difficulties inherent in conducting such studies in *The Big Fat Surprise*, one of the most thorough examinations of nutrition studies from the last fifty years: "Diet experiments are really always measuring two things at once: the absence of one nutrient and the addition of another. Sorting out the impact of one versus the other requires multiarm trials, and these are often prohibitively expensive."

If one component is removed from a diet, something else must replace it to maintain the same caloric intake. If we remove saturated fat, what should replace it? Carbohydrates? Fruits and vegetables? Some kind of processed oil? In a controlled study, monitoring every single variable is like juggling a hundred balls for five straight years and hoping no one secretly swaps out one of those balls as it's up in the air.

"Reading these studies in the literature, one is reminded of a game of telephone," Teicholz writes. "Maybe the first person in line says: 'Fewer heart attacks, but remember several important caveats.' Yet twenty years later, the message is simply remembered as 'Fewer heart attacks!'"

In the general American population, the results of this message are obvious: use of vegetable oils accelerates like it's aiming for the moon. In the course of the last hundred years (before which, most of these manufactured vegetable oils did not exist), soybean oil in particular skyrockets, and shortening from hydrogenated oil sees a sharp uptick just as lard slumps into obscurity. Margarine enjoys a few decades of popularity before sliding back downward again more recently—apparently at least some of us have gotten the memo that it's maybe not all that great. Taken together, though, the overall impact is huge: these vegetable oils make up 8 to 9 percent of all calories consumed by 1999. Almost a tenth of our calories from something that our bodies may not be equipped to handle, substances that didn't even *exist* until very recently.

Another correlation one could draw: since vegetable oils were introduced in the 1920s, their uptake mirrors the rise in heart disease with disturbing exactness.

You could perhaps see one small victory in the fact that many of us are turning away from margarine, realizing it may not actually be a very healthy replacement for butter. But fat is far from vindicated in the public eye. From a nation that once ate 18 pounds of butter per person a year, on top of copious amounts of lard, cheese, and meat, it's staggering to think how much the average person's diet has changed.

Why was it so easy for fat to take the fall? For all the bungled science and poorly controlled studies, I would argue that it was more of a misfire in what the public took for common sense that ultimately led to its woeful reputation. Fat just *seems* like it should be unhealthy. If nutrition were a slasher flick, fat would be the sweaty, balding, overweight mailman that delivers your mail at weird hours and then just kind of stands there, staring in your window.

Branding is important. Sugar got just the right packaging. It's "sweet," which happens to be a synonym for nice, pleasant, happy—all sunny good things.

Fat is called "fat."

Bad name, and it just looks bad for you. Fat actually looks like something that would make you fat. Pooling on your plate, congealing as it cools, glistening as it stains your napkin with a big smudge of grease. Watch it melt off your meat and it's easy to picture that stuff re-convening in your arteries, clogging, slowly but surely killing you.

I've tipped my hand at this point, and maybe there's no small bias involved on my part. It was certainly reassuring to read that research in recent years is stacking up in favor of butter's comeback, because it meant that my own diet for the next few months was slightly less likely to kill me. Not that there wasn't some lingering skepticism for a while, a nervous accounting of how much cheese I'd eaten in the last week, and did I really want to eat more today?

Others are noticing, though. More research is spilling out. Conventional wisdom regarding fat's ills seems to be melting away, like a stick of butter at slightly higher than room temperature.

In recent years, Michael Pollan has noted the comically shoddy science that led us to this point: "When the government decided to tell people to stop eating fat or cut down on saturated fat, the science was very thin then," he observed in February 2008, in an interview with alternet.com. He notes the sad paradox that resulted: a massive public health campaign to get people off of saturated fat and move them toward hydrogenated vegetable products, onto trans fats—only to discover, more recently, that trans fat shows the strongest correlation to heart disease of any fat.

Pollan points out, as well, something that had begun to bother me the more I scrutinized grocery store shelves: removing saturated fat and cholesterol will earn products a heart-healthy seal of approval even if they're packed full of carbohydrates. This blanket ostracization of fat, uncaring of what that actually leaves us to eat, is not in keeping with current scientific findings, as more and more research ties refined carbohydrates to issues once blamed solely on our fat intake. At best, touting the fat-lacking qualities of our snack foods is a shell game.

Animal fat doesn't just come in the form of butter, either. While meat gets a little trickier—the simple but almost inevitable act of charring red meat may be the primary contributor of carcinogens in your steak—many of the same misrepresentations apply.

In my research, I came across a tale that both illustrated our paranoia about fat and touched a bit close to home for me. It turns out that several decades back, two other men decided to live off of only one type of food entirely for a whole year. These crazy bastards chose meat.

The Meated Man behind the experiment was Vilhjalmur Stefansson, a Harvard-trained anthropologist, who had spent some time living with Inuits in the Canadian Arctic. Like other researchers studying similar populations at the time, before they'd felt the influence of Western culture and adopted its modern diets, Stefansson was struck by the health of the Inuits, their freedom from the Western diseases that plagued the rest of us, and their diet. For months, Inuits ate nothing but caribou. Other months, they ate almost exclusively salmon. In the spring: a whole lot of eggs. Three quarters of their calories came from fat. Puzzled by their health, Stefansson decided to run the experiment on himself: nothing but meat for a year. A game colleague even agreed to join him, with researchers monitoring their progress.

The news caught on to the story. The public, naturally, was skeptical. Friends warned them that they would die. Stefansson at least took the precaution of launching his experiment at Bellevue Hospital in New York City so that doctors could perform regular tests (an advantage I certainly couldn't have arranged, though I'm not sure I would have wanted to spend my year hanging out in a hospital, either). After three weeks on the diet, doctors determined the two men fit enough to return to their homes, where they continued eating nothing but meat for the year. Scientists anticipated that they might be in danger of coming down with scurvy, given that there was no obvious source of vitamin C in their diet. Yet they didn't, probably because they didn't eat meat the way most of us now do: slim, aesthetic cuts from what we view as the nicest parts of the animal. They ate it all: bones, liver, brain, everything. Their nutritional requirements were met. Stefansson became ill only one time, when the researchers monitoring the men convinced him to alter his diet to lean, low-fat cuts. To alleviate the discomfort and diarrhea that quickly set in, Stefansson prescribed himself a meal of fatty sirloin steaks and brains fried in bacon fat. It did the trick.

Doctors could find nothing wrong with the men at the end of the year, as confirmed by a number of papers published by the scientific oversight committee. Both reported that they felt extremely healthy, and Stefansson continued eating basically the same diet until he died in 1962, at the age of eighty-two, from complications of a stroke.

How can all these contradictions and confusion possibly exist? How absurd is it that we can swing between the absolute extreme ends of the dietary spectrum and yet still be unsure what's healthy and what's not?

Maybe it's because, as I've said, we have a bad habit of viewing diets and nutrition in absolutes. That's just now how these things work.

In 1980, Ancel Keys himself helps us to clarify the strange contradiction in the relationship between high-fat diets, cholesterol, and heart disease:

"The ten-year experience of the Seven Countries Study indicates that the importance of serum cholesterol as a risk factor varies among populations. In populations with a high frequency of coronary heart disease, the incidence of the disease, especially of death and [heart attack], tends to be directly related to the serum cholesterol level. In populations in which the disease is relatively uncommon, the cholesterol level in the blood seems to have much less, or even no, prognostic significance."*

From the man most eager to pin heart disease on dietary fat and cholesterol, this conclusion: high cholesterol is a risk factor for heart disease in populations that have high instances of heart disease. However, in populations that do not have a high instance of heart disease, the same levels of cholesterol are not a risk factor. Make sense?

It does if you consider that a third factor may be at work. Either this outside variable drives up both heart disease rates and cholesterol or acts as a necessary trigger before cholesterol is transformed into something harmful. Or, an alternate explanation: other factors of diet and lifestyle negate the risks of high cholesterol, so that certain populations do not suffer from higher rates of heart disease, even though cholesterol truly is a risk on its own.

Some research suggests that, perhaps, neither fat nor refined sugars are purely to blame for our modern ailments, but when consumed in excess together, collude to destroy our health. New research published in 2014 showed that even so much as doubling saturated fat in the diet won't drive up total levels of saturated fat in the blood. The straight and easy link to pin heart disease on fat that Ancel Keys set out to find just doesn't seem to be there. And yet, the culprit Keys never thought worth investigating looks more and more guilty. Diet subjects who increased their carbohydrate consumption for the study prompted a steady increase of a fatty acid linked to higher risk for diabetes and heart disease.

I don't want to demonize sugar after attempting to undemonize fat. As I've said, we need to be more careful where we aim our blame before shifting the diets of millions around. Trends and rushed observations should not dictate how we eat, and the conventional wisdom we should follow, as far as diet goes, should be that which took centuries to form, not ten years.

---

*Keys, *Seven Countries*, (Brouwer, 1994) 131–132.

Speaking only from my own experience, though, I couldn't help but notice how strange it was that I felt satiated on so little with my high-fat diet, and how, in my previous life, sugary drinks and rich, sweet foods would very quickly lead to flushed, jittery, light-headed sensations. There's a reason a "sugar high" is a thing. Our bodies aren't equipped for it. While "fat = bad" may also have seemed like common sense at one time, the questionable nature of sugar seems like a deeper sort of common sense to me. Refined sugar didn't exist until very recently, and now it's everywhere, in everything. Fat has always been with us. We've always eaten meat, and we begin our lives with dairy. So which should our bodies be better designed to handle?

There is so much irony, so much aggravation now in seeing a bag of pretzels on the grocery store shelf with a big circle proclaiming "Fat Free!" as one of its main selling points. Seeing yogurt brag of its low fat content, as if there couldn't possibly be anything worse inside. So much marketing continues to pile on fat as the deadly plague it probably isn't, an easy scapegoat that completely distracts from the fact that what the food is made of—refined sugar—is even more likely to be a deadly burden on our health.

I don't know what to tell my mother. I'm not confident recommending she eat anything in particular or avoid anything absolutely, and I definitely don't want to suggest that she follow any one diet. Yet it is a conflict—should I really be shrugging off her conviction that eating lean meat for heart health is the best approach? I'm not about to demand she eat a stick of butter per week, nor am I really convinced that would help. I still feel pretty sound in believing that a diet full of fresh vegetables and other largely vegetarian fare is going to treat her reasonably well. The evidence seems too elastic. Nudge the amorphous collection of data, push hard in one direction, and some unseen contingency bubbles out and knocks you off your feet.

I don't feel entirely certain of anything at this point. Certainly not in recommending dietary parameters to someone like my mother. But I feel totally fine about how I'm eating, and how I'm going to continue to eat. While I might eat less cheese when I'm off my fermented diet, I'm not going to be bothered by my fat intake in the least.

While I largely swore off exercise in 2014—my brain warning me not to waste precious calories on frivolous exertion—nothing would stop me from hiking. One such hiking venture in 2014 was to a small redwoods forest in northern California. It was my first time in that part of the country, my first visit to San Francisco. I only got to see a tiny fraction of the city, but nonetheless, I took an afternoon to skip out of town and spend some time among the trees.

By this point, three quarters of the way through the year, I'd gotten good at finding food on the go. I knew what kind of stores to seek out. I knew which aisles in those stores might offer some tasty, conveniently packaged snacks for lunch, and which broad swathes of the store were going to be entirely useless to me. This was all significantly easier in California, which is basically a foodie fantasyland and a beta test writ large for innovative counterculture food products. Californians could be counted on to hop aboard the fermented food train years before other chunks of the country had even an inkling of its benefits. So, foodwise, this was one of my easier trips. (Except for the airports at either end, that is).

Food stashed in my backpack, I found a stream off the trail through the redwoods and sat a few feet from the water on a large rocky outcrop.

Lunch was simply cured meat, a brand I hadn't ever seen before. The packaging detailed exactly where on the pig different cuts were from, a surprisingly illuminating and useful graphic. This particular charcuterie was thick with fat: broad, white rings of the stuff.

It was delicious. I ate the entire package for lunch and washed it down with some sparkling probiotic iced coffee (an idea I knew at once I would have to steal). I went on hiking. I realized I could eat meals like this anytime and feel great afterward.

I have conflicted feelings about eating a ton of meat in my diet, for various reasons. I'm fairly sure anything given the care and attention that such charcuterie necessitates is unlikely to be garbage meat from some antibiotic-slathered factory farm operation, but still, one never knows. But that meal in general, that type of meal, is, in some ways, perfect. Perfect for that setting, for that context, for that need. Simple and satiating.

Much of what I ate in 2014, in circumstances like those, was highly caloric yet small in volume. Dense calories. My stomach could rip through that tidy package of extra-efficient energy delivery, pass on the result to the rest of me, and be done with it. I could go on hiking after a couple minutes, hunger abated.

And that's the thing that really strikes me about the year I ate nothing but fermented foods, many of them high-fat dairy products: I felt good. Like, really good.

This isn't a scientific evaluation of my well-being. There was much about my diet and the way I ate that was far from ideal, as I've said. I spent much of the time unnecessarily hungry. I didn't eat on the regular schedule I should have, and I certainly could have eaten more avocados.

But considering the limitations of my diet, the fact remains: I felt great. I had a ton of energy. For as much as I was hungry, angry, stressed, mentally and emotionally broken from everything going on in my life, I should have been an exhausted, bleary-eyed mess. I should have collapsed. But I wasn't and I didn't. And most of the time, I felt a gnawing urge to sprint up a mountain. While I was watching my calories, it wasn't a defeat of my limbs that plagued me. It was a defeat of my mental energies, waiting for the next moment I could put this seemingly constant adrenaline rush to use, to buy a few minutes of relaxation and sanity. I had energy, I just didn't have peace of mind.

If only butter were more portable. I would take it on every hike, every mountain ascent I ever make. Butter and I, we're in this together now. There are so many trails to hike, so many new peaks to explore. And while everyone's body may be different, and may very likely handle nutrients differently, I can only do what feels good for me. Right now, my brain is telling me: butter for life.

# CHAPTER 11
# Eat Food, Not Too Much, Mostly Rotten Fish

'VE FOUND THAT THERE ARE ONLY A FEW THINGS THAT JUST ABOUT anyone can pinpoint as fermented, no matter how unfamiliar they are with the subject. Mostly beer and wine. Cheese, bread, and sauerkraut would all have to compete for a very distant second behind booze. I can just as easily pinpoint what would fall at the very end of the list of fermentation recognition too. Because no one ever thinks of meat.

Yet meat inevitably comes up, and when I mention that sure, of course meat can be fermented, the look on anyone's face is utter disgust. Immediately. I can imagine what they're picturing, so I elaborate quickly to help them out. Only one simple phrase is required to completely reverse the look on their face: "For instance, salami and pepperoni and prosciutto are fermented."

We are impressed on the importance of keeping all food fresh and cold and free of mold, but nothing more so than meat. If a block of cheese in your fridge started to show signs of going bad—maybe with a small spot of green mold on the open end of the package—you might just slice it off and inspect and eat the rest.

Lots of people assume fermented food is weird in general. I may not agree with that assumption, but some fermented foods are undeniably a bit odd. And given the extremity inherent in my project, I knew I had to get as weird as I could. I had to explore the far reaches of what fermentation was capable of. I had to push well past the line, past the safety of veggie jars, and go well beyond what any sane person would consider edible, appetizing food. If you're talking one of the most extreme fermented foods in the world, you're talking one of the most extreme foods in general. And you're likely to be looking for some type of meat.

Few people would consider salami or prosciutto extreme, despite the fact that these are thick hunks of flesh hung in the open air for months at a time, often developing crusts of mold that must be scraped off before they can be served. There's nothing in the end product to really evoke disgust: they smell good, they taste good. They retain the magic of inherent appeal.

But then I began reading about a different type of fermented flesh, the kind that comes from the sea. Naturally, you can ferment fish, because you can ferment just about anything. And one of the wonderful things about fish is that it is aggressively aromatic from the start and only smells stronger as it sits around.

Sometime around late summer, having survived my encounters with the weirdest fermented foods I'd managed to find stateside, I knew I would have to travel to eat something really extreme. Something really weird. Some kind of fermented fish.

There was one in particular that caught my attention in its outlandish extremity. Rotten shark meat. The Icelanders call it *hákarl*, and it's earned a bit of a reputation in recent years, with the advent of "food tourism" reality television. A number of celebrity chefs have tried it, mostly all coming to the consensus that it's one of the worst things you can put in your mouth and not die. While I couldn't help but feel that some of these reactions must be a bit overblown, the amount of people describing this food as thoroughly unpalatable was enough to capture my interest.

Maybe some exaggeration was in play, but a food doesn't have to be the worst-tasting substance in the world just to make you gag. Hell, I could barely get down my mom's meatloaf as a kid without smothering it in its own weight in mustard, and that was just poorly fashioned beef with some spices. (Apologies to my mother, but man, I really hated that meatloaf.) This rotten shark business would be an eye-opener, and I had to try it. It'd be a necessary education in the far reaches of fermentation, a fitting hoorah for the final days of my experiment and a good excuse to travel to a beautiful and fascinating country.

What else was I going to do in the quiet stretch of vacation between Christmas and New Year's, anyway? How better to mark the end of this long year, as I pined for my first bowl of guacamole, than eating one of the most extreme foods in the world?

I felt like I'd been unknowingly training for this quest for months. I roped my friend Dan into journeying with me, and we researched routes and plane tickets—it ended up cheaper to stop over in Oslo, Norway, for a day. That was fine with me: the Norwegians have their own intriguing fermentations worth exploring. Scandinavia in winter and all the weird food they could throw at me: I was hooked. To prepare mentally, I listened to hours of music from the Icelandic composers in my collection, who do a brilliant job of capturing the ethereal starkness of their land. Had to be in the right mindset. Rotten fish would not be gentle upon the weak and naive.

Scandinavians eat some undeniably weird stuff—boiled sheep head, for instance, served in full-head portions—but the closest thing to *hákarl* offered by the Norwegians is probably *rakfisk*, a fermented trout that sounded to me as if it might follow a similar method of fermentation, albeit minus the months of drying outside in a shack. It's brined in big crates, fermented at cool temps for months, up to a year, to sour in its own juices. It's often served as is, raw, though some eat it on *flatbrød*, or accompanied by raw onion, sour cream, and mustardsauce. It may be an obscure delicacy now, but it's the legacy of a meal that would have been incredibly common across the world throughout history. You preserve what you have, and for people near water, that's fish. Lots of fish.

But the loss of these fishy traditions isn't entirely the fault of our squeamish modern stomachs. Fermented meat doesn't just sound like it could be weird, it poses serious risks if done improperly, unlike other ferments. Meat runs a greater risk of unwittingly nurturing botulism. Almost any time an outbreak of botulism occurs in the United States in recent decades, it's usually in Alaska, linked to some traditional fermented fish or whale dish. The catch: these fish dishes weren't always a huge risk, but they've become so when made improperly by locals trying to adapt modern tools to ancient practices. Historic methods often involved wooden vessels or simply burying food in the ground, but using plastic buckets has become widespread in the preparation of such ferments now. Plastic, unfortunately, does not breathe, and meat sealed up in an anaerobic environment is prime breeding ground for deadly botulism spores.

When you are served a fermented fish—at least in the countries I visited—you are not witness to the methods of preparation. You do not know the sort of vessels it was fermented and aged in. You have to trust that these people have been doing it for a long time, and they aren't dead yet, so what's to get nervous about?

Oslo was pretty much how I pictured a Scandinavian city in winter. The countryside was pretty, and the inner city was stark, icy, and gray. The sun was just rising when our plane landed, and it was already starting to set soon after our short train ride into downtown. Exiting the train, the winter air hit hard. I hate to put on my literary hat and set the scene for you in such lurid, flowery prose, but I really need to get it across to you, so here it goes: Olso was very, very cold.

It was also strangely barren. Apparently most Osloans depart the city for the holiday, vacationing in the countryside. Walking the waterfront district of the town, observing the picturesque Oslofjord inlet backed by the afternoon sunset and a few of the forty islands within city limits, we shared the icy streets with only the wind. These northern realms can seem apocalyptic enough as it is in winter, the few hours of daylight carving an ominous finality in shadow, but the lack of crowds anywhere really tickled the strange sense that we'd wandered into a ghost town.

Unsurprisingly, in retrospect, the first stop on our quest for fermented fish was closed. An establishment called Fenaknoken had been described to me as part food shop and part museum, and I'd been looking forward to digging up some weird items there. Anything with a traditionalist bent, I figured, was bound to stock all sorts of Old World fermented goodies. Pictures show rafters lined with enticing cured meats, like *fenalår* (cured leg of lamb) and *pinnekjøtt* (dried sheep ribs), while the shop also stocked some of the obscure Norwegian cheeses that I was also on the hunt for. Alas, it was not to be: dark windows and an unreadable sign in Norwegian on the door indicated they were closed for the holidays.

Perhaps we'd made a mistake in not calling ahead before planning our trip?

At times I wasn't sure we'd survive the trek on foot, but our sightseeing tour of the city eventually found us across town at a market of the opposite kind: hypermodern and more than ready for holiday commerce. Fortunately, fermented fish is still enjoyed outside of museums, and it was at the gleaming artisanal market of Mathallen Oslo that we found *rakfisk*, right by the entrance, at the first vendor inside.

Whatever this fermented fish held in store, its appearance was strangely normal. It just looked like . . . fish. Plain, pink, prepared fish flesh. Edible and innocent, as any smoked trout or salmon might seem.

Standing over the display case, I inhaled, waiting for some noxious rotten aroma to work its way up my nostrils. Nothing. But there was a lot going on in this market. Plenty of competing smells. Evidently *rakfisk* wasn't the most potent-smelling fish around, as the urea-laced *hákarl* meat was said to be. Probably best not to start too extreme, anyway.

The fishmonger recommended we start with a small slice. *Rakfisk* procured, we picked up a few other dinner items around the market: a hearty loaf of dark bread and some of the strangest-looking cheese I'd ever seen. The market was even host to an elegant-looking beer bar, so we obtained beverages to wash it all down—especially important if the fish really did turn out to be as pungent as forewarned.

Still, up close, *rakfisk* maintained its seeming innocence. Warm in color, and hardly stranger smelling than . . . well, pickled fish that's maybe been left out for a bit. There's an unmistakable whiff of sourness and funk to it, but that's hardly intimidating compared to any number of cheeses I've had. At this point, I admit, I was no longer expecting a pungent, off-putting horror. The warning signs weren't there. It couldn't possibly be *that* weird.

They say seafood can be an acquired taste if you were raised landlocked, and the flat farm country of central Pennsylvania wasn't exactly known for ocean fare. Accordingly, the only period of my life in which I'd eaten much seafood at all was a brief stint working at Red Lobster in college. So yes, I would describe myself as fish-indifferent. If you gave me one to cook, I wouldn't have the slightest clue how to start. At this point, I'd probably turn to fermenting it first for lack of other ideas.

But I love eggs. I love dairy. I was realizing just how much I loved cured pork and beef. So if there was anything most likely to turn me off, it was a weird denizen of the sea. Or possibly a fermented version of my mother's meatloaf.

Considering all that, upon my first taste of the *rakfisk*, I will say, my reaction was pure shock: it was absolutely delicious. Dan and I briefly expressed our confusion at this development before rapidly devouring the pile of tangy, flavorful flesh. There was nothing very weird about the stuff at all. If you at all enjoy fish, I don't see how you wouldn't be okay with *rakfisk*. It wasn't putrid. It wasn't rotten. It was, I swear, just slightly funky fish. More complex than if you'd just marinated it in some vinegar, but still, in that realm of flavor.

While *rakfisk* hasn't necessarily picked up the extreme reputation that the *hákarl* of Iceland has earned, I'd read online that it was, at the least, on the spectrum. A BBC article from a few years back describes it as "the world's smelliest fish" and the author goes on to describe it as "not unlike a slice of sushi that has been on a rather long bus journey." That the stuff was so extremely enjoyable left me a bit concerned, frankly. Now, *rakfisk* can be fermented from a couple of months up to a year, so maybe, we figured, this was just a mild, lightly fermented example. But if it was any indication of what to expect with *hákarl*, there was definitely some concern that everyone else in the world was just being a bit too overdramatic when it came to the pungency of their seafood.

After all, the strangeness of *rakfisk* was easily trumped by another selection on our small, simple dinner plate. *Gamalost* is perhaps the oddest cheese I have ever encountered in my life: so peculiar, I still have my doubts that the stuff could really be cheese at all. It neither looks nor tastes like cheese, leaving the fact that it comes in wheels the most cheeselike thing about it. *Gamalost* is a brownish-tan color, heavily textured, as if it's made out of moss. And it's closer to moss in texture than cheese, too: it crumbles like bits of earth. It's bitter, dry, and most certainly not spreadable. It tastes like moss that's gone bad. Not wholly unpleasant, but incredibly strange. Your mouth can't quite register what sort of food you're eating. I had an easier time with it than Dan did, who generously left much of the *gamalost* for me while returning again and again to the fish.

We plucked tiny hairlike bones from our fermented fish and broke off crumbles of moss-cheese. The *gamalost* begged to be washed down with beer; it was far too dry and bitter to be eaten on its own the way that I normally eat cheese (like an apple). We finished it all. The bread and the *rakfisk*, we decided, were incredible. We debated going for seconds.

Up on the weirdness scoreboard: dairy: 1, fish: 0.

CHEESE GETS A PASS HERE IN AMERICA, AT LEAST IN OUR MODERN artisanal age. Even if we personally just prefer cheddar, most of us have come to accept that cheese can get pretty weird, and that's fine. But no matter what type of cuisine it is we're talking about, most of us would probably agree that the most off-putting thing that could happen to a food is having mold take it over. Except for blue cheese. Most of us seem fine with that. But any other food?

Which of the following is stranger: letting beans and rice grow moldy or aging dairy in a cave until it firms up into a meaty, pungent wheel?

Actually, it really depends where in the world you're asking the question.

Perhaps a moldy cheese—of which there are numerous, commonplace examples—would seem the worst of both worlds to someone out there. To me, blue cheese sounds totally harmless. Imagine this strange contrast: a society utterly terrified of mold growing on its food, which nonetheless wholeheartedly embraces a type of salad dressing based on moldy dairy. This salad dressing is so widely enjoyed, it's available in every diner throughout the land.

And yet, I won't deny it: going into a year of eating old microbial food, mold in most instances still sounded a bit uncomfortable to me. Nowadays, my distrust of moldy foods is slowly crumbling (like a brick of fine blue cheese). Tempeh—essentially moldy soy beans pressed into thin bricks—never bothered me at all, perhaps because no mold really remains evident by the time you go to cook with it. Like most soy products, it's relatively neutral in flavor, easy to work with, and thus extremely versatile. Tempeh bacon became a staple of my diet and lends itself wonderfully to Reuben sandwiches as well.

We Westerners fear mold, but this is not the case everywhere. Molds are put to great use elsewhere—and thus, because something apparently has to, other foods fill the niche of "disgusting." For many people in Asian cultures, a pungent, aged wheel of cheese is about the most off-putting, horrifying food they can imagine.

The reasons for this aren't particularly clear, though various explanations abound. Often said is that the population simply lacks the genes necessary to metabolize lactose, an issue shared by many people around the world to varying degrees. One could argue that lactose tolerance is the abnormality: most other mammals gradually lose it once their mother weans them, but various human populations have evolved what's referred to as lactase persistence, the convenient ability to easily digest dairy. While I'm no evolutionary scientist, this adaptation seems fairly common sense to me. The enzyme lactase, residing in the small intestine, enables us to enjoy all the dairy products we do, opening up a vast world of energy, a stable supply of nutrients and calories that have sustained human societies and adventurous writers for many years. If we can farm animals, why shouldn't we evolve to use them as a pathway to new caloric resources, without having to butcher them constantly? Such an adaptation would be of far less use to other mammals, who—lacking the brainpower, tools, and organizational abilities of humans—could not readily harness those sources that produce dairy in the first place. This ability, so taken for granted by cheese-fiends like myself, makes us freaks among our mammal brethren—"mampires," as a few paleoanthropologists termed it.

Still, as valuable as the ability to drink milk from other animals clearly would be, not every human developed it. Intolerance is more common globally than lactase persistence, and the variation is genetic. Some evolutionary trick, perhaps inspired by our quick and massive shift toward urban life, flipped a milk switch in our bodies sometime in the last ten thousand years.

I've heard it said that the unpopularity of cheese in China isn't strictly a matter of flavor. And it can't fully be an issue of digestion—aged cheese has almost no lactose remaining. The general disgust for it is psychological.

This is something I can relate to. I have flashbacks, regularly, to the image of that century egg. I have never eaten a second one. I don't think I could. It's not that the taste of it haunts me; I maintain that there was nothing especially bad about the flavor. And the texture, while strange, would have been completely acceptable from some other food. Except that it looked like that. It triggered some deep voice in my brain telling me, "That is not meant to be food."

Had I grown up in some province of China, of course, I would feel quite differently. Our disgust is extremely relative. This is what you realize in exploring the vast variety of fermented foods across the world: people throughout history were not squeamish, by necessity, and they were endlessly resourceful. We have become far fussier with our easy access to fresh salads, all year round, and only the choicest cuts of meat. But "picky" was not a good survival strategy throughout history.

Beyond their century eggs, the Chinese enjoy a number of unique and odorous foods, like fermented bean curd, generally served as a condiment for breakfast. Fermented bean curd has a unique texture that's suspiciously similar to some dairy products as a result of the breakdown of proteins during fermentation, much like in the process of cheese making. Like basic tofu itself, fermented bean curd remains mild in flavor, salty and subtly sweet, and is versatile in its ability to soak up the character of whatever liquid it's brined in. Many liken the texture and taste of fermented bean curd to that of a creamy blue cheese, to the point where this style of tofu is sometimes referred to as "Chinese cheese" by English speakers.

Why ferment tofu in this way, and not dairy, if the end result comes out so similar? And how could one develop a hatred for one yet not the other, when they seem to fill the same niche of flavor? From a nutritional standpoint, soybeans are another perfect candidate for processing through fermentation, as they are not particularly easy for the body to digest. Soybeans contain enzyme inhibitors and have the highest phytate content of any legume or grain. As with milk, and so many other foods, fermentation makes a raw but tough-to-crack source of energy far easier for the human body to utilize, expanding our options for fuel and food. While Western countries have lately been growing massive acreage of soybeans to turn into oil, fermented soy products have been a huge part of Eastern culinary tradition for thousands of years. We've latched on to soy in a tremendous way, but we may be missing a crucial middle step.

Tofu, bricks of coagulated soy-milk curds pressed into shape, is the most basic of processed soy options in the majority of grocery stores today. It originated sometime in Han Dynasty China, and theories abound to explain its invention. One hypothesis: the ancient Chinese borrowed the method by emulating the milk curdling techniques of the Mongolians or East Indians. Perhaps, the theory holds, applying this borrowed-knowledge to simply curdle dairy products themselves wasn't an option. There's an old Confucian taboo banning fermented dairy products and other so-called "barbarian foodstuffs," foods shunned as fit only for the Mongolians. China's lack of cheese, then, was not just a matter of distaste, but of cultural disdain.

We have no obvious cultural reason to shun moldy foods or stinky fish, so perhaps mere unfamiliarity is enough to explain these unspoken taboos too. Whichever fermented form of whatever stinky food you can tolerate, it seems that most cultures at least have something that fills this peculiar niche. Something that Westerners might wrinkle their nose at, grasping at adjectives and landing on "cheesy" as the closest comparison. Something pungent. Primal.

Not every weird fermented food ends up with the texture of cheese, though. Some bacteria species seem to have evolved with the specific intention of triggering visceral reactions of terror in humans. At least those of us, like myself, with a thing about the texture of our food. If the texture of something doesn't sit well with me, I'm out. It's easy for me to see how taste is psychological, because I'm well aware of how some of my own peculiar preferences have formed. I can think of a few foods that I know, objectively, taste perfectly fine, but they don't taste good to me, not anymore, because my dislike of their texture has warped everything else about the food in my head.

Toward the top of most lists of "weird fermented foods" would have to be natto, all because of its texture. And we're talking serious texture here: ropy, mucusy tendrils of slime. All from innocent soy beans, once more. The common theme throughout most of these foods is that it's not so weird what the food actually is, but simply how it's prepared.

Only a couple of ferments that I know of are alkaline. Century eggs are one, natto another. The fact that these fermentations dodge the signature tartness of so many other fermented foods and drinks and produce a more alkaline end product is strange to me, in an academic sense. I've mentioned that even a working definition of fermentation is remarkably hard to pin down, and this is another reason why. How do you define a force that flows in seemingly every direction? The slimy texture of natto is the result of a remarkable, unique species of bacteria—no mold this time. It's so niche, it even gives itself away in the name: *Bacillus subtilis var. natto.*

I had to work myself up for natto. Push down a few psychological obstacles I had in my head, like the fact that I generally avoid eating things that trail tendrils of slime. But once the natto was in my mouth, it wasn't so bad. You can't explain psychology, and I certainly can't explain why the green mucus of the eggs was so difficult when the stringy spiderwebs of the beans failed to horrify me. Maybe it was because I could tell myself it just looked like stringy cheese, half-melted, clinging to itself. Not a bad comparison. And the flavor was neither awesome nor awful, but a little intriguing, a little weird. Bitter, crunchy, unusual, but something I could see growing on me. Natto would be great in a taco.

Appearance aside, the pungent ammonia character of natto brings us yet again back to cheese. The universal object of comparison. Be it stinky blocks of tofu, slimy natto, old green eggs, raw fermented herring pickled in its own guts, or even odoriferous rotten shark meat: all have, by someone or other, been described as cheesy. "Cheesy" is to the world of fermentation as "tastes like chicken" is to everything else.

Interestingly, those who enjoy their particular traditions seem to have an easier time lining up an explanation for those things they don't like, rather than trying to parse out what makes the weird food they do enjoy so beloved. I can't tell you why a good super sharp cheddar or five-year-aged Gouda entices me so. But I can pick out exactly what bothered me about that century egg, and why natto took a long buildup of nerve before I was ready to dive in, even if I ultimately enjoyed it.

The Chinese even have phrases to explain the logic behind these preferences. Funky fermented foods originating from vegetables are said to be clean and clear in the mouth (*qing kou*), dispersing quickly so that any unpleasantness you may find in their flavor is fleeting. And it's true, I can't remember the century egg's taste lingering in my mouth, just its image in my eyeballs. Milky foods are greasy in the mouth (*ni kou*); they coat the tongue and stick around. I don't mind my cheese sticking around, but okay, point taken.

One man's rotten shark meat is another man's preserved aquatic treat, as my grandmother always says.

I didn't start eating lots of fermented food for the purpose of eating weird stuff. Sure, friends and family acted as if this was the essence of my quest, but I knew better. The whole point was that fermentation isn't weird; it's natural and ancient and tightly interwoven with health and culture. We take it for granted.

But I'll grant that fermentation can take food in uniquely weird directions. Sometimes, hungry people have gotten desperate. Had to innovate. Experiment. Not everyone would have survived these adventurous eating episodes, but eventually we figured out what straddled the line of edible and safe. Our ancestors occasionally had no choice but to sample some food that looked like maybe it was a bit off. Not quite meant for this world. We can all relate, can't we? Famished, desperate, perhaps limited to a roadside rest area on the highway, the dining concourse at the mall, or, God help us, an airport's fast food options. You eye that fossilized slice of Sbarro pizza, withering and limp in its own juices, and shrug your hungry shrug. Resigning yourself to your fate, you can be sure that your bowels will soon bang their angry gavel and let you know just how poorly you've chosen.

Whether you've found yourself in a particularly challenging geographic region or a particularly unappetizing annex of modern fast food dining, a general rule presents itself: the more inhospitable the environment, the bleaker your options.

Writer Hamid Dirar elaborated on the unusual-seeming but highly interesting world of Sudanese cuisine in her book, *The Indigenous Fermented Foods of the Sudan*, which, since its publication in 1993, sadly remains one of the few resources available in English on the culinary traditions of a people with some eighty different unique ferments. That sounds like a lot of variety—I could scarcely find more than a dozen unique fermented food products in the average American grocery store—but they are variations born out of scarcity.

"The struggle of man in these regions of the world against death as a result of hunger, malnutrition, and famine is so deep rooted that practically all aspects of life of an individual and of a community are completely shaped by this ever-present battle," Dirar writes.

Sudanese *shermout* is made out of dried and fermented strips of meat. Most fermented meats are given time to air-cure in a low-humidity environment. As the dry air dehydrates the flesh, the meat slips out of the grasp of the microbes that putrefy, while friendly microbes rearrange fat and proteins into enticing (or odd) new flavors. Think hunks of prosciutto on their way to becoming one of the most expensive and flavorful options in the meat cooler. Or think *shermout*, hung inside the household until it has a pronounced rotten character and is occasionally host to maggots.

But, delicious as maggoty meat may sound, herding communities like the Sudanese generally do not raise livestock for butchering. They're too valuable to wantonly kill, and certainly too valuable to waste any part of the animal once it does meet its fate. A dish called *miriss* is made by mixing pure fat into a paste and fermenting it until it develops a pungent aroma that clearly marks its presence at any market where it's sold. I've never smelled the stuff myself, but I wouldn't be surprised if it's "cheesy."

And when the Sudanese commit to using every part of the animal, they really commit.

*Dodery* is made from ground-up fresh bones (I mean, you would never even consider using not-fresh bones though, right?) left to soak in water and ferment for a number of days. Afterward, the liquid is kept for flavoring, and the bones, marrow, fat, and tendons are further blended into the consistency of paste, mixed with pot ash (a salt containing potassium derived from plant ash), and then fermented some more.

*Shermout, miriss,* and *dodery* are most frequently used to make sauce, which puts these ferments into an even more interesting light. Sauces and condiments are used to add flavor, not in spite of their flavor. You add flavorful sauces to bland dishes to make them more interesting. So while these dishes may have been born out of necessity, they continue through appreciation. These flavors are cherished, not tolerated.

It may seem odd that fermentation would work at all upon meat, or fat in particular. Even once you have dug into fermentation a bit, meat mysteries don't necessarily get any clearer. Most ferments, at their root, are based around carbohydrate sources. Bacteria and yeast love to consume sugar, which plant sources provide in ample quantities. Meat, not so much. It's simply not intuitive, and to make matters murkier, the line between a quickly cured corned beef, brined for a week, and a fatty aged salami isn't even that well defined. Where the microbial activity begins and ends is still very much up for argument.

But microbes are as versatile in their diets as we ourselves. Some friendly microbes, evidently, are happy to live on a high-fat diet rather than the sugars most of their cousins consume. In recent years, an English utility company began pouring vats of bacillus bacteria into its sewage network to clean up fat blockages. After the gluttonous holidays, the utility found that the excess of animal fat poured down drains was congealing in pipes and blocking up the system. Rather than cleaning out the buildup with high-pressure water jets, as they would have with a more typical volume of fat flooding, Yorkshire Water found that bacteria would perform the cleanup for free. Minimal human labor required.

It's amazing how many of life's problems can be resolved by just dumping the right bacteria on them, isn't it?

We have, throughout history, solved the greatest and most pressing challenges facing us with microbes. Without fermentation, humans would be a lot hungrier.

Fermented flesh as the base of a flavorful and pungent sauce is nothing new, and not even as exotic as it may first sound. Ever wonder how fish sauce is made? Hope you can guess by now: fish sauce is made by fermenting fish. It may be the oldest and most widespread condiment in the world, applied and reinvented by numerous cultures throughout history. A fermented fish condiment called *garum* was beloved by the ancient Greeks and Romans through the Byzantine Empire, and similar techniques have remained popular with seafaring countries everywhere.

How does one ferment fish into a black liquid sauce, you may now wonder (and then quickly wish you hadn't, once you visualize the answer)? Pack a bunch of small fish into a container so tightly with salt that eventually they begin to autolyze—a biological term for the self-destruction and digestion of a cell through its own enzymes. Just like honey will bloom into mead as soon as it is diluted with enough water, the saucifying of fish will begin spontaneously with enough salt. And really, could there be two liquids more similar than honeywine and fish sauce? As with many ferments, but especially critical with meat ferments, salt provides a crucial buffer between the flesh and the forces of putrefaction that also crave it. Where vegetables rely on only a small percentage of salt by weight, typically 2 to 3 percent, fish sauce can use 15 percent salt by weight, even up to 25 percent. Condiments seemingly can get away with a level of saltiness that would be borderline deadly in a side dish.

In the small Asian grocery in my town, some bottles of fish sauce resemble the pasteurized tame stuff available in any supermarket, an inscrutable black liquid reminiscent of soy sauce. Other bottles display visible sediment of indeterminable nature congealed at the bottom. A few, though, seem to have employed a very different straining process during packaging, and still contain semiwhole fish. I was under the impression that the autolysis and fermentation reduced the fish to pure liquid goop, so maybe these brands simply add whole fish back in for texture. Or as a subtle reminder of what you're buying. Their beady dead eyes stare out at you, imploring, *Splash me on your next stir-fry.*

Somehow I have walked by these bottles a number of times now and yet avoided their siren call. I do enjoy fish sauce, but I don't need to be so visibly reminded of its origins. It's, uh, a texture thing.

Almost every seafaring culture across the world has come up with a way to preserve fish through fermentation, usually in order to make it last longer and feed the family through harsh times. Other times because, as with soy and dairy, fermentation renders things more digestible. Sometimes it grants an even more basic benefit, like making things not poisonous. Which, you have to admit, is pretty useful. Would I choose a weird, no-longer-poisonous fermented fish or a poisonous and still-probably-weird nonfermented fish? Definitely the weird, fermented, not-poisonous option. No questions asked. Well, maybe a few questions asked. Like, What made this fish so poisonous in the first place? And, uh, how long did you bury it in the ground for, again? Also, is there a decent pizza place around, just for future reference?

A couple of cultures setting up their villages on rocky shorelines in cold northern climates got the double whammy of culinary conundrums, both *We better eat this rotten fish or we'll most likely starve to death*, and *We kind of have to let this fish rot first because it's super poisonous otherwise*.

Take the Greenland shark. The first settlers in Iceland to try eating the flesh from this monstrous shark, for example, would have shortly thereafter begun vomiting blood. The Greenland shark is a fascinating beast for many reasons—a genuine prehistoric monster that's adapted to inhabit waters far north of where other sharks can survive. These sharks can also live for some two hundred years, giving them plenty of time to practice and refine their inherent badassedness. With an impenetrable sandpaper skin and rotating deathblades of razor teeth capable of sawing prey in half, this beast happens to be about the same size as a great white shark and could probably kick the hell out of one in a fight, if the great white were even capable of bringing it to the Greenland shark's inhospitable home turf. At the shark museum I visited on my trip, we were shown various animal parts that had been pulled out of these animals' stomach: the leg of a polar bear, for instance; some wormlike deep-sea alien of a species never witnessed alive by human eyes; the skull of a small whale. Elsewhere, a Greenland shark was found with the body of an entire reindeer in its stomach.

One of its many incredible powers stems from the fact that the Greenland shark lacks kidneys and is thus constantly excreting urea throughout its own body. To survive the frigid temperatures in the waters it inhabits, the shark is thus equipped with a natural antifreeze: trimethylamine oxide. Between the full-body urea and its TMAO, the shark's meat simply can't be eaten without significant modification. Cooking over the ol' Viking bonfire wouldn't cut it.

And yet some lucky, hungry bastard figured out how to eat the stuff in spite of all this. Fermentation, followed by months of open-air dry curing, reduces the toxins enough that humans can safely eat the shark's flesh—though the potent smell of ammonia can't be scrubbed out entirely. It's a double whammy of peculiarity—funky rotten fish flesh and the lingering whiffs of once-deadly poison.

It's not hard to find *hákarl* in Iceland, at least not in Reykjavik. Some low-level hunting is required—I would certainly advise that you do basic Googling before you go exploring Reykjavik's restaurant scene, just to at least know where your options are. There are many restaurants with a focus on seafood, as one might expect, but most of them don't serve *hákarl* (or at least, it's not listed on the menu). Upon arriving in Reykjavik, Dan and I picked out a few potential restaurants to investigate, with a low-key, unpretentious spot called Café Loki up first. The spot is easy enough to find without even trying, as it's just across from the massive Hallgrímskirkja Church, which dominates the skyline and makes for one of the city's most visited tourist attractions.

The *hákarl* at Café Loki is served as part of various platters offering combinations of traditional Icelandic foods. Icelandic cuisine is big on Nordic staples like rye bread, preserved fish, butter, and cheese—the rare menu where a great many things were on the spectrum of what I could eat in my year of fermentation.

After our "Icelandic Delicacies II" platter was served, we went right for the *hákarl*. There'd been enough anticipation. We were ready.

The meat is served in the form of little cubes. It's a small serving size, so your first taste will be only a meager cube of flesh, and if it happens that you can't handle that, you won't be wasting much food. I'd guess that's the idea, anyway. I speared a cube with a toothpick and took a whiff. Lots of ammonia coming off, a good bit more than the *rakfisk*, but it wasn't a smell that should make anyone keel over backward. And like the *rakfisk*, everything about it appeared innocent: visually, the stuff was tame. I felt a jolt of confidence and adrenaline upon realizing I probably wasn't going to have to throw up in disgust that night.

After trying the first morsel, we immediately went for a second. The cubes were so small it was almost hard to get a good feel for the stuff. It was fishy, sure. This was funkier and fishier than most, but not putrid. It didn't smell like death incarnate. It was just unusual. Actually, after a few bites, the closest analogue I could come up with was a smelly cheese—it reminded me a lot of some particularly aromatic German cheeses I'd had recently. (Go figure.) Sure, weird, maybe even off-putting, but not horrifying.

But this couldn't be right. Were we just falling into a trap of tourist-baiting tame versions dressed up as traditional fermented fish?

We asked our server, who assured us it was pretty standard stuff. She was young, and I'd been told that the younger generation in Iceland wasn't quite as fond of the shark as previous generations had been. She did say that she would eat it on occasion, but this seemed more like a reassurance for our benefit than any genuine fondness.

Still, something didn't seem quite right. Café Loki was a lovely place for a meal, but there was clearly more to learn about the mysteries of rotten shark meat.

Only one way to find out beyond any doubt: visit the place where the stuff is made. Well, one of the places; there are four or five producers of *hákarl* in Iceland. The Bjarnarhöfn Shark Museum is a two-plus–hour drive north of Reykjavik, a drive we made the following morning through pouring rain. Driving around Iceland in winter, you wonder how anyone could have settled such a barren* island before the invention of greenhouses and electricity and reliable international trade. I knew the sun-deprived December landscape would be misleadingly gloomy during my brief visit— they get a concentrated summer full of sun, after all—but Iceland sure doesn't look like a place conducive to salads and fruit smoothies. Clearly, the diet of such a place was always going to consist largely of meat, fish especially.

Only kilometers from the ocean, the winds there had become focused into something like an arctic gale. Immediately, our tiny rental was buffeted like a cow in a tornado. Moving very slowly through this world of infinite gray and sideways rain, we soon found the entrance to Bjarnarhöfn. It would have been difficult to miss even in those conditions; there had been nowhere else to stop for long time, save for one small gas station and coffee shop a number of kilometers back that looked closed. Plus, the way was marked by a large metal fish. We took the gravel road a few more kilometers toward the ocean from there, hugging the side of a mountain that loomed above us despite the increasingly thick rain and clouds. The scene was already sufficiently ominous.

Eventually, buildings that must have been the shark farm emerged in the near distance, but so did a significant mound of murky white and dirty tan in the middle of the road ahead. Muddy snow and icy dirt. The car pulled to a stop in silence, and I thought, *Could we really have been thwarted by an actual avalanche?*

In retrospect, I wonder how the museum could ever handle vanloads of visitors in its busier seasons, as the road at that point was one lane at best, with zero shoulder and a fairly steep drop-off on either side. There was really nowhere to go from there, so we decided to just leave the car where it was, parked in front of the avalanche, and venture forward on foot. I certainly wasn't turning back.

I opened the car door and experienced an overwhelming force something like blowing out the airlock of a spaceship. Our map of

---

*Fun fact: you wouldn't know it now, but the island used to be covered in trees. Humans just broke them all, as we do. Currently, however, Iceland is making up for tree genocide by planting more per person than any other country in the world.

Reykjavik and a number of receipts were sucked out into the gray mist instantly, never to be seen again (save possibly by some fishermen in the Arctic Circle).

The headlights from a large truck lit up the road ahead of me as I worked my way past the snow from the avalanche. At first, I wasn't sure if this vehicle was actually trying to drive through the snowfield somehow and was just idling there in impatience, as even if it could clear the other side, our car would then be blocking it in. All I could really make out were the headlights, seeing as the sleet and wind had become so intense that it was physically impossible to look straight ahead without becoming instantly blind.

Working my way toward the truck, I realized that whoever was inside must be waiting specifically for us. The driver motioned for me to come around to the passenger side of the vehicle and open the door. An older man in blue overalls sat behind the wheel. I asked if the shark museum was still open, and when after repeated questioning he just kept gesturing at me to get in the truck, it became apparent that he didn't speak a word of English. There was no doubt as to who he was, though: he and his dock worker's outfit smelled distinctly of rotten sea life. It is not a smell you could fail to identify.

As it turns out, this was Hildibrandur of Bjarnarhöfn, the very man who performs the sharking. He gave us a ride back to the museum and led us inside accompanied by a gaggle of cats and a very puffy, very friendly dog. Evidently this was not a busy day at the museum, in spite of the lovely horizontally blown sleet storm raging outside, and Hildibrandur had to walk around turning on all the lights before we could explore.

The museum itself is a fascinating place, full of too many curiosities to describe here. Eventually, Hildibrandur's son Christian wandered in as our guide for the day. (His name was only something similar to "Christian," but I couldn't pronounce it for the life of me, and therefore have no idea how to spell it.) After some fun show and tell of the various showpieces surrounding us, with explanations of how they actually make the shark, Christian pointed to the slab of *hákarl* awaiting us on the table in the center of the room.

This was visibly far more serious shark business than the previous night's effort. For one, it looked like a piece of meat. There was a dark crust on the outside that appeared as if it could be the sandpaper-tough skin of the shark, but which was actually just a sort of brown rind (formed by microbes, presumably, just like a cheese) as the meat dry-ages in a shack. Unlike the featureless white cubes served at Cafe Loki, the flesh of this slab looked like flesh— with texture, color variation between unblemished white and darker, tougher-looking pink meat, and a general aura of fishiness.

This time, it actually looked like I was about to eat a piece of shark.

The most commented-upon feature of *hákarl* is probably the smell. Before a chunk of *hákarl* ever got close to my face, there was no mistaking the fact that this shark meat was next level compared to what we'd eaten prior. Leading up to the trip, this was the only thing that I really expected I might have a hard time with. Most people who consume the stuff remark that it doesn't taste nearly as bad as it smells, and the texture of it in your mouth isn't particularly disturbing, but the aroma alone will crush your ability to ever again experience joy. I would argue with this assessment. Yes, this stuff definitely had some funk in its game. Maybe it's because my ability to ever again experience joy was thoroughly crushed long before, but I just wasn't getting the sense that *hákarl* was worth barfing over. Here's the thing, too: everything within hundreds of meters of Bjarnarhöfn already smells deeply and distinctly of rotten shark. So by the time it gets to your face, it's not a totally new sensation. If you were really that turned off by its particular aromatic qualities, you would long ago be curled up in the fetal position on top of an avalanche, hakarling into the snow.

It's very difficult to actually capture what *hákarl* smells like. Fishy. Weird. Funky. It's not nearly as outright horrifying as I would have expected. It doesn't really smell like death, or full-on rot; you can sort of understand how some starving and confused Viking might have given it a little nibble after accidentally fermenting the Greenland shark for the first time ever. There's certainly a difference between the particular pungency of *hákarl* and meat that's gone south really badly. A very important difference.

I took a fairly big piece. I don't know, I was feeling cocky. (And it occurred to me that this was all I was going to have for lunch.) Unlike the first stuff, this meat was chewy, rubbery, but definitely fleshlike in texture. I tried to bite my chunk in half and realized that I was not going to succeed without extensive gnawing. So I just went for it. I pushed the whole thing into my mouth.

Dan and I agreed, chewing, it wasn't so bad. Flavorwise, we still kind of liked it. It definitely fell short of horrifying and possibly within the range of interesting. Just a very unique fish experience. Who doesn't want a very unique fish experience?

Definitely weird, though, especially the longer I gnawed on it. It tasted like you were chewing on raw fish along with a funky cheese at the same time. Like the strangest of cheeses, there was something thoroughly primal about the flavors, unwashed and bodily. An impression of inherent fleshiness that, for whatever reason, you don't get in domesticated land meat. Beef tastes like it evolved to be cooked and transformed into a hamburger. *Hákarl* remains stubbornly attached to being flesh.

It took a long time to chew the large piece. Eventually, I decided, okay, I need to get this down.

A strange thing happens as *hákarl* is in your mouth. (Only this *hákarl*, anyway, the flesh off the block; I didn't get any of the subsequent sensation from those mild white cubes.) A tingling begins to build in the back of your throat and up your nose. In your nostrils, it's a burning not unlike having taken a large bite of horseradish, but the feeling at the back of the throat is unlike anything I've experienced from any other food. It's a mixed feeling of stinging, burning, and tickling that does not quickly dissipate. I imagine it's close to how it would feel if a bit of acid were dissolving the layer of skin in your esophagus.

The burning in your throat eventually subsides after some time. The flavor lingers. And lingers. And hangs around after that. It comes in waves. You become intimately familiar with it. You are able to explore every nuance and wrinkle as the flavor of rotten shark meat evolves and unravels to get comfortable in your mouth. Together you are one; you are become deathshark, the destroyer of worlds. You really come to understand why it's traditional to wash down the meat with a chaser of *brennivin*, Iceland's national spirit.

We asked if we could see the Shark Shack where the meat hung to dry and cure. Christian simply pointed us in the right direction, though it had been impossible to miss; he just had no interest in venturing outside in this weather.

The Shark Shack is a shack full of shark meat. Just chilling. Hanging out there. The most incredible thing is that this shack is open-sided, all but exposed to the considerable elements. There is enough protection that the meat slabs weren't just blowing around in the wind, but not much more. I guess, though, such protection isn't really necessary. There are basically no insects in Iceland. There aren't many wild animals. When I asked Christian if their dog enjoyed the shark meat, he indicated that the pup would eat it if fed to him but seemed largely indifferent to it otherwise.

I showed Christian a picture of the mucus green, geodelike century eggs I'd eaten earlier in the year. He frowned and decided that that was a food he would never touch himself. And to be honest, I was with him: I would eat *hákarl* again well before I'd ever put another piece of century egg in my mouth.

After the perilous, even-more-icy trip back to our car, which involved a great deal of wind-propelled sliding on the ice, we reversed course tediously, a little nervous that our tiny rental would slide down an embankment and become a permanent feature of the Icelandic tundra.

Stopping at a fjord-side park a little way past the museum, and still lacking in *brennivin* to wash down the flavor that lingered faintly in our throats, we broke out some imperial stout from Borg Brugghús in Reykjavik. Garún Stout Nr. 19 clocks in at 11.5 percent ABV. When I'd had it previously, it was incredibly rich, with heavy flavors of licorice and fig and dark fruit. The type of beer that will dominate your palate. I needed something like that.

We debated a few theories as to why the *hákarl* from the cafe had been so different, so much tamer, than the *hákarl* from Bjarnarhöfn. As I'd find out later, *hákarl* can come in two varieties, which were never mentioned when we'd tried it either time: there's the chewy and reddish *glerhákarl* cut from the belly of the beast, which seemed like it could be what we had at Bjarnarhöfn, and then the white and soft *skyrhákarl* from the body, which was almost certainly what we'd had the first time. Whatever it was that explains the difference, it's important for adventurous foodies to know: you can't just try *hákarl* once. You're going to have to buckle up and eat it from a few sources, friend.

I took a few sips of the stout.

"Is it just me, or does this just taste like shark now?"

Dan took another sip and contemplated. "Yes. Yes it does."

Sweet, viscous, oily shark stout. Hours later, the lingering pungency of *hákarl* remained more potent than one of the strongest beers ever brewed in Iceland.

## CHAPTER 12
# After the Fermented Man

FOR A SOLID TWO MONTHS LEADING UP TO JANUARY 1, 2015, almost every single conversation I had included the question, "What's the first nonfermented meal you're going to eat?"

Of course you, dear reader, already know the answer. People seemed surprised how quickly I would respond "guacamole," with no hesitation. As if there were another option. As if I wasn't thinking about guacamole every single day since, I don't know, probably October. Nah, probably August. In my head, I wasn't even visualizing chips with the guac. No dipping, no superfluous accessories. Just a bowl of the stuff. And then planting my face into the bowl.

That isn't really how it went down, though, I swear. Even after all the cheese and shark meat, I did retain some semblance of dignity.

Iceland left me exhausted, which was actually good. Perhaps the first time in my life I thoroughly welcomed jet lag. I'd run the whole four-day trip on only one collective full night's sleep, and due to some tragic flaw in my personal character, I just can't sleep on airplanes no matter how eye-meltingly tired I am. After picking up a bottle of another Icelandic specialty in the airport duty-free—birch schnapps, complete with a birch twig in the bottle—I was tempted to drink half the stuff there and then just to actually get some rest during the flight. I held off and blinked my way through the next five hours as our plane chased the sunset.

My internal clock now thoroughly bewildered after this whirlwind arctic country-hopping tour, I stumbled through public transportation after landing, somehow not missing any train stops until I made it back home. From the dazed expression on my face and the faint whiff of fishy-ammonia that clung to my coat, I must have appeared to have fallen off a whaling boat or possibly through a time portal.

I slept through most of New Year's Eve. Like I said: for once, it was nice to be exhausted. That night, I went to a party hosted by a friend that manages a local artisanal grocery store. He had promised to procure exceptional guacamole, which was all I needed to hear to commit. I didn't even trust my ability to make the stuff anymore—this was not the time to get burned by botched guac. This was not the time to experiment with my own overly casual approach to spicing things.

By coincidence, one of the best meat ferments I'd ever had also awaited me at this party, a venison prosciutto made by my friend Chris. He's the brewmaster at Newburgh Brewery, but I hadn't known of his charcuterie skills until that night. More and more, fermentation love seems to be spreading across its myriad mediums, as a passion for one technique quickly leads to an embrace of the whole vast concept. These shared experiences with master fermenters in other realms have allowed me to accept that there are limits to what I can do myself. If I wasn't able to master meat and cheese ferments during a year of living off the stuff, it may just not be in the cards for me, at least not soon. I would rather focus on those ferments I've found I'm good at, and, with such a great community surrounding fermentation pursuits these days, make friends and share in the rest. Most of us don't live in a cabin in the woods, cut off from civilization, after all. Our food systems, our lives, are built on trade. I will defer to the mastery of others when needed— I keep offering Chris my remaining stash of century eggs in exchange for some cured venison, but he hasn't taken me up on it yet. Venison happens to be one of my favorite meats, and Chris's prosciutto is unlike anything I'd had before. Two years old, it was drier than most charcuterie, with a gamey, nutty, pungent flavor that reminded me of Parmesan cheese.

Ah, yes: it always comes back to cheese. Which I still ate that New Year's night, in great quantities as usual. I mean, it was there.

What else was I going to eat until the New Year?

The turn of the clock to midnight came up fast. Weirdly fast. There was no great feeling of release; the minutes just snuck by, and all of a sudden, I was done.

I shouted something guttural and vaguely Viking-like, to the great confusion of a good half of the party, who had no idea why this particular New Year's was a momentous cause to celebrate. I plowed through a bowl of guacamole perhaps a bit too fast. Realized I wasn't actually that hungry, and that my stomach had shrunk considerably since the previous January, and didn't entirely finish the bowl. This was shocking, but frankly, I was a bit worried about how my gut would take all this.

I felt fine the next day. Eager to eat just about anything I could get my hands on, I journeyed into New York City, land of infinite dining variety. Variety would be tough close to home on New Year's Day, when almost everything is closed, but at least somewhat easier in a city with a few thousand establishments to choose from. Many tacos were had and thoroughly enjoyed. I savored perhaps the tastiest burger of my life—not just because I hadn't had a burger in eons, but because it was a damn good burger. We're talking topped off not just with cheese, but with mac 'n' cheese. I owed it to my stomach to feel full for once—and yet, I still maintained enough self-control to not make myself feel *too* full. The motivation was partly selfish: I figured I could eat more different meals if I took it slow. But also, my eating patterns had changed, maybe for good. The thought of gorging myself until I was stuffed felt vaguely unsettling, suddenly. Some part of me now wanted my caloric intake in small and steady, efficient doses.

My options to stuff my face narrowed at dinnertime, anyway, when almost every destination I had in mind turned out to be closed. I was really in the mood for burgers, but, unfortunately, the second burger of the day was not the second-best burger I'd had in my life. I suppose it wasn't even fair competition after that magical first mac 'n' cheese burger. Even after a year away from fresh meat, a mediocre burger was still a mediocre burger. I would've preferred some of Chris's venison prosciutto and a ball of mozzarella, frankly.

And yet, still, my stomach did not rebel.

I explained this to friends: it's not like I was eating totally different substances, going in either direction. Meat was still meat. This wasn't quite the same as someone with severe lactose intolerance trying to eat a ball of mozzarella like an apple. This was far different than, say, if my vegan roommate all of a sudden converted back to the standard American diet and sat himself down in a corner booth at the local steakhouse for an evening. I realized that what I was craving was simply variations of preparation—that elusive, fancified meal that had eluded me almost all of the year. The illusion of some vibrant bounty of food.

But my friends' concerns weren't totally unfounded. Fermented foods are different. The greasy ground beef of a burger and the slim dried sausage of charcuterie may be, essentially, the same substance, but they have gone through very different lifetimes. The composition of the meat reaching your stomach is not the same. Not quite.

And what about sugar? I was curious how I'd feel about the stuff now. It's not as if I hadn't consumed a single sweet(ish) food in the past year. Plenty of food I'd consumed was carbohydrate-based, though fermented to various degrees. But now I could reach for a cupcake, if I wanted.

I brought back cream-filled doughnuts from central PA—one of our specialties. I indulged in an obnoxiously sweet concoction from one of our national coffee chains. I found that my tastebuds had shifted dramatically. What most Americans apparently consider a perfectly average amount of sugar to put in their morning beverage now tastes maliciously sweet to me, the sugary equivalent of the off-the-chart spicy buffalo wings they make you sign a waiver for before ordering. I realized something strange as I took my first bite: sugary sweets aren't much different from rotten shark meat. Both leave a lingering, mouth-coating sensation behind. Both *stick*. After half an hour or so, if you don't have anything to wash your mouth out with, the aftertaste becomes troubling. And if you eat too much of either, your body is going to tell you: buddy, eat too much of this stuff, you aren't going to feel well.

I rediscovered the crash you feel from a sugar rush, an hour or two afterward, when you get nothing more substantial in your stomach. Coffee and a doughnut do not a good morning make, come eleven a.m. or so. Or, for that matter, coffee and a croissant. Or coffee and a strudel. Or coffee and a bear claw. Why is it that almost every breakfast item is based around nutritionally useless refined white flour?

Everyone's body is different. No diet could possibly fit universally. Some may fare much worse with natural animal fats and dairy than I seem to. Maybe a diet of nothing but veggies and beans is ultimately best, even if fat ends up not being so bad. But in any case, my body seems pretty clear on the fact that refined sugar is not missed. It's not that I'll never eat a cupcake again or pass on a good doughnut. But looking around at the staggering number of foods we produce with white flour and a brief fermentation (if any fermentation), it seems more and more like the stuff is just glorified cotton candy.

For the first few weeks, eating (at least occasionally) foods like sugary cupcakes, generic deli sandwiches between generic bread, and the first plate of pasta I'd had in a year, I noticed changes. My appetite returned, and I was hungry far more often. There were times when my stomach decided, if not upon outright rebellion, than at least to send an ambassador to question exactly what the hell I thought I was doing. A few of these terse moments of negotiation might be blamed, in hindsight, on some questionable selections in the restaurants I frequented. I wanted to eat everywhere. I was in the mood for everything—understandably, I think.

But the food I was eating *was* different. And usually, probably, not better for me, even if I had salads and avocados back. I didn't cook much for a while, other than defaulting back to grilled cheese in moments of failed culinary imagination. I was still working through my latest batch of sauerkraut, a half-gallon jar of "pink" kraut (mix of white savoy cabbage and red cabbage) spiced with caraway and gochugaru (Korean red pepper flakes). I definitely wasn't sick of any of those things. Nor the cured meats that I still kept around. Or yogurt smoothies with coconut water (though I don't always take the time to ferment the whole mixture first, now).

Compared to the elementary meals I'd been eating for the last year, the sheer size and variation of "normal" meals, the meals that restaurants have trained us to think of as a standard serving size, seem truly gluttonous. I'm far from the first person, or the thousandth, to comment on the fact that Americans have an exaggerated concept of portion size. But when you are artificially limited to small, un-elaborate meals for a year, the abundance foisted upon you in almost any restaurant approaches comedy. Any attempt to clean my plate would leave me feeling horribly bloated and stuffed for hours afterward, drowsy, anxious to wake up the next day and not feel like I'd just swallowed a medium-size animal.

The fermentation diet demanded efficiency. No calories wasted, and all calories worthwhile. Cheese is a dense nutrient-delivery mechanism. It is predigested. Lactose is all but stripped out of it by the microbes that turned it into cheese. Whether you're lactose intolerant or not, it is simply a more effective mechanism for delivering the energy from dairy into your body.

After my return to the normal culinary realm, I've continued to eat simply. And I'm starting to think that this pattern of simple eating may actually be the greatest shift in my long-term diet, one that I wouldn't have expected before I began. The less complicated the food, the harder it is to overeat, and to overeat of things you maybe shouldn't be eating much of at all. Bread and butter remain my default breakfast, though now I can add eggs into that mix, from time to time (I do work at a brewery located on an operating farm, after all). Mealtimes have gotten more direct, especially on days when my hectic schedule gives me very little time to break for food. Some of my meals still consist of just a few simple, flavorful items grabbed from their jars and bags and applied directly to plate.

Breakfast: a slab of butter almost as thick as the bread beneath it. Sometimes, a light lunch in a pinch is no more than a few hard-boiled eggs. (That is, if I'm not thwarted by the memories of the four remaining century eggs still lurking in my fridge. Lead-free, vacuum fresh, health.) Sometimes, for dinner, those same ingredients end up layered onto a burger. Or often simply a grilled cheese, adorned with preserved vegetables, peppers, kimchi, and perhaps sauerkraut on the side. If I'm feeling especially fancy, maybe my eggs become hard-boiled and deviled: this is about as many ingredients as I think one can introduce before the food is no longer so simple. It's a hazy line, but I'm not claiming to have invented some new dieting rule.

That's the thing about diets: as profitable as it is to sell them, I've come to believe that the only real metric one can use to figure out your own is honed through intuition. Getting in touch with your own body, not the regulations set by someone who likely has an entirely different metabolism and health concerns. One doesn't have to live off of an extreme diet for a year to fine-tune one's own eating habits, though after it's all over, hard as it was, I'm glad I did. The experience forced me to strip my diet down to its essentials, to reexamine my food from scratch.

There's nothing wrong with cooking up an elaborate, multi-stage meal, but it surely doesn't need to be every single meal that's treated with such indulgence and zeal. I've realized how easy it is to overeat when presented with such complexity, and it seems that even my rare cooking efforts themselves are simpler these days. More rudimentary. Perhaps I'll return to a more creative spirit in the kitchen sooner or later, but my creative urges seem to be fulfilled in what I ferment. I'm eating well. I feel great. I haven't been stricken by food poisoning from any of my jars of ancient, ageless vegetables.

ANOTHER CHANGE IN HOW I EAT, THOUGH A SMALL ONE: I'VE BECOME a lot less scared of my food.

Maybe for better, maybe for worse, I've become a little flippant about leaving food sit out. It no longer particularly registers that something is sitting out; gone is the ingrained reflex to hustle every item back in the fridge the moment its use is up. And if something is perhaps a little older than what I should be eating, well, what doesn't kill me will make me stronger, right? Sometimes this new-found flippancy toward the storage of my food might just be laziness more so than enlightened preservation awareness, but nonetheless, whether I'm turning down hand sanitizer or debating my upbringing as a child on a farm, my cultured fear of "germs" is all but gone.

Fermented foods are getting a lot of attention these days for their probiotic benefits, and no small part of this is due to how very little we know to begin with. The microbiome in general has recently been the subject of endless press and of a great deal of research funding. Important work is being done exploring the human microbiome that, over the next few years, will illuminate much of how we ourselves interact with the unique microbial ecosystems that have terraformed us.

It's pretty clear at this point that *what* you eat affects the creatures that inhabit your gut. Eat mostly bread and cheese, and the ecosystem in your stomach will shift. Eat primarily vegetables, and they'll shift again—quickly, too. Diet has been seen to alter the makeup of your microbiome within a matter of days. No intense "eat only a certain type of food for one year" diet required. Bacteria respond to changes in their environment readily and dramatically.

So at the very least, the composition of yogurt may affect our microbiome simply in that it's composed of different stuff than a breakfast muffin. But what about the microbes riding into your stomach inside the avalanche of yogurt? Can we steer the direction of our microbiome by deploying invasion forces of *Lactobacillus* down our throat? Can we repair a damaged microbiome by summoning reinforcements?

Recently, research is picking up on the benefits of probiotics both in pill form and in their natural state, because science, of course, demands a little more than the anecdotal support of the last few thousand years. But speaking as someone who's invested enough in the wonders of fermentation to live off the stuff for a year, I'll warn you now: don't get your hopes up *too* much that fermented foods are some miracle cure-all. The fact that we seem so obsessed with miracle cure-alls and their popular dietary opposite, the singular scourge, is exactly the problem: health generally works much more quietly. In one small pilot study of twenty-eight individuals suffering from Irritable Bowel Syndrome (IBS), researchers observed that, upon intake of a probiotic fermented milk product, the abundance of butyrate-producing bacteria increased, though the global composition of the flora remained unchanged. Butyrate is known for its beneficial effects on gut health, and some studies have shown an association between IBS and a decrease in butyrate-producing bacteria. The scientists also observed a decrease of *Bilophila wadsworthia* bacteria, a species thought to be involved in the development of intestinal diseases.

But oddly, none of those bacteria are those knowingly added to yogurt in the making of the stuff, so where are they coming from? Are they riding in on the food itself, or there already, suddenly fed in such a way that allows them to proliferate? And phrases like "thought to be involved" are maybe fine when trying to unravel whether yogurt is "pretty good for you in general, I guess" but seem strangely ambiguous for the foundation of a multi-billion-dollar industry.

I've been curious about the probiotic potential of beer for some time, seeing as I've never seen it written about or discussed anywhere. Beer is commonly maligned as being an unhealthy vice, but consumed in moderation, most recent research makes such dogma look a little questionable. Studies have shown that beer, or at least certain beers, can offer as many nutritional benefits as wine, if not more. Sour beer containing an array of microbes is so niche even within the beer drinking community, it's no wonder this obscure genre of liquid never made its way to the probiotics discussion. But with *Lactobacillus* once again making an appearance, why not, I wondered? If sauerkraut is considered healthy for the *Lactobacillus* it harbors, and yogurt is considered healthy for the *Lactobacillus* it harbors, and kombucha has transformed into something of a fad for the diverse microbes living within, why not sour beer as well? Ultra-low-ABV table beers of this sort have been consumed throughout history—were they the kombucha of generations past?

So I partnered with Matthew J. Farber, PhD, a teaching post-doctoral fellow at the University of the Sciences in Philadelphia. Matt studies fermentation science and biotechnology, largely focusing on the effects of various proteases on beer quality. Our idea was this: to run a short dietary trial on Matt and analyze his microbiome at each stage of the way. (In retrospect, I wish I had been prepared to do this for my own yearlong dietary experiment, but I discovered the service too late to get accurate early samples in.) With only one subject, it wouldn't be the most thorough experiment ever performed, but we hoped it could serve as a jumping-off point for continued research.

I brewed two beers for Matthew: one with a single isolated culture of standard brewing yeast, and another with a cocktail of microbes, including numerous strains of *Lactobacillus* bacteria. Matt's diet for the duration of the trial underwent three phases. First, Matt endured a week with no beer in his diet at all, then followed this up with a second week of drinking two saisons per day that had been fermented with only a single strain of brewer's yeast. Finally, during the third week, Matt consumed two mixed-culture sour saisons per day, those containing an assortment of bacteria. The food he consumed for the three weeks of the trial was consistent and carefully documented; foods containing their own probiotics were excluded.

Even during such a short, one-man study, we saw results. The composition of Matt's microbiome shifted each week. But what those results meant, and how minor or major they might be, was much harder to parse out. We could not fully resolve our primary question: can beer be considered a probiotic if it contains lactic acid bacteria? What shifts we saw could perhaps be pinned on the microbes present in the beer, but whether those shifts were objectively good or bad or arbitrary were unclear. The possibility that some beers, containing a rich assortment of bacteria, might offer probiotic benefits still seems a likely possibility. But the shifts we saw in Matt's gut flora steered us to more questions, rather than clear answers.

Most of the research I've found is like this. Probiotics do produce results, or at least *changes*, though often the real-world benefits of those changes are hard to pin down in clear, scientifically credible terms. Eating more fermented foods for their health benefits is very likely a sound decision, but I don't know that we can make any firm conclusions on the exact nature of their probiotic benefit right now. Will you feel better as a result? Hopefully. Might probiotics make a drastic impact to improve your health in some specific way if you are an otherwise already-healthy person? Unclear.

Even after eating fermented foods for a year, I myself would be grasping quite a bit to give you some specific way they improved my health. My blood pressure went down, which was surprising. My cholesterol remained firmly on the recommended healthy range of the scale as outlined by the doctor's lab results, so presumably all the cheese really wasn't going to kill me. And for the first time in my life that I can remember, I wasn't clobbered by spring allergies—the generally watery-eyed months of April and May passed by mercifully, with only a few days of itchy eyes at the peak of the season. But maybe it was just a mild year. And as I've said, I had lots of energy, despite being hungry almost all the time. But "feeling like you've got a lot of energy despite being actually tired and stressed and hungry" is a very subjective outcome, missing seasonal allergies for one season is quite possibly coincidental, and none of my experiences add up to any hard scientific conclusions. That may be disappointing to some, but that's just the problem with fad diets and self-help gurus. Anything promising a magic bullet cure might involve a small kernel of truth, but undoubtedly it's all the appealing fluff surrounding it that draws us in.

Clearly there's more study to be done, and research into the microbiome has been dropping at a dizzying pace for the last few years, with bold new findings revealed seemingly every other week. But we're not at the point of knowing every cause and effect—not even close. In some sense, we're looking for solutions without fully having a grasp on the right questions to be asking. For instance, What is it we want the inhabitants of our gut to look like in the first place?

Dr. Lita Proctor is the head of the National Institutes of Health (NIH) Human Microbiome Project (HMP), established with the goal of identifying the microbial makeup of a "healthy" microbiome. A study published by the researchers in 2014 suggested there may be no such thing: even among people who were examined and found to be perfectly healthy, each person's microbiome is unique.

"We were going about it all wrong," Proctor explains. "It is not the makeup—these communities come together and they actually become bigger than the sum of their parts . . . It almost doesn't matter who is present, it just matters what they are doing."

The HMP discovered that the average human carries about a thousand species of microbes in the gut, though even that number is a misleadingly small glimpse of the possible diversity inside us. The project also found that there are about thirty-five thousand species that could exist within the gut—in varying combinations of species from person to person, making up the thousand-some each of us is host to. No two people have the same microbial community, meaning this intricate ecosystem of bugs is our own internal fingerprint. Fully grasping the intricacies of how the very foods we eat shift the balance of the microbes we're feeding will require a good bit more study and may very well turn out to be so individualized, so specific to each of us, as to be nearly impossible for most to navigate as a path to health. It may be that fad diets rise and fall by the dozens because each one of those twelve diets may work for one person and fail for a dozen others.

But we know enough about probiotics to say this: a single fermented food, like sauerkraut, couldn't possibly replenish most of the microbes in your gut. A few, perhaps, but the human microbiome is far more complex than any single fermented food. Probiotics, and the possibility that they might restore balance to a damaged gut ecosystem, are incredibly important, especially in our culture of rampant damaged health. But we need to look at the problem from another angle: how to eat in the first place. What to do before we need repair. It may not matter which exact microbes make up this ecosystem, so long as it is healthy and stable. And if it is? Your gut shouldn't need much in the way of reinforcements.

If there is anything we can know with certainty enough to confidently steer our diets—that human societies have known for some time—it is that feeding microbes outside of our personal, fluctuating microbiome makes for an easier time once food does reach our gut. In feeding them, we have an easier time feeding ourselves.

The lesson is learned with almost every food I've written about in this book. Most dramatically, perhaps, it is the lesson of the rotten shark meat. Fermentation, predigestion of our food, makes our food easier for us to process. And often safer to eat.

Fermented foods are good for us in so many ways. There's the possible probiotics. The nutrients added by fermentation alone make them important and worthwhile. The awareness they impart, bringing us closer to the microbes that shape our world, and inspiring research into this long relationship. Ending the War on Germs that is eroding our most powerful weapon against infectious disease, rendering our life-saving antibiotics impotent.

We only ever seem to think about how our food affects our health. *Our* guts. As if we're the only one living inside us. But there are many more of them than there are of us. Maybe we shouldn't always be the only priority. What are we feeding them?

It's a quietly strange revelation: it may be equally (or more) important to think about the composition of our food in terms of feeding bacteria than how that food nourishes us as a single organism. Because we aren't a single organism, not unless you happen to be a Bubble Boy. Because it is the microbes inside us (and outside of us, breaking down our fermented foods) that determine, to a large extent, which nutrients are available to us. What foods might sustain us. Our health. Our moods. Our diseases. Which foods we crave.

Fermenting your food feeds the microbes outside and inside. Maybe they survive the journey into our gut or maybe not. But looking at it in the most simplified terms possible, you know for sure that fermented foods are microbe-friendly foods.

Our war on bacteria is misguided. Some primal part of our brains can't move past its Us-versus-Them instincts. In that primal part of our brains, it's always us with our backs against the wall, guns blazing as we stand alone in opposition to the overwhelming enemy mobs. We do not have to always frame the world in the framework of this lonely battle. We can make allies. We can inspire our allies to defeat our enemies for us without waging such a gruesome and unwinnable campaign. Instead of trying to nuke the vague and unspecified "germs" out of our lives, the better approach would be to feed the microbiome, to support it, to nourish it in order to promote diversity and stability. A healthy microbiome will naturally suppress harmful interlopers.

But as probiotic pills and yogurt sales boom, an understanding of the prebiotic benefits of fermented foods seems to remain stuck on the fringe of the discussion. You'd think anything involving microbes would be equally weird to the general germ-averse public, but having bacteria predigest our food for us apparently just doesn't have the sexy ring to it that putting bacteria in our stomachs does. Or maybe it's because of novelties like fermented shark meat, where the predigestion takes a food from a default position of horrifyingly inedible all the way to just generally off-putting. Still, you have to admit, such a health benefit is quite significant—we've gone from vomiting blood to not vomiting blood, a significant leap in the quality of our lunch. *Hákarl* is a showcase of extremes, but the same dramatic effect can be equally important with many more traditional substances. Just because something may lack overt probiotic qualities doesn't necessarily negate its value as a fermented food.

We should not miss, or fail to educate others, in the important ways fermentation transforms foods like cheese, bread, butter, and beer. Modern society does not view these items as health foods, so they often fall out of the discussion when "health" and "fermentation" come up. By default, vegetables are seen as the healthiest of foods, and generally, much of the attention surrounding "fermentation is healthy" is thus limited to veggie ferments. The notion is not wrong— veggies are certainly healthy, and fermented veggies especially so—but you still sometimes have to eat other stuff too. And that other stuff is what's going to make or break your diet. You can't live off of just sauerkraut.

I know, I've tried.

# Acknowledgments

THE JOURNEY TO TURN *THE FERMENTED MAN* PROJECT INTO THE book you hold now owes a great debt of gratitude to many people. But especially to Dan Crissman, without whom *The Fermented Man* would have never come to life in any form at all. Besides being an excellent editor, Dan has a remarkable ability to sort out which of my ideas are dumb but worth pursuing, and which are just dumb.

Thanks to Peter Mayer, Allyson Rudolph, Erik Hane, Mark Gompertz, and everyone else at Overlook Press who helped pull this book together, and kept me on track through an undertaking that would have been enormously intimidating had it been my fifth book, much less my first.

Thanks to the many, many friends and family members who patiently and amusedly listened to me explain and expound upon my idea for this project. I appreciate how supportive you all were, though in retrospect I'm a little concerned that more of you did not try to talk me out of this.

Thanks to Colin McGrath and Sprout Creek Farms for a fascinating glimpse behind the cheese-making process. Fermentation often needs to be seen to be fully understood, and now I understand just how beautiful a room full of mold can be.

Thank you to Blair Marvin and Andrew Heyn of Elmore Mountain Bread for their insight and openness. Blair and Andrew are among the most passionate and hard-working people I have ever met. Keep changing the bread world, one stone mill at a time.

Thank you to Barry, David, Yoni, Noah, and Farmer John for welcoming me into the ambitious venture of the Food Cycle, and giving me a playground of wild microbes and rustic farmhouse terroir with which to make increasingly weirder beers.

Thank you to the people of Iceland for keeping that shark meat around.

Matthew Farber endured a task almost as challenging as my Fermented Man diet: drinking beer that I made exclusively for a number of consecutive weeks. In consuming all that saison, we hoped to answer questions we both had about the resulting effects on the human microbiome, but really, Matt did all the hard work. Many thanks to Matt for his valuable research, and for applying a scientific mind to results that would have been well over my head.

Thank you to Aubrey, Barry (both of you), Bill and Lorie, Christopher, Cindie, Dan, Danielle, Dante, Dave and Linda'Lee, David, Debra, Fuj, Jeff (both of you), Jesse, Jordan, Justin, Kelsey, Lena, Lilly, Lindsey, Matt and Kim, Mattias, Max, Michelle, and Shawn for supporting the book early on and helping to make the most epic of my adventures possible.

And thanks to my parents, for the above, and also for being weirdly supportive of this whole thing.

# Recipes

# CHERRY TOMATO PICKLE

MAKES 1 QUART (1 liter)

If you're dabbling in fermentation for the first time, I can hardly think of an easier start than fermented cherry tomatoes. They're so easy to make, you may not even want to give me credit for considering this a "recipe." It takes about five minutes to prepare, and requires you to do no more than fill a jar.

Tomatoes, of course, can be fermented in a number of ways. I started out pureeing normal-size tomatoes and fermenting them for pizza sauce, but later realized that these fermented cherry tomatoes worked just as well, and were even easier to prepare. Use them in any recipe that calls for tomato, or just eat them on their own—the fermentation and acidity gives each tomato a refreshing zing.

## INGREDIENTS:

> *Enough cherry tomatoes to fill a quart (liter) jar*
> 3–5   *basil leaves*
> 1.5   *tablespoons (23 ml) sea salt or pickling salt*
> *Water, as needed*

## INSTRUCTIONS:

1. **Wash**. Gently wash tomatoes with lukewarm water in a colander. Thoroughly clean the jar you'll be using, and your own hands.

2. **Jar**. Fill up a quart-sized mason jar with tomatoes until just below rim. Distribute the basil leaves and salt throughout the jar, though you don't need to worry about getting the distribution exactly even—the brine will take care of that.

3. **Brine**. Top off the jar with filtered water until tomatoes are covered.

4. **Ferment**. Place the lid on the jar and tighten, but not all the way—you don't want the jar completely sealed, as $CO_2$ still needs to escape. Place jar out of direct sunlight and ferment at room temperature for about one week. If you use the "loose lid" method, monitor the ferment in the first few days, burping the jar a few times a day and ensuring that the tomatoes stay submerged beneath the brine.

5. **Enjoy**. Ferment to taste—I find the tomatoes are good after about a week. When ready, the jar can be sealed and kept in the fridge.

# CARROT AND PARSNIP PICKLE

MAKES 1 QUART (1 liter)

The humble parsnip is so similar in appearance to the carrot (other than its whitish-gold color) that, in historic literature, the two vegetables were often confused. Parsnips have a sweet yet tangy flavor that lends itself perfectly to the bright acidity of lacto-fermentation, especially when paired with their orange doppelgangers. With the addition of a bit of grated ginger, this pickle has a surprising kick of horseradishy spiciness. As it's incredibly easy to prepare and returns a powerful flavor from two vegetables that I never really knew what to do with before, this has become one of my favorite ferments to make at home.

## INGREDIENTS:

1    pound (0.5 kg) carrots
1    pound (0.5 kg) parsnips
1    teaspoon (5 ml) freshly grated organic ginger
1.5  tablespoons (23 ml) sea salt or pickling salt
     Water, as needed

## INSTRUCTIONS:

1. **Wash**. Gently wash parsnips and carrots with lukewarm water in a colander. Thoroughly clean the jar you'll be using, and your own hands.

2. **Slice**. Trim off the tops. Using a clean knife or a mandolin slicer, slice the vegetables into discs.

3. **Mix**. Using clean hands or a spoon, mix everything together in a bowl until the salt and ginger are well distributed throughout the vegetables.

4. **Jar**. Take the vegetable slices and pack them into the jar. You don't need to pack them firmly enough to extract liquid, as you would when making sauerkraut. Simply squeeze them in until there's about an inch of space at the top of the jar.

5. **Brine**. Top off the jar with cool water until vegetables are covered.

6. **Ferment**. Place the lid on the jar and tighten, but not all the way. Place jar out of direct sunlight and ferment at room temperature for about one to two weeks. If you use the "loose lid" method, monitor the ferment in the first few days, burping the jar a few times a day and pressing down the veggies with a fork to ensure they mostly stay submerged beneath the brine.

7. **Enjoy**. Ferment the carrots and parsnips to taste—about one or two weeks. When ready, the lid can be tightened and the jar kept in the fridge for long-term storage (or devoured right away).

# SPICY RED PEPPER KRAUT

MAKES 1 QUART (1 liter)

Sour and salty fermented cabbage is delicious on its own, but I'm a firm believer that everything is better with a little heat. While I love kimchi and its complex, infinitely rearrangeable mosaic of flavors, most kimchi recipes involve a dozen ingredients and an elaborate, multistage production. This recipe combines the simplicity of traditional Western sauerkraut with the unique pungent spice of Korean kimchi, and maintains a crunchy texture that's an added, greatly appealing bonus.

## INGREDIENTS:

> 5    pounds (2.25 kg) green cabbage (approximately 2 medium-sized heads)
> 2    teaspoons (10 ml) caraway seeds
> 3    tablespoons (45 ml) gochugaru (Korean red pepper flakes)
> 1.5   tablespoons (23 ml) sea salt or pickling salt
>      Water, if needed

## INSTRUCTIONS:

1. **Wash**. Gently wash cabbage with lukewarm water in a colander. Wash your own hands well, and any other implements you may be using to press down the cabbage.

2. **Slice**. Cut off the root end of the cabbage, then remove the tough outer leaves. Chop the cabbage into quarters and slice off the hard white core. Slice each quarter down its length into wedges, then chop each wedge into very thin ribbons.

3. **Mix**. Dump the ribbons of cabbage into a mixing bowl and add salt. Using your hands, work the salt into the cabbage. Eventually, the salt will begin to draw liquid from the cabbage. Continual massaging will make this process go faster, or you can choose to simply distribute the salt throughout, walk away to let it sit, and return in an hour when the salt has done the work on its own. When the cabbage appears noticeably wilted and liquid has pooled at the bottom of the bowl, add caraway seeds and gochugaru and mix again to distribute.

4. **Pack**. Pack the cabbage into a jar. Firm pressure will extract even more brine from the strips of leaves. Continue to fill and press down on the cabbage until there are no air bubbles in the jar, and the level of brine is near to the top of the cabbage. The jar should be full to within an inch of the top, with brine covering everything. If some cabbage is still peering out, the brine can be topped off with water or a splash of vinegar.

5. **Ferment**. Place the lid on the jar and tighten, but not all the way—you don't want the jar completely sealed, as $CO_2$ still needs to escape. Set jar out of direct sunlight and ferment at room temperature for about two weeks. If you use the "loose lid" method, monitor the kraut in the first few days, burping the jar a few times a day and pressing down the leaves with a fork to ensure they mostly stay submerged beneath the brine.

6. **Enjoy**. After about two week—or up to a month, if more sourness and funk is desired—fermentation should be complete. The lid can now be tightened and the jar kept in the fridge for long-term storage.

## KIMCHI SOURDOUGH PANCAKES

MAKES APPROXIMATELY 12 PANCAKES

When combining ingredients that had already, on their own, required a serious dedication of labor, I found I didn't exactly want to spend more time in the kitchen putting a meal together than necessary. Turning my sourdough starter into creative pancake-like breakfasts was perhaps a lazy way through morning meals, but also delicious and versatile. Adding kimchi to the mix bumps this recipe into the "any meal, any time of day" category. For even more flavor, experiment by topping these off with various fermented condiments: sour cream or yogurt, butter, soy sauce, or hot sauce.

### INGREDIENTS:

2 cups (500 ml) of sourdough starter
¾ cup (180 ml) kimchi, or spicy red pepper kraut
½ cup (125 ml) Greek yogurt
1 egg (if on an all-fermented diet, you can leave the egg out)
1 tablespoon (15 ml) honey (see honey-fermented garlic recipe)
½ teaspoon (3 ml) of salt
1 teaspoon (5 ml) baking soda
Butter to grease pan

### INSTRUCTIONS:

1. **Pulse**. In food processor or blender, pulse kimchi until it's the consistency of relish—you can go finer or chunkier based on your own preferences.

2. **Mix**. Combine the sourdough starter, kimchi, Greek yogurt, egg, honey, salt, and baking soda in a large bowl. Mix together well.

3. **Heat**. Melt butter in a large pan or griddle on medium-low heat.

4. **Cook**. Spoon or ladle ¼ cup (60 ml) per pancake onto pan or griddle. Cook the pancakes until they are golden brown, flipping once, when the tops are full of bubbles.
5. **Enjoy**. Top with any additional condiments and enjoy.

## HONEY-FERMENTED GARLIC

MAKES 1 PINT (500 ml)

While I've found myself taking an increasingly skeptical view of sugar over the last few years, there are a few substances I can never resist: maple syrup and honey. Fortunately, raw honey is something of a miracle substance, with numerous health benefits and self-preservation qualities that grant it, essentially, eternal shelf life. While sealed, undiluted honey will never go bad, raw honey is nonetheless an environment rich with microbes, locked into stasis by honey's low moisture content, low pH, and the preservative hydrogen peroxide imparted by the metabolism of the bees that produce it.

This ferment is a bit of an odd one, as there's no real brine involved. Simply adding a few cloves of garlic to raw honey will dilute it sufficiently to initiate fermentation. I like to let this sit for about a month before I dig into it. The garlic is good in any dish that calls for it, and great on bread or crackers with a smear of the honey itself. As both honey and garlic are associated with immune health, many see this ferment as a cold-fighting remedy of sorts. But health professionals warn against feeding raw honey to infants due to their weak immune system, so it's probably best to play it safe and keep this treat adults only.

### INGREDIENTS:

12 *ounces (355 ml) raw honey*
5–8 *cloves garlic*

### INSTRUCTIONS:

1. **Peel**. There's a secret technique to save you time peeling all those garlic bulbs: you can basically shake the skins off. Smash each bulb apart by placing it on the table and striking it with the heel of your hand. Then drop the cloves into a metal bowl, place a cutting board or plate (or another bowl) over the first to enclose it, and shake vigorously for about ten seconds. Now your bowl should be littered with the discarded skins of garlic and conveniently peeled garlic cloves. Or at least, mostly. I always still have to pry a few stubborn skins off.
2. **Mix**. Drop the peeled garlic cloves into a pint-sized fermentation vessel. Pour the raw honey overtop, covering the garlic cloves completely. Fill until the honey is about an inch below the rim of the vessel.

3. **Ferment.** Place the vessel on a plate or pan to catch any spillover as the honey begins to ferment, usually within a couple of days. The garlic will refuse to stay submerged. You can prod it back down with a fork, or, depending on the type of fermentation vessel you're using, simply flip the jar upside-down so that the garlic floats to the "bottom" of the jar. You'll likely get some leakage with this method, of course.

4. **Age and Enjoy.** After about a month, move to the fridge and consume as desired.

# FERMENTED HOT CHILI PEPPER SAUCE  MAKES 1 PINT (500 ml)

**H**ot sauce is great. Fermented hot sauce is, obviously, greater. Of course, it's no great leap to make hot sauce this way, and some of your traditional favorites perhaps already are. A long fermentation produces natural acidity to balance out the heat, and impart smoky, funky complexities. A great hot sauce, however it's made, should always be more than just straight heat. Most modern hot sauces are made with vinegar as the source of acidity, achieving an easier-to-produce and more shelf stable hot sauce at the expense of complexity and flavor. But if you're going to the trouble of making your own hot sauce at home, why rush it? Once ready, your fermented hot sauce should age gracefully for a long time, even after you begin using it. I've had an open jar of homemade hot sauce in my fridge for well over a year, and it's remained incredible.

## INGREDIENTS:

1   pound (450 grams) fresh chili peppers (you can use any peppers, but I like a blend of cayenne and serrano)
½   parsnip (can be fresh or fermented)
1   tablespoon (15 ml) honey
1   tablespoon (15 ml) sea salt or pickling salt

## INSTRUCTIONS:

1. **Blend.** Cut the stems off peppers and add to blender along with half a parsnip, one tablespoon honey (with fermented garlic optional—see fermented honey garlic recipe) and one tablespoon salt. Blend until mixture forms consistency of a thick, chunky liquid.

2. **Ferment.** Pour into fermentation vessel. Ferment for two weeks, monitoring vessel for spillover or mold.

3. **Blend Again**. To really achieve the proper consistency, I've found you need to blend both before and after fermentation. After two weeks, pour the mixture back into a blender and let run for at least one minute. The resulting liquid should pour with the consistency and texture of, well, hot sauce.

4. **Age and Enjoy**. Move to the fridge and let the hot sauce continue to age as desired, or begin sprinkling it on everything and anything.

## FERMENTED SWEET POTATO FRENCH FRIES

ENOUGH FOR TWO TO THREE PEOPLE, AS A SIDE

Under any strict diet, you're probably going to replace or attempt to replicate certain foods that have always just been a part of your culinary roster. For me, losing the ability to eat a burger and fries was a hard blow. Even vegans can fashion a burger replacement pretty easily, but a fermented patty with an appealing texture and form was a challenge beyond my abilities. Fortunately, the classic French fry was easier to tackle. Broken down, fermented French fries can be made much the same as the regular variety, with only an added step and a few extra days of preparation. There's no getting around the fact that these fries will have a weirder, funkier flavor than what you're used to, but whether you love or hate them, they make for a unique new experience worth trying. On top of that, they're healthier, too: fermentation helps to prevent the formation of acrylamide, a carcinogenic chemical found in certain cooked foods, especially potato products.

### INGREDIENTS:

2 medium-size sweet potatoes
1 tablespoon (15 ml) salt
Dash of rosemary and pepper, or any other spices of choice
Big dash of corn starch
Sprinkling of olive oil

### INSTRUCTIONS:

1. **Rinse**. Gently wash potatoes, but do not peel. Slice into fries, then place into bowl or jar full of cold water for half an hour. This wash will draw starch out of the potatoes.

2. **Jar**. Drain water and place potatoes in fermentation vessel. Add tablespoon of salt and fill with lukewarm water to rim of vessel.

3. **Ferment**. Store in a cool dark place for three days. Warmer temps will favor a more aggressive fermentation with more diverse microbes, including yeast that favor the starchy snack offered by the potatoes. Fermentation at cellar temps is ideal. If fermented too long or too warm, you may see a pellicle develop, but it is harmless.

4. **Prepare**. After three days, dump potato wedges into a colander to remove liquid, then arrange on paper towels to dry. Preheat oven to 425 degrees F. Once dry, add potatoes to large bowl with spices, corn starch, and olive oil. Mix well.

5. **Bake**. Arrange on non-stick baking tray. Make sure fries are single layer and not crowded together, to ensure they get crispy. Bake for 15 minutes, or until crispy, with edges beginning to brown.

6. **Enjoy**. Pair with dipping sauce or condiment of your choice.

# NO-COOK BEET BORSCHT
MAKES 1 QUART (1 liter)

**B**eets are often said to be among the world's healthiest foods, and they certainly do pack a vitamin punch: they're a good source of folate, manganese, potassium, copper, dietary fiber, vitamin C, iron, and vitamin B6. While Westerners mostly seem to consume beets in the form of salad topping, in Eastern Europe, the earthy, distinctly flavored vegetable is often consumed as a soup. Borscht can be made hot or cold, but while cooking degrades the beet's many nutrients, fermentation will preserve and enhance them. Fermented beets can be eaten (and the brine drank) on their own, as a pickle and a tonic, and this is often the way I go. But with only a little blending, you can also create a hearty soup, ideally topped with some Greek yogurt or sour cream for another fully-fermented meal.

## INGREDIENTS:
- 2 *pounds (900 grams) beets*
- 2 *large slices horseradish*
- 1.5 *tablespoons (23 ml) sea salt or pickling salt*

## INSTRUCTIONS:

1. **Slice**. Gently wash beets. Peel off skins, then cut into slices or cubes. Dice horseradish.

2. **Combine**. Add beets and horseradish to fermentation vessel. Add salt and fill with cool water to rim of vessel.

3. **Ferment**. Place the lid on the jar and tighten, but not all the way—you don't want the jar completely sealed, as $CO_2$ still needs to escape. Set jar out of direct sunlight and ferment at room temperature for about two weeks.

4. **Blend**. If a cold borscht is your goal, you can now blend the fermented beets in their brine to make a cold borscht soup. Top with sour cream and serve with hearty bread.

5. **Drink.** Or, if soup isn't your thing, try drinking the beet brine on its own. A couple ounces every day makes for a potent and healthy tonic, with an intriguing flavor unlike anything else—earthy, salty, and tangy.

## LACTO-FERMENTED SALMON    MAKES 1 QUART (1 liter)

Fish probably isn't the first thing you'd think of when contemplating fermentation, yet fermented fish concoctions are some of the oldest and most diverse culinary traditions on the planet. Fish sauce was a popular Roman condiment, and cultures from around the world have evolved traditions to preserve fish by burying it in the ground. This recipe for lacto-fermented salmon is a much simpler and safer approach to enjoying raw, microbe-made fish, performed more for flavor than preservation. Indeed, this one is best enjoyed relatively fresh, after only a few days of fermentation.

### INGREDIENTS:

Approximately 1 pound (450 grams) wild-caught salmon
1    cup (250 ml) chopped red onions
1    tablespoon (15 ml) raw honey
1    lemon
2    sprigs fresh dill
2    teaspoons (10 ml) fish sauce
¼    cup (60 ml) whey
2    tablespoons (30 ml) sea salt or pickling salt
Water, as needed

### INSTRUCTIONS:

1. **Assemble.** Cut salmon into strips. Red onions can be chopped or diced any way you like, and, optionally, previously fermented onions can also be mixed in for an additional boost of bacteria to start the fermentation.

2. **Combine.** Mix everything in a large bowl. After making sure salt and spices are evenly distributed, pack everything into a jar. Pour any liquid remaining in the bowl into the jar, then top off with dechlorinated tap water or spring water until the contents of the jar are submerged in brine.

3. **Ferment.** Place the lid on the jar and tighten, but not all the way—you don't want the jar completely sealed, even though this fermentation probably won't generate nearly as much $CO_2$ as others. Leave the jar at room temperature for 24 hours, then transfer to the fridge.

4. **Enjoy**. The salmon can be consumed after an additional 24 hours in the fridge or given a few extra days for flavors to develop. However, unlike most other ferments, the salmon won't stay good forever and should be eaten within three weeks.

## BAGEL KVASS                    MAKES APPROXIMATELY 12 BOTTLES

Kvass can impart a tasty second life to any stale bread product, but its unique and refreshing flavors are worth the purchase of even fresh bread, if necessary. Regardless of stale or fresh, feel free to get creative with different bread and bagel types and unlikely flavorings, though the traditional Eastern European approach, with hearty rye, makes for an especially flavorful tonic. Like kombucha, kvass contains trace amounts of alcohol—around 1 percent ABV generally—but will grow more pungent and sour the longer you let it sit.

### INGREDIENTS:

10–12 stale pumpernickel bagels

2.25 gallons (8.5 liters) water

1 cup (250 ml) sugar or raw honey

Handful of fresh mint leaves (optional)

2 tablespoons (15 ml) sea salt or pickling salt

¼ cup (60 ml) sourdough starter or

1 tablespoon (15 ml) dry bread yeast or

¼ cup (60 ml) whey

### INSTRUCTIONS:

1. **Stale**. Help your local bakery or bagel shop unload some stale bagels at the end of the day, and cut into cubes while still soft. If your bagels are on the fresher side, you can always let them sit around for a bit longer after cubing (just don't let them sit to the point of growing mold). Once your bagels are nice and inedible, toast them in the oven on a low setting until dark and crispy. While the bagels are toasting, fill a stockpot with 2.25 gallons (8.5 liters) water and bring to a boil.

2. **Soak**. When the water has reached a boil, turn off the flame. Dump in the hunks of stale bagels and stir until every piece has soaked up all the water it will take. You'll be left with a soggy bread soup. Cover the pot with a lid and let sit overnight.

3. **Juice**. Using a colander or cheesecloth, drain the liquid from the bagels

into a large jug or jar. You don't need to extract all the juice to the point where the bagel-mush is again dry, but they'll have soaked up quite a bit, and you want to extract most of it.

4. **Sugar and Spice**. After the liquid is done draining, pour sugar or honey into the jug or jar containing the bagel juice. Add the mint leaves if desired (I find they add to the refreshing quality of the drink and round out the tangy, doughy flavor) and salt. Sourdough starter, dry bread yeast, and whey can all be used to successfully make tasty kvass, but sourdough provides the most ideal mixture of microbes.

5. **Ferment**. Place an airlock and stopper on the jug, or screw the cap on the jar (just don't tighten it all the way), and let your fermentation vessel sit at room temperature for two to three days. This fermentation shouldn't take long, but you'll see the telltale signs: the hazy, brownish liquid will summon a ring of foamy bubbles at its surface. How long you let it sit is partly a matter of taste: for sweeter kvass, a shorter fermentation will leave some sugar behind, but after that, the bacteria will run through all the food they can find to create a brisk sourness.

6. **Enjoy**. After fermenting, the kvass can be packaged in individual bottles or consumed right from the fermentation vessel. However you choose to enjoy it, you should now store the kvass in the fridge and enjoy it cold. While best consumed fresh, I've had nine–month-old kvass (kept in my fridge the entire time) that was still fizzy, tangy, and delicious.

## WILD-FERMENTED SQUASH BEER

MAKES 48 BOTTLES

Beer is not hard to make, but the process can be difficult to compress into the short standard format of a 30 minute dinner recipe. There's the question of missing equipment, for one thing. A recipe for chili can safely assume that the reader already owns pots and a stove, at the least, but in order to make beer, you're likely going to need to spring for some extra stuff. How much extra equipment depends on the beer-making approach. There's "all-grain brewing," the traditional route, in which you're mashing grains in a specialized vessel and then running off the sugary liquid to boil and ferment. Easier, though, is "extract brewing," in which the sugars have already been converted and condensed out of the grains. Since the focus for this project is on the unique approach of initiating fermentation with wild microbes off of squash, I've elected to go with the simplest possible recipe. If you wish to brew this as an all-grain beer, and are set up to do so, simply replace the extract with 6 pounds (2.75 kg) Pilsner malt and 2.5 pounds (1.25 kg( white wheat malt and mash around 150 degrees F (65 C).

## INGREDIENTS:

1    *large squash or pumpkin (use whatever variety you prefer)*
     *Water as needed, for brine*
2    *tablespoons (30 ml) sea salt or pickling salt*
6    *pounds (2.75 kg) wheat Dry Malt Extract*
½    *ounce (15 grams) Cascade hops*
6    *gallons (23 liters) water*

## INSTRUCTIONS:

1. **Prepare**. Gently wash squash or pumpkin, but do not peel. Cut into cubes, then place in large fermentation vessel. Add 2 tablespoons salt. Fill with lukewarm water until vegetables are completely covered. Weigh down, if necessary, to keep below level of the brine.

2. **Ferment**. Set in cool dark place and ferment for 7–10 days.

3. **Brew**. After 7–10 days, the squash should be fermented adequately to use as a starter for your beer fermentation. Heat 3 gallons (11 liters) of water in extra large pot on your stovetop. When water has begun to simmer, cut off the heat and add malt extract. Stir well, until there are no clumps. Return to a steady simmering boil. Add 0.25 ounces (7.5 grams) of Cascade hops, and continue to boil for 60 minutes. At end of boil, add remaining 0.25 ounces Cascade hops.

4. **Chill & Combine**. At end of boil, remove pot from stove and place in ice bath. Chill until liquid is at room temperature. Pour liquid into clean, well-rinsed homebrew carboy or bucket. Top off with room temperature, distilled water until volume totals 5 gallons (19 liters). Pour fermented squash and brine into fermentation vessel. Seal with stopper or lid and airlock.

5. **Ferment**. Place fermentation vessel in cool place—a temperature range of 65 to 74 degrees F (18–23 C) is ideal. Airlock should begin to bubble within a few days. Let ferment for a minimum of four months, up to six months. Ideally, you should measure the gravity (sugar in solution) of the beer over this period, in order to accurately gauge exactly when fermentation is completed. To do so, purchase a hydrometer from your local homebrew shop, and begin taking gravity readings every three weeks, starting after the second month of fermentation. When there is no change in gravity between three subsequent readings, fermentation has completed.

6. **Bottling Equipment.** When visiting your local homebrew shop to obtain that hydrometer, also ask them to help you collect the equipment you'll need to bottle a beer. This should include a bottling bucket with a spigot, a spring-tipped bottling wand, siphon, two cases of bottles, bottle caps, and a bottle capper.

7. **Priming Sugar.** Measure ¾ cup (150 grams) sugar and stir into hot water until dissolved. Allow a few minutes to cool.

8. **Bottle.** Pour sugar solution into empty, clean bottling bucket. Use siphon to transfer beer from fermentation vessel into bottling bucket. The sugar solution will become evenly distributed throughout the beer by the action of the liquid transferring through the siphon. Once transfer is complete, place bottling bucket on a table and fill bottles using bottling wand, then immediately cap.

9. **Conditioning.** Once bottled, a refermentation will occur in the bottles due to the added priming sugar solution. Yeast and bacteria will consume this additional sugar and create carbonation, which is now trapped in the bottle. In order for this to happen, bottles need to be stored at room temperature (refrigerating them will only hamper fermentation). After 3–4 weeks, try a bottle to see how it's developing. It should be carbonated, and hopefully, delicious.

10. **Enjoy.** After about a month, your whole batch should be ready to drink. It may still taste "young," as this is a wild ale, and will continue to develop and improve for months, possibly even years to come. Even if it tastes great from the start, I recommend drinking the batch slowly to witness how it changes over time.

8/16